Valuing Cultural Heritage

Valuing Cultural Heritage

Applying Environmental Valuation Techniques to Historic Buildings, Monuments and Artifacts

Edited by

Ståle Navrud

Associate Professor of Environmental and Resource Economics, Agricultural University of Norway

Richard C. Ready

Assistant Professor of Environmental and Natural Resource Economics, Pennsylvania State University, USA

Edward Elgar

Cheltenham, UK • Northampton, MA, USA

Published by
Edward Elgar Publishing Limited
Glensanda House
Montpellier Parade
Cheltenham
Glos GL50 1UA
UK

Edward Elgar Publishing, Inc.
136 West Street
Suite 202
Northampton
Massachusetts 01060
USA

A catalogue record for this book is available from the British Library

ISBN 1 84064 079 0
Printed and bound in Great Britain by MPG Books Ltd, Bodmin, Cornwall

Contents

List of figures

List of photographs

List of contributors

Wiktor Adamowicz Department of Rural Economy, University of Alberta, Canada

Trine Bille Institute of Local Government Studies (AKF), Copenhagen, Denmark

Peter Boxall Department of Rural Economy, University of Alberta, Canada

Marina Bravi DICAS, Politechnico di Torino, Italy

Richard T. Carson Department of Economics, University of California at San Diego, USA

Lauraine G. Chestnut Stratus Consulting, Boulder, CO, USA

Michael B. Conaway Institute for Social Science Research, University of Alabama, USA

Alexi Danchev Department of Economics, University of Portsmouth/International University Franchise in Bulgaria

Jeffrey Englin Department of Applied Economics and Statistics, University of Nevada at Reno, USA

Guy Garrod Centre for Research in Environmental Appraisal and Management, Department of Agriculture, Economics and Food Marketing, University of Newcastle-upon-Tyne, UK

Andreas Kontoleon Centre for Cultural Economics and Management, University College London, UK

David Maddison Centre for Cultural Economics and Management, University College London, UK and University of Hamburg, Germany

Robert C. Mitchell Graduate School of Geography, Clark University, USA

Edward R. Morey Department of Economics, University of Colorado at Boulder, USA

Susana Mourato Environmental Policy and Management Group, Imperial College of Science, Technology and Medicine, London, UK and Centre for Cultural Economics and Management, London, UK

Ståle Navrud Department of Economics and Social Sciences, Agricultural University of Norway, Norway

David Pearce Centre for Cultural Economics and Management, University College London, UK

Marilena Pollicino Centre for Cultural Economics and Management, University College London, UK

Shannon Ragland   Science Applications International Corporation, Denver, CO, USA

Richard C. Ready   Department of Agricultural Economics and Rural Sociology, Pennsylvania State University, USA

Patrizia Riganti   School of Architecture, Queen's University of Belfast, UK

Kathleen Greer Rossmann   Department of Economics, Birmingham-Southern College, Birmingham, AL, USA

Walter Santagata   Department of Economics, University of Turin, Italy

Riccardo Scarpa   Universita della Tuscia, Viterbo, Italy and CREAM, University of Newcastle-upon-Tyne, UK

Giovanni Signorello   Dipartimento di Scienze Economico-agrarie ed Estimative, University of Catania, Italy

Gemma Sirchia   DICAS, Politechnico di Torino, Italy

Jon Strand   Department of Economics, University of Oslo, Norway

Ken G. Willis   Centre for Research in Environmental Appraisal and Managment Department of Architecture, Planning & Landscape, University of Newcastle-upon-Tyne, UK

Preface

While non-market valuation techniques have been applied in thousands of studies of environmental goods worldwide over the past 40 years, the interest in applying these techniques to cultural heritage goods is quite recent. Throsby and Winters (1986), see table 15.1, seems to be the first study applying these environmental valuation techniques to performing and visual arts, while a contingent valuation study of the Nidaros Cathedral in 1991 (Navrud and Strand, chapter 3) seems to be the first study of cultural heritage buildings, monuments and artifacts. During the 1990s the number of studies have increased to about thirty, but we are still very much in the initial phase of applying these valuation techniques to cultural heritage. Since many of these studies were unpublished, we got the idea of collecting these studies in a book, to present a state-of-the-art review of cultural heritage valuation and draw some conclusions from this initial phase of applications. We presented our idea to many of the contributors to this book at a meeting during the First World Congress of Environmental and Resource Economists in Venice in June 1998, and they were all very enthusiastic about the idea. Edward Elgar later that evening endorsed the idea. We were all inspired by the ambience of Venice, which turned out to be the perfect place to launch this book project!

Part of our work with this book was undertaken in connection with the project 'Rationalized Economic Appraisal of Cultural Heritage' (REACH); 1998–2001. We are indebted to our European colleagues on the REACH project for providing us with an inspiring working arena, and the European Commission for providing financial support for our work on the REACH project (Contract ENV3-CT98-0708). We are also grateful to the staff at Edward Elgar Publishing for their support throughout this project. Most of all we would like to thank all contributors to the book for their keen interest and enthusiasm about this project, and for the big effort that went into the writing of this book.

Ståle Navrud
Drøbak, Norway

Richard C. Ready
State College, Pennsylvania, USA

PART I

Introduction

1. Why value cultural heritage?

Richard C. Ready and Ståle Navrud

The readers of this book will be well aware of the challenges facing our built cultural heritage. Agencies and organizations whose mission it is to protect and preserve historic and culturally important buildings, monuments, and artifacts from the ravages of weather, pollution, development, and even use by the general public must compete for needed resources with other social goals. Should we raise taxes to increase spending on cultural heritage, or should we divert resources away from some other worthy cause such as education, health care, or aid to the poor? What is the proper level of expenditure on cultural heritage? Given limited resources, priorities must be set among competing preservation and restoration goals. Given the myriad different types of cultural heritage and the myriad pressing problems, which problems should be addressed first? At the same time, some question the proper role of government in providing cultural heritage goods. Should preservation and restoration efforts be supported by tax revenues, or should cultural heritage goods be self-supporting, either through user fees or donations and subscriptions?

These challenges and questions are remarkably similar to those faced in another area of public policy—environmental policy. In that arena as well there are issues of what resources to dedicate to protecting and enhancing environmental quality, which aspects of environmental quality to spend those resources on, who should provide those resources, and how. The field of Environmental Economics has developed to address these issues, and provides a consistent, coherent way to frame these questions. Consideration of cultural heritage goods could benefit from applying such a framework, if only because it provides another perspective on these issues.

CULTURAL HERITAGE AS A PUBLIC GOOD

Cultural heritage goods are similar to environmental goods in that they are typically *public goods*. Economists have a very precise definition of what a public good is. In order to be a pure public good, the good must have two properties. First, public goods are *non-excludable*. That means it is technically infeasible to keep users from enjoying the good. Cultural heritage goods vary in their degree of excludibility. Viewing an artifact in a museum is an excludible activity—it is easy for the museum to keep you out if you don't pay. However, sightseeing in an historic area of an old city is typically not an excludible activity—it is impractical to try to charge admission to a living part of a city. In between these two extremes are a range of possibilities, where it is feasible to exclude use of the cultural heritage good, but may be costly to do so.

Excludibility is an important consideration, because economic theory tells us that private, profit-driven, markets will not produce enough non-excludible goods. It is easy to see why. If you cannot keep people from enjoying the good you provide, then you cannot force them to pay for it. If you cannot get your customers to pay you, then you cannot make a profit. If you cannot make a profit, then you do not provide the good in the first place. If we rely on private providers to preserve our cultural heritage, only those goods with high market demand will be protected.

This result is fairly straightforward, but it can have subtle implications. Consider a land-owner who has a beautiful example of period buildings on his farm. The land-owner knows that passers-by on the road enjoy looking at these buildings, but he cannot extract any payment. The buildings are generating social benefits, but those benefits are accruing to the passers-by, not to the owner. That owner has no incentive to preserve the buildings, and indeed may not have the resources necessary to do so.

Even where a private provider can charge some fees, those fees may not represent all of the benefits being generated by the good. Consider a castle on a hillside overlooking a town. The owner of the castle may be able to charge tourists who want to go into the castle an entry fee, and therefore may have some incentive to preserve the condition of the castle. But even though he can capture some of the value that the castle generates, he will not be able to charge people who enjoy looking at the outside of the castle. Indeed, if the castle is sufficiently important, there may be people far away who gain some enjoyment just from knowing that the castle is in a good condition. The owner will not be able to capture those values, and may allow the castle to deteriorate even though the benefits, to all those who receive them, are sufficient to justify the costs of preserving the castle.

The second characteristic of a public good is that it is *non-rival* in consumption. That means two different people can enjoy (consume) the public good at the same time without interfering with each other's enjoyment. A perfect example would be a statue in a public square. I can look at a statue, and enjoy it, at the same time that you do the same. As long as there are not too many of us trying to do the same thing at the same time, we can consume the good simultaneously without diminishing the value that each receives from the good. This aspect of cultural heritage is important because if a cultural heritage good is non-rival in consumption, then it will always be better to allow more people to enjoy it than fewer. Even if exclusion is feasible, it is not desirable as it reduces the total number of people enjoying the good, and so the total enjoyment that the good provides.

Many cultural heritage goods exhibit intermediate levels of rivalness. A cathedral that receives many visitors may become so crowded that each visitor's enjoyment of the experience becomes diminished. Such a cathedral would be a *congestible* public good. Or, the presence of the visitor may actually damage the cultural heritage good itself. In either case, in contrast to the pure public good case, it may be desirable to limit the number of people who visit the site. One way to limit visitation is by charging an entry fee. As compared to other means of limiting entry, such as queuing, an entry fee has a couple of advantages. It generates revenues that can be invested in the cultural heritage good, and it assures the limited number of entry slots go to those who place the highest value on the experience.

If we do not trust private for-profit providers to supply enough cultural heritage goods, then it is up to the government and not-for-profit organizations to do so. But what is the right amount of cultural heritage goods? We live in a world with limited resources, and must make tradeoffs among competing objectives. Here, again, the theory of public goods can help guide us. This theory states that the correct amount of a public good is determined by comparing the marginal cost of providing more of the good with the marginal social benefit of providing more of the good. How would this work in practice? Suppose there are 100 culturally-significant sites in a city, and that we don't have money to protect them all. We would calculate the cost of protecting one site, two sites, and so on. We would then compare those costs to the benefits of protecting one site, two sites, and so on. The socially-optimal number of sites to protect is the number where the additional cost of protecting one more site is equal to the additional benefit from protecting one more site, so that the cost–benefit ratio for the last site considered is equal to one. The same type of analysis can also help guide the decision of how much to spend on each site.

Clearly, in order to use this framework, we need to be able to estimate the benefits and costs of providing cultural heritage goods. This book does not consider in detail the issue of estimating costs. That is best done by experts in the provision of cultural heritage goods. This book is concerned with estimating the values generated by cultural heritage goods, i.e. the benefits. There is a large body of literature and experience in estimating values for environmental public goods. Because these goods are not traded in markets, the methods developed for valuing them are referred to collectively as non-market valuation techniques. The purpose of this book is to explore how these methods, developed for estimating environmental values, can be applied to cultural heritage goods.

These methods provide information that can be of use when addressing a variety of policy issues related to cultural heritage. First, values estimated using these methods can help inform decisions over the level of funding of cultural heritage. Public values for cultural heritage goods can provide a strong argument in favor of public funding for those goods. Second, public preferences can help when making decisions among cultural heritage goods. While there is always a central role for expert opinion in deciding which types of cultural heritage goods will receive attention, information about the general public's preferences over such decisions is a useful complement to expert judgement. The methods discussed in this book allow measurement of those preferences. Finally, the same methods can help inform decisions about funding of cultural heritage goods. They can show the possibilities and limitations of relying on contributions or access charges in supplying a good that generates values to a much broader set of people than just those few who choose to visit the good or donate to its preservation.

WHAT IS "VALUE"?

In the preceding section, the terms "value" and "benefits" were used in a very loose way. But economics has more precise definitions of these terms. In Chapter 2, these terms will be defined formally. Here, we wish to give the reader an intuitive understanding of how economists define the "value" that someone receives from a cultural heritage good.

The guiding principle in defining what is the value of a public good, such as cultural heritage, is that the definition should be logically consistent with how we measure value for a private, market good. Market goods have a market price, but that price is not always a good indicator of value. There are many reasons why the price may overstate or understate value, including the imposition of distortionary taxes, quotas that limit the quantity supplied or purchased, and price controls. More generally, we define the value that a consumer gets from using a market good to be the largest amount of money that the consumer would willingly pay to get the good. So if a consumer is willing to pay £10,000 for a new car, but the price is £12,000, the value to that consumer is his willingness to pay (WTP) for the car, not its price. If someone else decided to give him the car for free, the benefit to the recipient of receiving the car would be £10,000, not £12,000 (assuming he is restricted from selling the car).

For a public good such as cultural heritage, we adopt the same general definition. The value that a person gets from being able to enjoy a cultural heritage good is defined as the largest amount of money that person would willingly pay to have that opportunity. For a cultural heritage site, then, the use value that a visitor receives would be defined as the largest amount of money the visitor would be willing to pay, over and above any actual entry fee, to gain access to the site. We find the total use value generated by the site as the sum of all the individual visitors' WTPs.

Use Value vs Non-use Value

In the above paragraph, *use value* is defined as the maximum WTP to gain access to the site. However, a cultural heritage site might generate values even to those who do not visit the site. *Non-use value* includes benefits that people enjoy because they know the site is being preserved. These benefits might be motivated by a desire that the site be available for others to visit (*altruistic values*), that the site be preserved for future generations (*bequest values*), that the current non-visitor may decide to become a visitor in the future (*option value*), or simply that the site be preserved, even if no-one ever actually visits it (*existence values*). This last category of non-use benefits might motivate why, for example, we may want to expend resources to protect cultural heritage goods that are considered too fragile to be opened for viewing by the general public.

As with use values, we can define the size of non-use values using our market analogy of WTP. The non-use value that a non-visitor receives from preservation of a cultural heritage good is the largest amount he would willingly pay to be assured that the cultural heritage good is preserved. This is not the same as the amount he would donate to its preservation. When the resources for provision of a cultural heritage good are being generated through donations, there is a strong incentive to free-ride on the donations of others. Economic theory tells us that the amount of the donation we observe will be lower than the full value the person receives from the good. The challenge is to measure the full WTP for the good in situations where the user or non-user is not required to pay anything. We discuss this challenge more in Chapter 2.

Extent of the Market

The total value of a cultural heritage good will then include both use values and non-use values. The relative importance of these two categories of values will vary widely among cultural heritage goods. Another related issue is determining the "extent of the market", that is, the total population holding values for the good. A local cultural heritage good may generate values only for those who live in close proximity to the good. An example might be an historic building in a small town. While such a good might generate both use and non-use values for the residents of that town, or visitors to the town, we would not expect large values for people who live some distance from that town. In contrast, a national cultural heritage good may hold some importance for all citizens of a country. An example might be the building where an important national document was signed. Such a site could also generate both use and non-use values, but here we could expect non-use values for preservation of the building even among those who live some distance from the building, and who never plan to visit it. Finally, there are some global cultural heritage goods. Many of these, but certainly not all, have been designated as world heritage sites. Goods such as Buckingham Palace, Machu Picchu, or the Great Wall of China generate values for people who live in distant countries and never plan to visit those sites.

Consideration of the extent of the market is important because, when measuring the value associated with a cultural heritage good, we must decide whose values to include. Most cost–benefit analyses are conducted either at the national level or some regional level. This is done to match the jurisdiction of the body making the decision and spending the money. If it is a national government committing money to the preservation of a cultural heritage good, then that government will want to consider the benefits enjoyed by all of its citizens, but will likely not care as much about the benefits enjoyed by citizens of other countries (except to the extent that those benefits flow back to the host country as tourism revenues). Likewise, a local government that has power to tax only the local population will want to be sure that the benefits to the local population exceed the costs of an investment. This natural tendency of funding agencies can lead to problems, though, when considering global cultural heritage goods. If the national government of a less-developed country that contains a globally-significant cultural heritage good decides issues of preservation based only on benefits to the citizens of that country, it may conclude that preservation is too costly. In such a situation there is a clear need for an analysis that includes both values accruing outside the country, and investment in the good from sources outside the country. Studies such as those contained in this volume can help international organizations decide what resources to expend on such global goods, and where.

THE ROLE OF VALUES IN DECISION MAKING

The techniques and results described in this book provide a consistent way to measure the benefits provided by cultural heritage goods. These can then be compared with the costs of providing those goods. However, that comparison is not sufficient for making policy decisions. If a cost–benefit analysis using non-market valuation shows that a specific investment in a cultural heritage good has a positive net benefit (benefits exceed costs), that is a useful piece of information to the decision maker, and a powerful argument in favor of committing funds to the project, but it is not sufficient information for making the decision. Likewise, a negative net benefit is not sufficient to determine that an investment should not be made. There may be good reasons for investing in the public good even though it does not generate positive net benefits. We may wish to provide the good so that less-advantaged members of society can enjoy it, even though those members have low WTP for the good due to their limited resources. We may wish to preserve certain types of cultural heritage even though the tastes of the current generation do not favor that particular type of good. Finally, we may feel compelled to preserve cultural heritage goods out of a sense of duty and moral purpose, regardless of the preferences of the general population. Even so, information about that population's preferences can only improve decision making.

The availability of techniques for measuring the values of cultural heritage goods is not a substitute for expert analysis and opinion. The general population values cultural heritage goods in the context of what they know about it. Expert opinion of the relative importance of different goods will inform public preferences, and public values. Likewise, the expert has an important role in framing the decisions—determining what the options are and where and when the decision points lie. Finally, the expert informs the decision directly. The decision maker should treat both the expert's judgment and the public's preferences as valid pieces of information when making decisions about cultural heritage goods.

OVERVIEW OF THE BOOK

The remainder of this book looks in detail at how non-market valuation techniques can be applied to cultural heritage goods. In Chapter 2, we present the most important techniques used in valuing public goods, and discuss some of the challenges and opportunities associated with applying those techniques to cultural heritage. In Chapters 3 through 14, we present case studies where these techniques have been used to value specific cultural heritage goods in a wide variety of contexts and countries. Chapter 15 reviews most of the cultural heritage valuation studies that have been done to date, and attempts to draw some general conclusions about both the results of those studies and the utility of valuation of these types of goods.

2. Methods for valuing cultural heritage

Richard C. Ready and Ståle Navrud

In this chapter, we review various non-market valuation techniques that can be used to estimate a monetary value for cultural heritage goods. The literature on these techniques is vast, and growing quickly.[1] We cannot hope to provide a complete review of the latest methodological advancements. Instead, we have two objectives in this chapter. First, we hope to introduce non-economists to these techniques, providing sufficient background for them to understand the case studies presented later in the book. Second, we hope to point out the unique challenges and opportunities involved in applying these techniques to the valuation of cultural heritage goods.

WHAT IS VALUE?

Before we can begin to measure the value of a good, any good, we must first decide what we mean by the concept "value". Here, we take a very neoclassical economic perspective. Within that perspective, the "value" of a good is defined as either (1) the amount of money the potential consumer would be willing to pay to get the good (willingness to pay, WTP), or (2) the amount of money the owner of the good would have to be paid in order to induce him or her to part with it (willingness to accept, WTA).[2]

In the case of goods that are traded in markets, consumers can compare their own value for the good (their WTP) with the market price, and decide whether or not to make a purchase. If the consumer does purchase the good, then we know that their value for the good must have been larger than its price. Owners (or producers) of a good can compare their value for the good (their WTA) with the market price, and decide whether or not to sell. If an owner sells, then their value for the good must have been less than the market price. In a market equilibrium, the marginal consumer and the marginal producer will have WTP and WTA respectively for the good that are just equal to its price. For that reason, we can view the market price as a signal of the good's marginal value to both consumers and providers.[3]

When we apply this conceptual framework to issues involving cultural heritage goods, we immediately face two problems. The first is in defining what we mean by "the good". It is rarely useful to consider a building or monument itself as the good to be valued. Rather, it is often more useful to value some change in the characteristics of the building or monument, for example a change in its appearance, authenticity, or accessibility. If we let Q^0 represent a complete physical description of the building or monument, and Q^1 represent some different physical description, then we can define the good to be valued as the difference between Q^0 and Q^1. For example, if we are interested in soiling of a cathedral from airborne pollutants, Q^0 could represent a more-soiled facade, while Q^1 represents a less-soiled facade.[4]

The individual whose value we are interested in has some utility function that ranks different sets of outcomes. This utility function will logically include as an argument the individual's wealth or income, Y, as well as the physical state of the cultural heritage good, Q, so that the individual's utility is given by $V(Y, Q)$. Combinations of Y and Q that yield higher levels of utility are preferred to combinations that yield lower levels. The value that the individual places on the change from Q^0 to Q^1 (in this case the individual's WTP for a change from Q^0 to Q^1) is then the largest amount of money the individual would willingly give up in order to achieve Q^1 instead of Q^0, and is given by:[5]

$$V(Y, Q^0) = V(Y - \text{WTP}, Q^1). \qquad (2.1)$$

It is this measure of value that we hope to estimate empirically.

This brings us to the second difficulty when trying to apply the market model to cultural heritage goods, namely they are rarely traded in markets, and thus have no observable price. There are very good reasons why cultural heritage goods are not traded in private markets. Cultural heritage goods are typically public goods, meaning they have two precisely-defined characteristics. First, the benefits (values) generated by cultural heritage goods are typically non-rival, that is the benefit enjoyed by one individual does not come at the expense of the next individual's enjoyment. This is in contrast to market goods, where a given unit of the good can only be consumed by one individual. Second, it is often difficult to force people to pay a price before they can enjoy the benefits from the cultural heritage good. Even where entrance to a building can be regulated by an entrance fee, non-user benefits accrue regardless of whether they have been paid for. We say that the good, or enjoyment of the good, is non-excludable. These two conditions lead to a situation where markets cannot be trusted to provide an adequate supply of cultural heritage goods. It is for this reason that such goods are usually provided collectively, either by governments or by groups of people working cooperatively.

The absence of a price means that we cannot observe values for cultural heritage goods directly. Instead, we must, like detectives, look for clues that tell us something about value indirectly. Non-market valuation is a term used to describe a variety of techniques for looking for and interpreting these clues about value for goods that are not traded in markets. There are two broad categories of non-market techniques: revealed preference techniques and stated preference techniques. As the name implies, revealed preference techniques involve searching for those clues by examining an individual's past behavior. One type of behavior that can be examined is purchases of market goods that are closely tied to the non-market good of interest. The hedonic pricing method uses this approach. A second type of behavior that might be examined is decisions made about where to go to spend one's free time. The travel cost method utilizes this type of information. Whereas revealed preference techniques make use of past behavior, stated preference techniques make use of the individual's own guess about what future behavior might be, in a world different from the present day. The contingent valuation method (and other variants[6]) asks individuals what they would do in a hypothetical world that does not now exist, and then infers value from that hypothetical behavior.

In the following sections, each of these techniques will be discussed. The basic strategy motivating each will be presented, along with a discussion of the practical difficulties involved, especially with regard to valuation of cultural heritage goods.

THE HEDONIC PRICING TECHNIQUE

The hedonic pricing technique for valuing non-market goods is based on the characteristics value approach of Griliches (1971) and Rosen (1974). While the hedonic pricing technique is commonly used to value a variety of environmental goods and urban amenities, there have not been, to our knowledge, any previous studies that have used this technique to value cultural heritage. There is no theoretical limitation of this technique for such a purpose, but there are some practical problems in implementing the hedonic pricing method for cultural heritage goods, which we discuss at the end of this section.

The basic idea behind the hedonic pricing method is to look for situations where the purchase of a market good includes the opportunity to enjoy a given level of the non-market good. The analyst then looks for price differentials between units of the market good that have high levels of the non-market good associated with them, and units that have low levels. The price differential provides information, then, about the value of the non-market good.

In the context of cultural heritage goods, the most likely market good for such an analysis is housing, either privately-owned houses or rental units.

Consider a city with several residential areas. The housing price of a given unit will depend on the physical characteristics of that unit (size, age, quality of construction, etc.) but will also depend on the characteristics of the neighborhood (proximity to shopping, quality of schools, amount of greenspace, etc.). One neighborhood characteristic could be the amount and quality of cultural heritage goods. For example, neighborhoods could vary in how many restored historical buildings they contain. If residents value living in proximity to restored historical buildings, then price differentials should develop among the neighborhoods due to differences in that cultural heritage good. These price differentials are signals about the value that residents place on living in a neighborhood with a higher level of cultural heritage goods.

The actual mechanics of using the hedonic pricing method in a situation such as this are as follows. First, the analyst would collect information on a large number of housing units. The information would include each unit's price (sale price or rental price), the physical characteristics of the unit, and the unit's location. From the unit's location the analyst would determine the characteristics of the neighborhood, including the level of the cultural heritage good. Second, the analyst would use statistical regression techniques to estimate a model explaining differences in housing unit prices. This is commonly referred to as the implicit price function. For example, the analyst may estimate a model of the form:

$$\text{Price} = \alpha + \beta_1 \, (\text{Size}) + \beta_2 \, (\text{Age}) + \gamma_1 \, (\text{School Quality})$$
$$+ \, \gamma_2 \, (\text{Historical Buildings}) + \varepsilon. \tag{2.2}$$

Here, the slope parameters of the equation represent the marginal increase or decrease in price that would be expected from a change in the housing unit's characteristics. These parameters are called the marginal implicit prices (or sometimes simply the implicit prices) for the characteristics. In our example, γ_2 is the marginal implicit price for historical buildings.[7]

It remains necessary to demonstrate why these marginal implicit prices contain useful information about value. We assume a housing market where consumers are mobile and there exists a variety of housing units with different combinations of characteristics. The individual housing consumer chooses the house that maximizes his or her utility. In making that choice, the individual makes tradeoffs between price and the various characteristics (how much more am I willing to pay to get more living area, etc.). If there are enough different types of housing units available, then each of these tradeoffs will be optimal, i.e. they will reveal the consumer's preferences. In particular, the consumer will tradeoff the price of the unit against the level of the cultural heritage good, and will find a housing unit in the market where his or her willingness to pay for an increase in the cultural heritage good exactly equals the marginal implicit price of purchasing that increase. Each individual consumer will prefer a different housing unit, due to differences in preferences and income, but each will "purchase" additional cultural heritage up to the point where their marginal WTP equals the marginal implicit price. Thus, the consumers' own optimization assures that the marginal implicit prices are equal to the residents' marginal willingness to pay for more of the cultural heritage good. For small changes in the level of the cultural heritage good (for example the preservation and restoration of one or a few historic buildings), the value of the change could be measured by multiplying the marginal implicit price for that cultural heritage good by the size of the change.[8]

The use of the hedonic pricing method to value cultural heritage goods will be limited to those situations where "consumption" of the cultural heritage good is closely tied to consumption of the market good, in our case the housing unit. In other words, this technique will capture the value of the cultural heritage good only if the benefit from the cultural heritage good accrues only to those who live close to it. However, cultural heritage goods tend to have important visitor use values and non-use values—values that cannot be captured by a housing price analysis. You do not need to live close to a cathedral to visit it or to value the fact that it will be available for future generations. Any price gradient that exists around a cathedral will capture only the value of seeing the cathedral day-to-day, on your way to and from your home, which is likely to be a very small part of the cathedral's total value. The proportion of total value that would be captured by a housing price analysis will depend on how local the cultural heritage good is. A restored building facade may be valued most by local residents, and may be effectively valued using this technique. There, the only limitation will be in finding suitable variation in the cultural heritage good across neighborhoods. However, this technique is not well suited to valuing a cathedral with national significance.

There is a variation of the basic hedonic pricing method that might prove more viable in valuing cultural heritage goods. That variation takes advantage of differences in the level of cultural heritage goods among different cities. Here, an individual's choice of city in which to live is modeled. Two important factors in that decision are the characteristics of the cities (including the level of cultural heritage goods) and the prevailing housing prices. Here, an implicit price function is estimated for city-average housing prices as a function of city characteristics. One complication is that, in addition to differences in housing prices, differences in prevailing wages must also be incorporated.[9] For cultural heritage goods where the bulk of the benefits accrue to residents of the city in question, this approach could capture most use values. The challenge would be to find enough different cities with enough variation in the cultural heritage good to identify the implicit housing and wage price functions, and control for other differences that make the cities more or less attractive as places to live and work.

THE TRAVEL COST METHOD

The most observable source of value associated with cultural heritage goods is that accruing to people who visit historical buildings, monuments, or areas during their free time. Clearly, a visitor to the Tower of London or Notre Dame Cathedral derives some benefit from the visit. Simply by turning up at the site, a visitor shows that the visit has positive net value (i.e. the total value to the visitor of the visit exceeds its cost). The travel cost method is a technique that attempts to learn something about the size of that net value, by looking at visitation patterns.

The first applications of the travel cost method were to value changes in people's opportunity to engage in outdoor recreation, where the recreationists must travel to reach the recreation site, but it has since been used to value other goods that involve travel. The basic unit of analysis is the "trip" or "visit". In the context of a cultural heritage good such as an historic building or group of buildings, the "visit" would include all travel from the visitor's home to the site and back, plus all time spent at the site. A visit may last a few hours, or it may stretch over several days, depending on the nature of the site and the distance the visitor must travel.

The strategy of the travel cost method is to view each visit as a good that the visitor purchases. For good reasons, most cultural heritage sites charge no or low entry fee. Even where a fee is charged, it tends not to vary over time, making it impossible to trace out a demand curve for visits based solely on the entry fee. However, the total cost, or price, of visiting a site includes much more than the entry fee. It includes all costs incurred traveling to and from the site, as well as possibly lodging and food costs. Luckily, from an analytical point of view, these travel costs do vary from visitor to visitor. By looking at differences in visitation behavior across persons facing different visit prices, we can trace out a demand curve for visits to the site.

There are two types of travel cost models that take advantage of these differences in visit prices. The first type models how often an individual (or group of similar individuals) visits a given site. These will be called visitation frequency models. The second type models which of several sites a given individual will choose to visit on a given occasion. These will be called site choice models.

Visitation Frequency Models

To apply a visitation frequency model to a cultural heritage site such as an historic building, the simplest approach would be to survey a large number of individuals living at different distances from the site, and ask each how many times they had visited the site during a specified period (the previous year, 10 years, or such). The total price of visiting the site would be calculated for each individual in the sample, usually by multiplying the distance that would have to be driven by some constant cost per mile of operating a car, and then adding any entrance fee the visitor would be required to pay. A "trip generating function" would be estimated, where the number of trips taken is estimated as a function of the total visit price, along with any other relevant explanatory variables (income, ethnicity, etc.).[10] An example of such a trip generating function is shown in Figure 2.1. This trip generating function can be viewed as a demand curve for visits to the site. In the example shown in Figure 2.1, a potential visitor who lives very close to the site (and has zero total visit cost) will visit the site five times. Visits per person will decrease as distance to the site increases, with no-one visiting from a distance where total visit cost is $70 or higher.

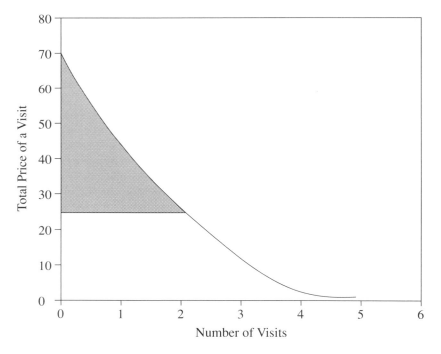

Figure 2.1   A trip generating function for a cultural heritage site

From this demand curve, the analyst can calculate the total consumer surplus (benefit) each visitor receives from being able to visit the site. For an individual with costs of $25 per trip, the estimated trip generating function predicts a visitation rate of two trips. However, the value of those trips is something more than the $2 \times \$25 = \$50$ that the visitor pays in trip costs. The extra benefit the visitor receives from the two trips, over and above what he actually pays, is called the visitor's consumer surplus for the site, and is given graphically by the area under the trip generating function, above the per trip costs (the shaded region in Figure 2.1). In this example, this visitor's consumer surplus from the site is $42. The calculation would be repeated for every potential visitor to arrive at the total consumer surplus (net visitor benefits) generated by the site.

The trip generating function can also, in some cases, provide information about impacts from a change in the quality of a site. Suppose that visitation frequencies are measured before and after site quality changes (for example because of a restoration or cleaning).[11] It would then be possible to include site quality as a separate explanatory variable in the trip generating function. Site quality then becomes a demand shifter. Consumer surplus would be calculated both before and after the change in quality. The benefit (or cost) caused by the change in quality would then be the difference between these two consumer surplus values.

The basic approach outlined above is, of course, more complicated in actual practice. We mention here just a few of the challenges faced in applied studies, and the refinements often made to address those challenges. First, for many destinations, most potential visitors visit the site zero times in a given year. For this reason, it is common to aggregate visitors into groups, usually geographically based on their home address, and to model instead the average visitation rate from a region or zone of origin. The zonal travel cost model approach simplifies sampling as well, as it is then possible to take a random sample of visitors only, at the site, rather than interviewing a random sample of the general population, in their homes. Second, an important category of trip costs is very difficult to measure, namely, the opportunity cost of the time used for the trip. Travel to and from the site is costly both because of the direct costs of the journey, and also because the time spent traveling could be used in some other utility- or income-generating activity. Unfortunately, it is impossible to observe the value that each visitor places on his or her own time. A common approach, based on results from the transportation literature, is to value travel time at some fraction, usually ¼ to ½, of the visitor's wage rate. Third, it is important to account for other recreation opportunities faced by the potential visitor, including other cultural heritage goods. Persons who live in a town with a prominent cathedral may be less likely to visit some other town to see its cathedral. Failure to account for the availability of substitute sites will cause biases in the estimated trip generating function. Unfortunately, it is difficult to know what other sites and activities will compete for the potential visitor's attention.

Site Choice Models

The second set of travel cost models model the potential visitor's choice of where to go on a particular trip. The idea behind these models is that, on a given occasion—a given Saturday, say—a potential visitor considers several sites, and then chooses one to visit. This forward-thinking visitor considers all of the characteristics of the candidate sites, as well as the cost of reaching each, and then chooses the one site that provides the best combination of characteristics and price.

The theoretical model underlying this method assumes that some utility function exists that ranks the different sites, based on the characteristics of each site and the total cost of visiting each site. On each occasion, the individual potential visitor calculates the utility from each site, and chooses the one site that gives the highest utility on that occasion. The utility function includes a random component that varies across sites and across individuals and is unobservable to the analyst. Because of this random component, the analyst will never know with certainty which site the individual will visit, but can state the probability that each site will be chosen. This random term also varies from one occasion to another, something which explains why a given individual does not always visit the same site on every occasion. As a group, these models are called random utility models.

The strategy for using a random utility model to describe visitation behavior is as follows. First, a sample of potential visitors is asked which sites they visited during a given time period. The measurable characteristics of each site are collected, and the total visit price for each individual to each site is calculated. A specific functional form is chosen for the site utility function, and its parameters are estimated, using specialized statistical regression techniques. Once the utility function is estimated, the WTP for continued access to a site, or for a change in the quality of a site or group of sites, can be calculated directly, according to a modified version of equation (2.1).

Random utility models of site choice are uniquely capable of investigating changes in site quality. Unfortunately, they are not well suited to predicting total visitation at a given site. For that task, methods that model visitation frequency will be more reliable. Random utility models share with visitation frequency models the difficulty in measuring the opportunity cost of travel time, and they introduce a number of difficult statistical issues. The results received can often be very sensitive to the assumptions made in the statistical analysis. Still, for cultural heritage goods, it will often be aspects of site quality that are most policy-relevant. For that reason, the site choice models look to be a more promising technique for these applications.

Applying the Travel Cost Method to Cultural Heritage Goods

There are several features unique to cultural heritage goods that limit the potential for using the travel cost method. First, many of the visitors to cultural heritage sites undertake the visit as part of a longer trip that includes several destinations. For example, suppose that we discover an American visiting the Tower of London. That American may visit the site as part of a longer visit to London, or even as part of a visit to several European countries. The visit is possibly an add-on to a business trip. In either case, the site visit is not necessarily the single primary purpose of the trip. The difficulty with such a visitor is that it is theoretically impossible to divide total trip costs and apportion them to each activity in the trip. There is no correct way to determine that $X\%$ of the airline ticket should be considered a cost of visiting the Tower of London, while some other portion should be assigned to visiting Buckingham Palace. Because the cost of the visit is unmeasurable, the travel cost method cannot be applied to that visitor. While the above example is extreme, it points out a common problem with the application of the travel cost method. The travel cost model is valid only for visitors whose sole purpose for traveling is to visit that one site.[12] Many cultural heritage sites are not the kind of good that people take single-purpose trips to see.

An exception to the above statement might be a museum in a city, where local residents take single-purpose trips to visit the museum. However, such a situation raises its own difficulties. Travel costs within a city are often somewhat independent of the location of the visitor's residence. If the mode of travel includes public transportation, out-of-pocket travel costs (the fare itself) are often the same for everyone living within a rather large area. The only differences in travel costs that can be used to estimate a visitation model are those caused by differences in travel time, which is something that we have difficulty valuing.

A second problem that can occur within a city is the self-selection of residential location. Those residents who value visiting cultural heritage sites most highly will choose to live close to those sites. For example, a resident who cherishes walking through a restored old-town area, and feeling its ambiance and history, will be likely to choose to live in or near such an area, reducing the cost of reaching it. The total cost of visiting the site is then, in part, self-determined, causing problems in estimating either a trip generating function or a random utility model.

Finally, it should be remembered that the travel cost method will only capture those benefits that accrue as part of a visit to the site. Any non-use value attached to a site will be excluded. Still, knowledge of visitor use values can be very important when considering for example tradeoffs between access to a sensitive site, which generates use values, and preservation of the site, which maintains non-use values.

STATED PREFERENCE TECHNIQUES

By far the most common method employed for valuing cultural heritage goods has been contingent valuation, and its variants. In this section, we present and discuss primarily the basic contingent valuation technique, and then mention some of the variations that exist. Ideally, we would observe individuals in situations where they must make tradeoffs directly between their own wealth and the quality of the cultural heritage goods they derive value from. That is, we would watch people make decisions whether or not to "purchase" improvements in cultural heritage goods. Unfortunately, such situations rarely exist. Even if we consider an individual's decision whether to contribute to a charitable organization dedicated to preserving cultural heritage goods, the tradeoff is muddied by the potential for free-riding behavior, where an individual enjoys the fruits of others' contributions, without contributing themselves. This stems directly from the fact that most cultural heritage goods are non-excludable.

While situations may not exist in the real world where such decisions must be made, it may be possible to imagine such situations. In the contingent valuation method, survey respondents are asked to imagine that they face a situation where they must make such a tradeoff. In a typical application, the respondent is asked to imagine that he or she must choose one of two courses of action. One action will give the individual higher monetary wealth, but a lower level of the cultural heritage good, than the other. The respondent tells the interviewer how he or she would behave in that situation. The value that the respondent places on the cultural heritage good is then inferred from their hypothetical behavior.

An example will help demonstrate how this works. Suppose we observe a tourist exiting a cathedral that has no entrance fee. We know that the tourist's visitor use value is positive, because they undertook the visit, but we don't know how large that value might be. We could stop the tourist and ask them the following question: "Suppose you had to pay an entrance fee of £3 to go inside this cathedral today. Would you have done so?". The tourist would then have to tradeoff the enjoyment they received from touring the cathedral with the loss of £3. If the tourist answers "yes", then we know the value from the visit was at least £3. If the tourist answers "no", then we know the value from the visit lies somewhere between £0 and £3. While we still do not know exactly the value of the visit, we know quite a bit more from having asked the question.

In the above scenario the respondent was trading off visitor use values and money. We learn nothing about non-use values. The difficulty in trying to measure non-use values is that it is hard to construct scenarios where an individual can have a large influence on the level of provision of a public good. Fortunately, it is not necessary that the individual's choice be decisive. It is only required that the individual's choice increases the likelihood that one or the other course of action is followed. Thus, we can propose to a respondent a public program to increase the level of provision of a cultural heritage good (or slow its decrease) that will cost each individual money, possibly in the form of higher taxes. We could ask, if there were to be a referendum on such a program, would they vote for or against it.[13] Hoehn and Randall (1987) show that if the individual's value for the program exceeds his own expected cost, then (1) it is optimal to vote for the program, and (2) it is optimal to say as much in an interview. There is no strategic advantage to answering falsely, and we can use the answers as reliable indicators of the respondent's value.[14]

The Hypothetical Scenario

It is worth taking the time to discuss some of the design decisions that must be made in creating a contingent valuation scenario. The most important of these are the description of the good to be provided, the payment vehicle, the method of exclusion for non-payment, and the value elicitation method.

Describing the good to be valued

In order to make an informed decision within the context of the contingent valuation scenario, the respondent must fully understand what it is he or she is "buying". It is vital that the respondent knows what the level of the cultural heritage good will be under both courses of action. It is not sufficient, for example, to tell the respondent that a preservation program will preserve a statue in its present condition. The respondent must also know what the statue would look like without the program.

There is a tradeoff between overloading the respondent with too much information, making the interview too lengthy and burdensome, and providing enough detail to allow a well-informed response. With cultural heritage goods, where many of the quality aspects are aesthetic, visual aids such as photographs or videos can be used to convey important information in a way that is quick and interesting to the respondent. New advances in digital photography techniques allow the analyst to create "with program" and "without program" photographs showing the program impact visually.

It is also important to describe how the good will be provided, and by whom. This is because the method of provision often has its own consequences. If a statue will be protected from air pollution by reducing the level of pollutants, the program will have very important consequences other than for cultural heritage. Indeed, the respondent may value such a program mostly for the improvement in health and visibility that it would invariably provide. A restoration project that covers a site with scaffolding for 12 months will be worth less than one that disrupts the site for a shorter period of time. It can be challenging to construct a provision mechanism that elicits exactly the values that are of interest.

The payment vehicle

The respondent must also know how they will forfeit the money involved. Here, the vehicle used for collecting the money must be realistic, given the provision mechanism. A government program might logically be funded through taxes. A project undertaken at a single site might logically be funded through entrance fees. In addition, the payment vehicle must not itself be objectionable to the respondents. If the mechanism is not credible and appropriate, the respondent may object to the entire scenario. For example, a respondent may think it is unfair to pay for restoration of a cultural heritage good with national significance using only local taxes, and may state opposition to the plan, even if his or her value exceeds the projected cost.

The exclusion mechanism

In order for the question to involve a tradeoff, there must be a mechanism by which the level of the cultural heritage good is linked to the individual's payment, i.e. the level will be higher if and only if the individual pays the money. An entrance fee easily satisfies this requirement—if the entrance fee is not paid, then the respondent cannot visit the site. A referendum involving a tax increase also satisfies this requirement—if the program is adopted, the respondent will pay higher taxes. A payment vehicle that does not include an exclusion mechanism is contributions to a charitable organization. The economically-optimal strategy when a public good is provided through charitable donations is to free-ride on the contributions of others. Thus, actual donation behavior does not reveal preferences. Hypothetical donation behavior does no better.

The elicitation method

Having set up the provision scenario and payment vehicle, there are several ways to ask the respondent about their preferences. The examples given so far in this chapter are examples of the dichotomous choice method, where the respondent is faced with two options, and the costs of the options differ by a fixed amount of money, chosen by the researcher. This approach is commonly used, because it is believed to be easiest for respondents to answer reliably. It is most like an isolated purchase decision, where a consumer sees a product in a store and must decide whether to forfeit the listed price in order to gain the product. Any one answer to such a question provides limited information about that individual's WTP for the good. However, by asking many respondents the same question, using different prices for different respondents, it is possible to trace out a distribution of the value of the cultural heritage good across the entire population.

Alternatively, the respondent could be asked directly the price that would make them indifferent between the two courses of action. For example, a tourist visiting a cathedral could be asked "what is the largest entrance fee that you would pay, right now, in order to visit this cathedral?". This is an example of an open-ended valuation question, where the respondent reports their own maximum WTP for the good. The advantage of this approach is that it generates full information about WTP from each respondent, increasing the precision possible from a limited sampling budget. The disadvantage is that it is a difficult question for respondents to answer reliably. It is not similar to any everyday decision process that people go through. We are rarely required to calculate the absolute maximum we would pay for a market good. Lacking that experience, answers to an open-ended valuation question may be highly variable, or may even be biased upward or downward, depending on the decision heuristic adopted by the respondent.

An approach that uses the familiarity of the dichotomous choice method, but that generates more information, is the double-bounded dichotomous choice method. Here, the respondent is asked a standard dichotomous choice question, with a set price. If the respondent says "yes", then he or she is asked a second question, identical to the first but with a higher price. "No" respondents are given a follow-up question with a lower price. In this way, the analyst learns more about the respondent's WTP, but each question takes the familiar purchase/don't purchase form. This process can in principle be repeated several times, resulting in an iterative bidding exercise, but there are two reasons why it typically is not. First, the amount of additional statistical information provided by additional rounds of questions falls off dramatically after the first two. Second, there is evidence that the answers to later questions are influenced by the prices posed in earlier questions. So-called starting point bias occurs when respondents are more likely to answer "yes" to a price if they have previously been asked a higher price, and less likely if they have previously been asked a lower price.

Finally, there are some other variations of the contingent valuation method that differ in how the value is solicited. A simple extension of the dichotomous choice approach involves asking the respondent to choose from among more than two possible courses of action. The multiple alternatives differ in the level of provision of the cultural heritage good, and in the cost to the respondent. The respondent is asked to pick the most preferred course of action (the contingent choice method), or to rank the courses from most to least preferred (the contingent ranking method), or to attach a numerical rating to each course of action (the conjoint analysis method). A second extension of the dichotomous choice method is to present several dichotomous choice situations sequentially, with the price and/or level of provision varying from pair to pair (the paired comparisons or stated choice method). The answers to such questions are analyzed using a random utility model similar to that used in the travel cost method.

Reliability of Contingent Valuation Responses

There has been some concern over whether respondent statements about their behavior in hypothetical situations are reliable. Here, the basic question is whether respondents would actually do what they say they would do, if faced with the described situation. There are three reasons why they might not.

First, respondents may lie to the interviewer. The questions themselves may provide the respondent with an incentive to not answer truthfully. For example, if the respondent knows that he or she will not personally pay the costs of providing the good, but the amount of the good provided will depend on the total value expressed in the survey, there is a clear incentive to overstate WTP. It is the job of the analyst to construct a scenario where it is in the respondent's best interest to answer the valuation questions truthfully. Even so, the respondent may feel some pressure to express value for the good in question, in an attempt to please the interviewer. This concern is very relevant for cultural heritage goods, where a respondent may feel that it is seen as churlish to oppose provision of such a good. When writing the survey instrument, the analyst must describe the choice in a balanced way, such that the respondent feels free to choose either course of action without feeling guilty.

Second, the respondent may not invest enough effort into thinking about his or her own preferences. In a purchase decision for a market good, there is a clear incentive to think through the consequences of the decision. A mistake costs real money. In a contingent valuation survey, however, a mistaken answer due to inadequate attention or effort is costless to the respondent. The only incentive respondents have to expend any effort on answering the questions accurately is their desire to help the interviewer, and their desire to help guide public policy. In some studies respondents are given a gift or cash as a token of appreciation (and an incentive to participate). It is hoped that they will then feel some compulsion to provide higher quality responses. Otherwise, it is wise to keep the burden on the respondent as light as possible, while still generating useful information.

Third, respondents may make random or systematic errors in how they answer valuation questions. These can have dramatic impacts on the inferred WTP values. For example, if 5% of respondents in a dichotomous choice study check the wrong box (i.e. say "yes" when they should have said "no", or vice versa), that will dramatically increase the mean estimated WTP for the population. This is because the WTP value implied by a "no" response is bounded from below by zero, while the WTP implied by a "yes" response is unbounded from above. The analyst must be very careful to try to identify respondents who make errors in answering the valuation questions.

Because of the potential for unreliable answers, there has been a good deal of research on the validity of contingent valuation method (CVM) estimates of value. Two ways to assess validity are (1) to compare CVM estimates of value to other, trusted estimates (criterion validity), and (2) to look for patterns in CVM estimates of value that are predicted by economic theory (construct validity). The evidence to date from these efforts has been mixed. There are many studies that show problems with the CVM method. For example, some studies have shown large differences between stated purchase intentions and actual purchase behavior in similar situations (for example Neill *et al.*, 1994 among others). Other studies have shown large differences between estimates of WTP derived using different elicitation methods in the same CVM survey (for example Ready *et al.*, 1996 among others). Other studies have found estimated CVM values to be insensitive to important changes in the good being provided (for example Boyle *et al.*, 1994 among others). At the same time there are studies that have shown convergence between stated and actual purchase behavior, convergence among different elicitation methods, and sensitivity to the good being provided. The conclusion is that CVM can be done poorly, and give poor results, but can also be done well, giving reliable results (Carson and Mitchell, 1993; Carson *et al.*, 1996).

Application of Contingent Valuation Method to Cultural Heritage Goods

Most of the studies to date that have valued cultural heritage, including most of the studies in this volume, have used a stated preference technique. There are good reasons for this, directly related to the difficulties mentioned in applying revealed preference techniques to cultural heritage goods. In order to apply the revealed preference techniques, an observable decision must exist that reveals the individual's value for the good. For reasons discussed above, these situations are rare for cultural heritage goods. In contrast, the CVM and other stated preference techniques are very flexible with regard to the goods they can value. The only limitation is that a credible scenario can be devised where the respondent can imagine making a tradeoff between money and the level of the cultural heritage good. The scenario does not even have to be realistic or likely. Respondents are generally willing to suspend disbelief and consider an unlikely scenario, as long as it is imaginable and unobjectionable.

Cultural heritage goods are also well suited to contingent valuation studies because most respondents accept the idea of public provision of these goods. Contingent valuation does not work well if respondents feel that provision of the good is "someone else's" responsibility. For example, clean-up of a polluted river would be seen as the responsibility of the polluters, and a contingent valuation scenario involving payment by individuals is often rejected by respondents. In contrast, the experience of most studies involving cultural heritage goods is that the general public sees it as natural that the costs of provision be borne widely.

Contingent valuation is also well suited to valuing cultural heritage goods because it is the only valuation method that can capture non-use values. The extent to which non-use values dominate the total value generated by a cultural heritage good will vary from case to case, but it is clear that for at least some of these goods, non-use value will be very important.

There are also some unique challenges associated with applying contingent valuation to cultural heritage goods. An important issue is the sampling frame for the study—how large a population should be sampled? For a less-than-well-known cathedral in England, will the relevant population be limited to those who live close by, or to all who live in England, or could people in other countries hold value for the cathedral? This question is important because a contingent valuation study can generate an over-focusing effect within respondents. A respondent who had never heard of the cathedral prior to the interview may think that if the good in question is so important that it is worth doing interviews about, then he must have some value for it. Careful design of the survey should minimize this effect, but the fact that WTP is bounded from below by zero means that errors will tend to bias estimated WTP for distant sites upward, and the very large populations that these values would be applied to can result in very large aggregated estimates of WTP. Caution should be applied when using these methods to value goods that are not widely known to the respondents.

Finally, application of the CVM to cultural heritage goods can be made difficult due to the complexity of the issues involved in its provision. A typical program to improve the quality of cultural heritage goods often includes both positive and negative components. Cleaning a cathedral might bring out detail that was covered by soot, but might make the cathedral look too "new", reducing its aesthetic value. Moving a statue indoors might preserve it from deterioration, but will alter its relationship to its surrounding space. Restoring a damaged facade will improve its appearance, but at a cost of lost originality. Contingent valuation in a simple situation where the good is unambiguously desirable is a difficult task for a respondent. Valuation of a good with both positive and negative aspects is that much more challenging.

CONCLUDING COMMENTS

In general, economists prefer to rely on actual behavior consumers undertake in response to price signals, as opposed to hypothetical statements about behavior. The presumption is that actual decisions involving real money carry penalties for mistakes, and are therefore more reliable indicators of value. Unfortunately, there are few good situations where observed behavior reveals preference for cultural heritage goods. In those isolated situations, the presumed preference for revealed preference techniques applies to these goods as well as any other public good. However, stated preference techniques are often the only practicable approach to generating value estimates for cultural heritage goods.

ENDNOTES

1. For good surveys of non-market valuation methodology, we recommend Freeman (1993) and Braden and Kolstad (1991). The review in this chapter covers techniques based on individual preferences. However, there are also methods based on expert preferences, e.g. delphi techniques and multicriteria decision analysis, etc.
2. It should be noted that this approach gives complete sovereignty to the individual. Goods have value only because individuals want them, and are willing to trade money in order to get them. In particular, this definition of value rules out intrinsic values for goods that are independent of people's preferences for those goods.
3. Whether price also represents the good's marginal value to society depends on whether there are any externalities in consumption or provision.
4. In extreme cases, Q^0 could represent the complete loss of the building or monument, but complete elimination of a building or monument is rarely policy-relevant.
5. In the economics literature, this measure of value is called the individual's compensating variation for the change, or less precisely their consumer surplus.
6. There are many different ways to ask stated preference questions, and each approach has a different name. These include conjoint analysis, choice experiments, paired comparisons, and contingent ranking.
7. In a simple linear model, the regression coefficients are the marginal implicit prices. More generally, a non-linear model will fit the price data better. The marginal implicit prices are then given by the derivative of the implicit price function.
8. For larger changes in the level of the cultural heritage good, this approach will generate errors due to declining marginal utility. It will overstate WTP for large increments, and understate WTA for large decrements.
9. For an example of this approach, see Blomquist *et al.*, (1988).
10. A statistical regression method that accounts for the integer nature of the dependent variable is typically used. Examples include the Poisson and negative binomial models.
11. Or, visitation frequencies could be measured to a number of similar sites, that differ in quality. With the multisite approach, however, it is difficult to control for all relevant differences among the sites.
12. In some cases, the cultural heritage good can be viewed as an attribute of a site that provides several services. The value of the cultural heritage good can then be measured by looking at its impact on site choice. This is the approach taken in Chapter 8.
13. If referendums are not a common means of making public decisions where the interview is being conducted, the respondent could be asked which action he or she would prefer.
14. This result depends on the respondent believing the cost estimate that is given.

REFERENCES

Blomquist, G.M. Beger and J. Hoehn, 'New estimates of quality of life in urban areas,' *American Economic Review*, 78: 89–107, 1988.

Boyle, K.J., W.H. DesVousges, F.R. Johnson, R.W. Dunford and S.P. Hudson. "An Investigation of Part–Whole Biases in Contingent Valuation Studies". *Journal of Environmental Economics and Management* 27(July 1994): 64–83.

Braden, J.B. and C.D. Kolstad, eds. *Measuring the Demand for Environmental Quality.* New York: North-Holland. 1991.

Carson, R.T. and R.C. Mitchell. "The Issue of Scope in Contingent Valuation Studies". *American Journal of Agricultural Economics* 75(Dec 1993): 1263–7.

Carson, R.T., N.E. Flores, K.M. Martin and J.L. Wright. "Contingent Valuation and Revealed Preference Methodologies: Comparing the Estimates for Quasi-public Goods". *Land Economics* 72(Feb 1996): 80–99.

Freeman, A.M. *The Measurement of Environmental and Resource Values: Theory and Methods.* Washington, DC: Resources for the Future. 1993.

Griliches, Z., ed. *Price Indexes and Quality Change.* Cambridge, MA: Harvard University Press. 1971.

Hoehn, J.P. and A. Randall. "A Satisfactory Benefit Cost Indicator from Contingent Valuation". *Journal of Environmental Economics and Management* 14(1987): 226–47.

Neill, H.R., R.G. Cummings, P.T. Ganderton, G.W. Harrison and T. McGuckin. "Hypothetical Surveys and Real Economics Commitments". *Land Economics* 70(May 1994): 145–54.

Ready, R.C., J.C. Buzby and D. Hu. "Differences Between Continuous and Discrete Contingent Valuation Estimates". *Land Economics* 72(Aug 1996): 397–411.

Rosen, S. "Hedonic Prices and Implicit Markets: Products Differentiation in Perfect Competition". *Journal of Political Economy* 82(1974): 34–55.

PART II

Case Studies

3. Social costs and benefits of preserving and restoring the Nidaros Cathedral

Ståle Navrud and Jon Strand

INTRODUCTION

The main purpose of this study was to elicit the value of protecting and restoring the Nidaros Cathedral in Trondheim, Norway, which is the oldest medieval building in Scandinavia. Thus, a contingent valuation (CV) survey of visitors to the cathedral was carried out in the summer of 1991.

This valuation exercise is of interest for several reasons. First, the Nidaros Cathedral is a major, and perhaps even the most important, cultural monument in Norway. A value of this monument may serve as a benchmark against which other Norwegian and international monuments can be valued, especially at the time of the study since this was one of the very first applications of CV to cultural heritage. Second, by its design, the study provides information about the relative value of retaining the cathedral in its present state, versus restoring it in the future. Almost certainly, the value of the latter alternative will provide a lower bound for the value of the former. Restoring the cathedral is in principle always an actual future option (given that it is not completely deteriorated), while retaining it in the present state is not, whenever further future damage will be inflicted.

Third, the study provides information on methodological aspects of the CV method in an area of application where few studies had been conducted at the time. This in particular concerns embedding and scope, which deal with the question of whether respondents are able to identify their value of one particular cultural monument, versus the values of all cultural monuments, or an even more encompassing category of public goods. Another methodological issue dealt with in the study is whether it matters if the proposed payment is to be made in the form of a tax or in the form of a voluntary payment into a fund designed to protect and restore the cathedral. Theoretically, the former should be the more incentive-compatible payment mechanism and yield a lower mean value than the latter case, where individuals might act strategically and state a high willingness to pay (WTP) just to get the fund set up, and then free-ride when actual donations are collected. On the other hand, it is generally recognized that utilizing a tax payment mechanism may yield values that are biased downward, since many individuals are sceptical toward increased taxes in general and therefore protest at the payment mechanism by answering zero even when they have a positive WTP.

In the study we distinguish between two different types of protective measures:

1. Through reduced air pollution it is presumed that the present degree of originality of the Nidaros Cathedral can be retained.
2. If air pollution is not reduced, it is conceded that the cathedral will deteriorate gradually over time, and thus lose more of its original structure. In such a case we propose that the cathedral can be protected through increased maintenance and restoration.

In both cases we preserve the Nidaros Cathedral, but in the latter case it loses more of its originality, which is an irreversible effect. All respondents were asked about their WTP for each of these two types of protective measures.

THE SURVEY

The CV survey was conducted outside the Nidaros Cathedral during the summer (June–August) of 1991. 237 persons were contacted, of which 163 were willing to be interviewed in person. The main reasons for not wanting to be interviewed were a simple refusal (52%), and problems with the language (29%), having mastered neither a Scandinavian language nor English. Open-ended WTP questions (without a payment card) were used. The survey sample was split into four subsamples, in order to test for effects of different payment vehicles, and sequence and scope.

The first three questions posed to subsamples 1 and 2 were designed to make respondents aware of negative consequences of air pollution other than the corrosion and soiling of cultural monuments. They were also reminded that air pollution is just one problem among several potentially serious environmental concerns facing our society. By giving this information we wanted to put this issue in a broader context to avoid embedding effects, i.e. respondents stating their WTP for a more comprehensive good than the one they were asked for.

In the first WTP question, respondents in subsample 1 were asked for a voluntary donation to a fund, while subsample 2 was asked for increased taxes:

What is the most you are willing to pay per year, into a fund (in increased taxes), in order to protect the remaining originality of all cultural buildings and monuments in Norway?

The second valuation question to these two subsamples was then:

How much of the total amount you stated you were willing to pay in order to protect the remaining originality of all cultural buildings and monuments in Norway, do you wish to allocate to the protection of the Nidaros Cathedral?

This sequence of valuation questions implies a "top-down" approach starting with valuing the more inclusive category of public goods before valuing a single object. The main purpose of such sequencing of questions is to reduce embedding effects, by making respondents aware that the particular good valued is just one item among a larger class of goods, all of which may be valued positively. This can also be viewed as a scope test, to test whether respondents are stating a higher WTP for more than for less of a public good.

Subsamples 3 and 4 were not given any initial information about other environmental problems, nor were they subjected to the first question above. Instead, their first question was as follows:

What is the most you are willing to pay per year into a voluntary fund, in order for the entire remaining originality of the Nidaros Cathedral to be protected?

Subsamples 3 and 4 faced identical questions (where for both a voluntary contribution was used as the payment vehicle). The only difference between the two was that subsample 3 consisted of Norwegians, and subsample 4 were foreigners (whereas subsamples 1 and 2 consisted entirely of Norwegians). Thus, the only differences between subsamples 1 and 3 were the amount of information provided and the initial valuation question posed to subsample 1, both of which were designed to reduce embedding effects. Comparing the WTP from these two groups should thus potentially provide information on the impacts from the embedding problem in our survey. Subsamples 1 and 2 differ only in terms of the payment vehicle, and comparing these provides information on the effect of the payment vehicle on WTP. Correspondingly, a comparison of subsamples 3 and 4 would show potential differences in WTP between Norwegian and foreigner visitors to the cathedral.

The next question posed to all was:

You have now expressed the maximum amount you are willing to pay. How would you distribute the amount you stated to be willing to pay in order to protect the remaining originality of the Nidaros Cathedral, among the following alternative motives:

i. *The experience of visiting the Nidaros Cathedral.*
ii. *The value of protecting the Nidaros Cathedral, for others to visit it and in order to leave it intact for future generations.*
iii. *Other motives; please specify.*

This question gives an informal measure of the relative sizes of the use and non-use components of value.

The next question concerned the other specified way in which to preserve the Nidaros Cathedral, namely restoring it. The question posed was whether the value attached to restoring was greater than, less than, or the same as the value of preserving the present degree of originality. If the valuation was stated to be either greater or less, we asked a question about the most they would be willing to pay into a fund for restoration of damage inflicted on the cathedral from air pollution

After these WTP questions, a number of other questions were posed concerning the purpose of their visit to the Nidaros Cathedral, the number of visits to the cathedral in recent years and planned future visits, the nature of the trip and travel costs related to the visit, and the beliefs of respondents concerning what fraction of the cathedral's facade is original.

RESULTS

We attempt to value two different qualities of the same good: the Nidaros Cathedral preserved for the future in its current condition, and the cathedral restored to its current external (but less original) state after some future deterioration due to air pollution. These values are represented in the study by estimated WTP to prevent the cathedral from deteriorating, and for restoring it, respectively. In welfare economic terms these values represent equivalent variation measures of consumer surplus, EV. For a particular respondent this is defined as:

$$U^* (Y, Q_1) = U^* (Y - EV, Q_0) \qquad (3.1)$$

where U^* is a particular utility level for the respondent, Y is his or her income, and the quality of the good deteriorates from quality level Q_0 to Q_1 if nothing is done to reduce air pollution. Q_0 must here be identified with the two alternative qualities, namely the preservation and the restoration quality respectively, and with EV in principle taking different values in these two cases.

Table 3.1 shows that the mean WTP for protecting all cultural monuments in Norway was 1160 NOK per year (in 1991–NOK), and mean WTP for preserving (WTPP) and restoring (WTPR) the Nidaros Cathedral comprises 27 and 24% of this amount, respectively. This is of course a considerable fraction, and it may appear unreasonable that one particular building absorb one fourth of the value allocated to all Norwegian cultural buildings and monuments. On the other hand, the Nidaros Cathedral may well be the most important cultural object in Norway. In addition, the individuals surveyed have shown a particular current interest in the cathedral by actually visiting it during the time of the survey. We therefore feel there is no obvious reason to suspect serious embedding effects in our survey, although the possibility cannot be completely ruled out.

Table 3.1   Willingness to pay (WTP) for preserving or restoring the Nidaros Cathedral (NC) and all cultural monuments in Norway. WTP per respondent per year, in Norwegian Kroner (NOK), 1991 values. 1 NOK = 0.12 euro = 0.11 USD

WTP for:	Mean WTP	Standard deviation	Min WTP	Max WTP	No. of observations (N)
Preservation of all cultural monuments in Norway (WTPALL)	1,160	1,749	0	12,000	86
Preservation of NC (WTPP)	318	475	0	3,000	161
Restoration of NC (WTPR)	278	440	0	3,000	157
WTPP divided into:					
i. WTPP-USE Own experience visiting NC	44	133	0	1,000	160
ii. WTPP-NON-USE Protect NC for others and future generations	252	406	0	3,000	160

Note: A third category includes motives like the historic importance and religious value of the Nidaros Cathedral as a place of worship. These "other motives" accounted for the remaining mean WTPP of 22 NOK.

Interestingly, we note that only 44 NOK out of the mean WTP of 318 NOK to preserve the Nidaros Cathedral (WTPP), or about 14%, is on average motivated by use value. Since visitors by revealed preference are likely to be among those with the highest relative use value from the cathedral, one may suspect that this fraction is even lower in the population at large.

When comparing mean WTPP and WTPR, we see as expected that the former is greater, but only slightly; 318 versus 278 NOK. The difference is not significant at the 5% level. Concerning respondents' beliefs about the originality of the present cathedral, the fractions that believed 100, 75, 50 and 25% of the current facade is original were 3, 24, 22 and 45%, respectively. Roughly 35–50% of the facade is actually in its original state. We also found that stated WTP amounts are greater for those who believe the current facade is more original; a doubling of this share (e.g. from 25 to 50% or from 50 to 100%) raises WTPR by 47%, and WTPP increases by 31%.

On the question about the relative value of preservation versus restoring, 65% of respondents stated that preservation in the current state was more valuable, while 35% stated that the two values were the same (as expected, none stated that restoring is more valuable than preserving). Although a large majority thus prefer preservation, the mean WTPs for these two alternative protective measures were not statistically different (at the 5% level). Since a preservation question was posed to all respondents before the restoring question, there may be some anchoring from the first to the second, which may bias the stated WTPR value in the direction of stated WTPP. Another possible issue is lack of realism of the preservation alternative. This alternative requires the immediate elimination of all effects of air pollution on the facade of the cathedral, which is probably impossible to carry out in practice.

Concerning other variables, we found no significant effect on stated WTP from an increase in the number of visits to the cathedral during the year in question (1991), nor was there a significant difference between men and women.

A comparison of subsamples 1 and 3 (Table 3.2) should yield information on possible embedding effects, since the only difference between these subsamples was that information about additional possible cultural goods to be valued was given only to sample 1, and that one has also tried here to "embed" the WTP answers for the Nidaros Cathedral by first requesting WTP for a more inclusive set of cultural goods. The natural prior hypothesis is then that the embedding effect should tend to increase WTP answers from sample 3 relative to sample 1 (and relative to sample 2 as well, although the payment vehicle here was different). Correspondingly we see that average WTP figures are about 20–25% higher in sample 3 than in sample 1, pointing to possible embedding effects. It turns out that when formally tested, these differences are not statistically significant. The results in this respect are thus tentative, but indicate that a certain but perhaps not very large embedding effect is present in the material.

A comparison of samples 1 and 2 makes it possible to measure the impact of different payment vehicles, since the payment vehicle is the only difference between the surveys used for these two groups. We find that the answers here are practically identical, indicating that whatever vehicle bias is present in our survey must be equally strong for both vehicles applied.

The third type of comparison invited by the figures in Table 3.2 is between WTPP and WTPR. The prior hypothesis here is that WTPP figures should

Table 3.2 *Willingness to pay (WTP) preserving (WTPP) and restoring (WTPR) the Nidaros Cathedral for the four subsamples. In subsamples 1 and 2 the respondents were reminded that air pollution had other negative effects, and that air pollution was just one among several environmental problems. Subsamples 3 and 4 were not given this information. WTP per respondent per year, in Norwegian Kroner (NOK), 1991–values; 1 NOK = 0.12 euro = 0.11 USD*

Subsample no.	Payment vehicle	WTP measure	Mean WTP	Standard deviation	Zero WTP answers (%)	No. of observations (N)
1	Voluntary fund	WTPP	313	495	11	44
		WTPR	276	494	9	43
2	Increased taxes	WTPP	324	399	14	42
		WTPR	279	370	20	41
3	Voluntary fund	WTPP	410	623	17	35
		WTPR	400	535	15	34
4	Voluntary fund	WTPP	238	368	38	40
		WTPR	174	329	49	39

exceed WTPR figures, since the former measure the value of a presumably more valuable good, namely the Nidaros Cathedral in its present state of originality, versus the latter which express the value of the cathedral in a future, restored, state, after being exposed to air pollution damage over a more recent future period. As already commented on above, this hypothesis appears to be proven true in our data. No respondent stated WTPP lower than WTPR, while 65% of respondents gave a higher WTPP. Looking in more detail at the different samples, we find that for all samples the average WTP is greater for preservation than for restoring, but the difference is relatively small for all. It is greatest for sample 4 (foreigners) which may not be unreasonable, since it is difficult to find good reasons why foreigners should attach a particularly high value to a restored cultural monument in Norway.

A comparison of samples 3 and 4 reveals differences in valuation between Norwegians and foreigners who visited the cathedral in 1991. We see that the WTP of Norwegians is clearly higher, but this is largely due to the far greater fractions of foreign respondents stating zero WTP.

AGGREGATED BENEFITS

To calculate aggregate, annual social benefits we assume that our sample is representative of all visitors to the cathedral that year. From Table 3.1 we find that the mean WTPs per person per year for the entire sample were 318 and 278 NOK (in 1991 values) for preservation (WTPP) and restoration (WTPR), respectively. The number of visitors to the Nidaros Cathedral in 1991 was approximately 165,000. Using these WTP amounts and visitation numbers the annual benefits to all visitors of preserving and restoring the cathedral were 52.5 million and 48.9 million NOK, respectively. These estimates include both use and non-use values for the visitors.

To derive the total social benefits of the Nidaros Cathedral, we have to add the benefits to all those who attach a positive value to the cathedral but did not visit it in 1991. Note that aggregate use values among visitors were only about 14% of their aggregate WTP to restore it (Table 3.1), or approximately 7.5 and 7 million NOK, respectively, when the results above are applied. Since we do not have any data on the valuation of Nidaros Cathedral among non-users, assigning WTP values to these must be speculative since visitors are a self-selected and not a random sample of the (Norwegian and foreign) populations in this context, and not likely to be representative with respect to such valuations.

Assuming that the non-use values for non-visitors do not exceed the corresponding values for visitors, we can however derive an upper bound on total social benefits of the Nidaros Cathedral among Norwegians. Using the figures above, the annual mean non-use values among Norwegians for preserving (respectively restoring) the cathedral in 1991 were approximately 300 NOK and 275 NOK per person respectively. With about 3 million adult Norwegians (above the age of 18), the upper bound on the aggregate non-use value among all Norwegians is 900 million NOK for preservation, and 825 million NOK for restoring, respectively.

In fact it may be appropriate here to base the valuation among Norwegians not on the average figures in subsamples 1–3 as done above, but rather on the most "conservative" of these, namely the figures from subsample 1. The difference between values from subsamples 1 and 3 is likely to be due to greater embedding effects in subsample 3, biasing these figures upward (or biasing them upward more than the figures in subsample 1). Using subsample 1 alone, the mean, annual preservation and restoration values are 270 and 235 NOK per adult, respectively. This corresponds to total social benefits among the Norwegian population of 810 and 710 million NOK, respectively.

These are formidable figures, and likely to be too high for at least two reasons. First, as already noted, non-use values are most likely greater for visitors than for non-visitors on average. Second, it is possible that the visitors interviewed are not a random sample of all visitors. Remember that approximately 30% of those approached by the interviewer were unwilling to be interviewed. It is likely that the WTP among these non-respondents is lower than the WTP among respondents. This implies that the estimate for overall social benefits is biased upward, by about 30% as a maximum.

In addition there are values accruing to foreigners. The number of foreigners visiting the cathedral in 1991 can be estimated from our sample, where approximately one fourth of all persons interviewed were foreigners. Given that also one fourth of all visitors were foreigners, this means that approximately 41,000 foreigners visited the cathedral in 1991. Using the average WTP amounts of 238 and 174 NOK for foreigners from Table 3.2, sample 4, the total valuation of preserving, and restoring, the Nidaros Cathedral was approximately 10 million and 7 million NOK, respectively. Use values constituted 18% of these figures for foreigners, or about 1.8 and 1.3 million NOK, respectively, leaving 8.2 and 5.7 million NOK for passive-use values accruing to visiting foreigners under the two alternatives. However, benefits to foreign visitors would not be included in a social cost–benefit analysis (which focuses on the welfare effects on the national population).

COST–BENEFIT ANALYSIS AND POLICY IMPLICATIONS

These social benefits of preserving and restoring the Nidaros Cathedral can be compared to the social costs of preservation and restoration. Preserving the cathedral in its current state requires that air pollution be eliminated such that the facade of the cathedral is not exposed to pollution in the future. For one thing, this is practically impossible in the very short run. In the longer run a significant reduction in air pollution is possible, but we do not have any figures to indicate the relevant costs, which can be compared to preservation values.

For restoring, the calculations are simpler. There has for a long time been a restoration program for the Nidaros Cathedral, which aims to retain the outer appearance of the facade of the cathedral. In 1991 the expenditure related to this program was 9.5 million NOK. Taking this as typical of the annual cost of restoring, it is clear (given that preservation is not undertaken) that restoring the cathedral is socially beneficial, even if we only count social benefits to visitors to the cathedral. The benefit–cost ratio seems to be at least 5, meaning that each 1 NOK spent on restoring the cathedral creates 5 NOK in social benefits. Thus, restoration must be viewed as a very profitable project. The results from this analysis could be used to argue in favor of increasing the restoration budget if that was necessary to achieve a fully restored cathedral. Before opting for the restoration project, data collection for a complete cost–benefit analysis of the preservation option should also be undertaken, in order to identify the more profitable option of the two.

4. Northumbria: castles, cathedrals and towns

Guy Garrod and Kenneth G. Willis

INTRODUCTION

The United Kingdom has a rich history and many reminders of the country's past and the culture it has engendered exist in our towns and cities and in the wider countryside. These reminders range from World Heritage Sites such as Stonehenge and Hadrian's Wall, to an array of historic houses, monuments and archaeological sites, and cherished landscapes such as the Lake District, Snowdonia and the Scottish Highlands.

Like many nationalities the British are fiercely proud of their cultural heritage, while at the same time taking many of its physical manifestations somewhat for granted. Most of us rely on government agencies, charitable organizations or property owners to maintain the buildings, landscapes and other relics of our past that are the most vivid reminders of our heritage, though we may be happy for a small proportion of our taxes and charitable donations to go towards the cost of this maintenance.

If we place a high value on a particular cultural good then we may be prepared to pay to experience it. Thus, we may pay to see a production of 'As You Like It' by the Royal Shakespeare Company or to visit an art exhibition at the Tate Gallery. Similarly, where the appropriate producer property rights exist, we may choose to pay an entry charge to visit an historic building or site. If we have a high preference for such sites we may join an organization such as English Heritage or the National Trust, which will entitle us to visit the many historic buildings and sites that these organizations manage on behalf of the nation.

Clearly the demand for many aspects of culture can be measured and valued in the market place like any other economic good, and in practice many cultural goods are no different from the millions of private goods which are traded every day. For example, Bovaird et al. (1984) undertook a recreational demand analysis of historic houses in England owned by the National Trust and were able to calculate price elasticities of demand for these sites. Other cultural goods may benefit society but do not attract a market price and have more in common with environmental goods such as amenity woodland or rivers.

This chapter concentrates on Northumbria, an area in the North East of England with a distinctive character and history, and attempts to estimate the value of three sites that have particular cultural associations for people in the area. Each of the sites investigated is different in terms of its similarity to conventional marketed goods. In the first case, Warkworth Castle, access to the castle interior is only available after the payment of an entrance charge whereas visitors to the second case site, Durham Cathedral, are only asked to make a voluntary donation. By contrast the third case, Newcastle's Grainger Town, is a commercial area with a wealth of historic buildings, the exteriors of which can be enjoyed free of charge. Non-market valuation techniques permit aspects of the cultural benefits of each of these sites to be estimated.

These three cultural goods are static, and their market is bounded by how far people are prepared to travel to experience them. All are extremely expensive to maintain, a cost which is principally borne by their owners or occupants. However, visitors to these areas can enjoy the exterior ambience of the buildings free of charge. The fact that owners of these historic buildings cannot charge for the 'public good' benefits they provide means that these historic sites attract a lower rate of return from their private use, compared with their total value to society, and too little may be spent on maintaining them. Thus for cultural goods, with 'public good' characteristics, society faces the dilemma of assessing what they are worth, how they should be paid for, and who should pay for them. The studies reported in this chapter use a contingent valuation approach to address some aspects of the first two questions.

WARKWORTH CASTLE

Where visitors have to pay for access to a cultural good, a considerable amount of information exists from which to calculate demand curves and price elasticities. What is less certain is the magnitude of any consumer surplus that visitors may derive over and above the amount they pay and the number and value of any additional visits that would accrue if the entry charge was reduced. Such information may be of considerable importance in terms of pricing policy or in justifying support payments.

If contingent valuation studies are to prove useful in such cases, they should provoke responses that are similar to the behaviour that would be observed if the scenario used were enacted in reality. This is the criterion validity test outlined by Mitchell and Carson (1989) and discussed in Chapter 2. This issue was examined in a study that investigated differences between individuals' actual and stated behaviour when faced with the decision to purchase a cultural good. The study measured willingness to pay (WTP) to enter Warkworth Castle in Northumberland, a former stronghold of the powerful Percy family.

Warkworth Castle is located in a picturesque village on a popular coastal route and, although largely a ruin, retains an attractive facade; most of the early thirteenth century gatehouse and fifteenth century castle keep remain intact. Warkworth Castle attracted some 63,000 visitors in 1994; it is owned and managed by English Heritage, a government agency.

The main problem in testing the criterion validity of WTP estimates lies in devising a criterion that is better than the measure (the contingent valuation estimate), the validity of which is being assessed. In this case a real economic commitment provided such a criterion, and offered the opportunity to conduct an illuminating experiment. From their experiences of visiting similar properties most visitors to historic properties can make a reasonable estimate of the likely entry charge. Some households and individuals never attempt to visit such properties, being deterred by their perception of the entry charge. However, a number of potential visitors throughout the course of a day approach historical properties with a view to entering, and can be observed looking at signs detailing the entrance charges and deciding whether or not to enter. These prospective visitors were the subject of the Warkworth study.

Although the majority of individuals decided to pay the entrance charge and enter Warkworth Castle, a significant minority were observed who made a decision not to enter because of price, which at the date of the survey (1994) was £1.80 per person (see Willis and Powe, 1998). These potential visitors were asked their maximum willingness to pay to visit the castle and then offered a ticket, at the price they stated, that would permit them to enter the castle. This take-it-or-leave-it approach provided a real monetary test of whether potential visitors were truly willing to pay what they said they would pay. *A priori*, it was hypothesized that if the respondent did not accept the tickets at his or her stated price, then expressed WTP would be biased, or the behavioural intention flawed.

The survey was designed so that visitors who were prepared to pay the full entrance charge were not able to purchase reduced-price tickets through the survey. In order to be interviewed as a potential visitor, a given respondent had first to look at the sign detailing the entrance charges but not enter the castle. Respondents were then interviewed in the ordinary way, and after some introductory questions were asked if they had considered entering the castle today. If they were potential visitors, their maximum WTP to enter the castle was elicited and at the end of the questionnaire they were offered the tickets at their stated price. If they did not accept the tickets then their reason for not accepting was noted. If they accepted, the respondents were discretely given the tickets and asked not to discuss the transaction with other visitors. Furthermore, caution was taken not to conduct the survey on the same day each week to avoid strategic behaviour. By adopting such measures respondents had no prior knowledge of the possibility of obtaining cheap entry tickets.

The results of this real monetary test are provided in Table 4.1. These results cast some doubt over the usefulness of benefit estimates for cultural and heritage goods based on WTP to gain access. Of the 97 respondents fulfilling the potential visitor criterion, 54 did not consider themselves as potential visitors on the day interviewed. Although each respondent approached had first looked at the sign detailing the entrance charges and then walked towards the entrance of the castle and looked inside, this did not prove to be a sufficient test for those considering entering.

Table 4.1   *Responses to real monetary test of potential visitors' maximum willingness to pay to enter Warkworth Castle*

	Frequency	Mean WTP (£, 1994)	Standard error (£)
Accepting tickets	17	0.94	0.11
Not accepting tickets	17	1.17	0.03
Intending to enter later	9	2.40	0.29
Not potential visitors	54	0.69	0.13
Total	97		

Of the 43 respondents who considered themselves as potential visitors, 17 refused the tickets at their stated maximum WTP, 17 accepted, and nine gave a maximum WTP in excess of the entrance charge and stated that they intended to enter later. The most common reason given for refusing the tickets (nine respondents) was that they did not have enough time to enter the site. This would clearly suggest that, although they initially stated they were potential visitors, when subject to a real test this was not the case. Whilst the respondents spent some time considering whether to enter, in the final analysis they were ambivalent about their behavioural decision and about their stated WTP value.

The Warkworth Castle study suggests that at least some of the respondents (40%, i.e. 17/43) may have correctly indicated their maximum WTP to enter the castle, and made a real economic commitment by entering the castle at that price. The usefulness of the other 60% of responses was questionable. The mean WTP responses of this latter doubtful validity group were higher than for those who accepted the ticket. However, the difference between the 'accepting ticket' and 'not accepting ticket' groups was not statistically significant; although mean WTP between these groups and the 'intending to enter later' group was significant at a 95% probability level.

In assessing the 'truth' of contingent valuation model (CVM) responses there are two questions of relevance: how accurate is the respondent's stated WTP amount; will the intention to participate or consume the environmental good be translated into actual behaviour?

Fishbein and Ajzen (1975) suggested conditions where the similarity between intention and behaviour is likely to be maximized. They postulated that accuracy will be greatest where there is: (a) correspondence between the question asked and the inference drawn; (b) proximity between the survey stage and the behavioural intention stage; and (c) familiarity with the consequence of the change in the quantity, and quality, of the good. The Warkworth study came close to meeting the Fishbein–Ajzen conditions: individuals were teetering on the brink of purchasing the good in the real world, one or two minutes prior to the survey. Yet despite this, the study suggested that a substantial proportion of WTP values elicited were neither very robust nor reliable, and subject to considerable ambivalence. So even when the survey was juxtaposed to the behavioural intention stage, a substantial proportion of stated WTP values were not translated into real economic commitments and purchases. Perhaps this should not be surprising from a knowledge of the actual market place. Individuals often make a purposeful trip to purchase a good only to inspect the good closely and decide not to buy. The problem is that some contingent valuation surveys treat such individuals as valid respondents and count their WTP as an element of the total utility of the good. As a consequence, non-market goods may be overvalued in aggregate. Contingent valuation studies need to adopt stringent criteria in deciding the legitimacy of responses, especially if they cannot be judged against real economic commitments.

While these results are somewhat negative regarding the reliability of individual WTP responses, they are more supportive of the aggregated responses. Suppose that hypothetical WTP (aWTP) is some random variable correlated to actual WTP (hWTP), for example hWTP = aWTP + e, where e is some error term. In a well calibrated model in which e has zero mean, such that $E[hWTP] = E[aWTP]$, about half the respondents will overstate aWTP, with the other half understating aWTP. This is precisely what is observed. For those who can visit the castle immediately, exactly half overstate aWTP and half understate aWTP, with no statistical difference in mean stated WTP between the two groups. Clearly, not everyone will accept the offer, otherwise, if there is any error at all, the aggregated values would be too conservative. The point is analogous to that in standard gamble experiments where utility is estimated with respect to the point of indifference; where the outcome can be decided on the toss of a coin. This implies that half the respondents will choose the good, whilst the other half keep the money to spend on other things.

DURHAM CATHEDRAL

Many buildings of architectural and historical significance in the UK permit entry free of charge. This is the case with many of the country's finest cathedrals, including York Minster, Gloucester, and St. Giles, Edinburgh. Another such building is Durham Cathedral, founded in 1093 as a Benedictine Abbey and a shrine for the body of St. Cuthbert, and now part of a World Heritage Site. Visitors entering the cathedral are, however, confronted with a large donation chest, and a prominent notice informing visitors that the ancient building is expensive to maintain and repair, with a suggested donation amount (in 1993, £1 per visitor and in 1997, £2). On most days, an additional visitor to the interior of Durham Cathedral will not reduce the utility that others derive from visiting the cathedral, and in such circumstances the optimal admission charge is zero. Nevertheless, given ownership rights by the Dean and Chapter of the cathedral, visitors could be excluded and a price charged for admission as at Salisbury Cathedral.

Because of the fixed nature of supply, it is possible to estimate the value of visiting the cathedral by modelling the effect of a price change on visitor behaviour. To this end a contingent valuation survey attempted to measure consumer surplus by asking visitors as they left the cathedral the maximum they would have been willing to pay to gain access for their current visit (excluding those areas for which a charge was levied). Any increase in price would lead to a welfare loss, so an equivalent variation measure was employed to measure the change. In effect, the difference between the current price (i.e. the voluntary donation) and the maximum WTP gives a measure of the maximum that the individual would be prepared to pay to avert the introduction of an admission charge.

Of 92 respondents with fully completed questionnaires in the survey, 51% stated they had made no voluntary contribution for their visit. Only 12% of respondents had contributed in excess of the suggested £1 donation level for their current visit; although 27% had contributed between 50 pence and £1. The average reported contribution made was 43 pence. When asked, if they had to pay an entry fee to gain access to the cathedral, what would be the maximum they would be willing to pay, only 36% said they would be unwilling to pay anything; 31% stated a maximum WTP in excess of £1 for their current visit, compared with only 12% of visitors making a contribution of that magnitude. Overall, the mean stated WTP was 77 pence.

Clearly, the current management arrangement permits a certain amount of free-riding for what is in reality a private good. Despite an attempt to engender a sense of moral obligation on the part of visitors to make a voluntary contribution, the level of contributions falls short of that which would be attained if the Dean and Chapter behaved as a perfectly discriminating monopolist and took full advantage of the private good nature of access to the cathedral. Of course, unlike God, the Dean and Chapter lack omniscience, and would be unable to fulfil this demanding role. One alternative would be to charge a single compulsory price which maximized revenue. The price at which revenue is maximized depends upon the elasticity of demand with respect to price; with revenue being maximized where the price elasticity of demand equals -1. This position is illustrated in Table 4.2, which shows the aggregate contributions under various price levels, assuming an entrance charge at the mid-point in each contribution level. From a position of no entry fee, the nominal visit rate of 100 declines as price increases and aggregate revenue increases then declines, reaching a maximum at 87.5 pence, which yields an aggregate revenue of £42.88.

Table 4.2   Aggregate revenue per 100 visitors at various entrance price levels

Entrance charge (£, 1993)	Visit rate	Aggregate revenue (£, 1993)
0.000	100	0.00
0.125	64	8.00
0.375	61	22.88
0.625	52	32.50
0.875	49	42.88
1.125	31	34.88
1.375	23	31.63
1.625	19	30.68
1.875	15	28.13
2.250	8	18.00
2.750	5	13.75
3.250	3	9.75
3.750	0	0.00

As Table 4.2 shows, a compulsory charge of 87.5 pence would result in visit numbers declining to 49% of their current levels. Moreover, existing aggregate voluntary contributions per 100 visits at the current zero entry charge amounted to £43.52. Thus the current policy of voluntary contributions results in the same marginal revenue as that which would be generated under a compulsory entrance charge (though even with an entry charge it is anticipated that some donations would continue to be made, reflecting consumer surplus above the entry charge) (Willis, 1994).

Of course, it may be possible to increase aggregate income by introducing a differential price structure, for example by allowing different groups (e.g. the unwaged) admission at a lower price set to maximize revenue from that group. Price discrimination offers a mechanism to maximize revenue which is relatively undeveloped in admissions to buildings of architectural and historic interest compared to its use in other areas, and the work of Bovaird *et al.* (1984)

suggests that there is considerable scope for increasing the use of such mechanisms. Frequency of visits is another obvious candidate for price discrimination, with the possibility of introducing season tickets for frequent visitors. Indeed, the Durham Cathedral study suggested that frequent visitors contributed less per visit, although they were willing to pay more in aggregate. In cases such as this, price discrimination by frequency of visit could yield a higher revenue than the voluntary contribution, though increased transactions costs could reduce the net benefits of such an approach to the cathedral.

GRAINGER TOWN, NEWCASTLE-UPON-TYNE

The renovation of an area of historic buildings may generate a number of economic benefits. Some of these benefits will be derived from the increased commercial value of the property; whilst non-priced benefits will arise to local people and visitors. In Newcastle-upon-Tyne, although many of the buildings date back to the first half of the nineteenth century, the layout of the Grainger Town area of Newcastle's city centre has its origins in the original medieval street pattern. Large scale replanning of the city centre was undertaken by the developer Richard Grainger and the architect John Dobson between 1834 and

Photograph 4.1   The Grey Street area of Grainger Town

Photograph 4.2   Decline in the Clayton Street area of Grainger Town

1839, when a new city centre was inserted into the northern area of the medieval walled town. This development, now termed 'Grainger Town', is considered one of the finest examples of town planning in England and, unlike earlier examples of town planning which were primarily aimed at the residential sector, the area was designed principally for commercial use (see Photograph 4.1).

One of the main problems of the Grainger Town area is the underuse of the historic buildings, principally their upper floors, due to the changing needs of the occupiers; a problem exacerbated by changing shopping patterns associated in part with the development of a large indoor shopping centre immediately to the north of the Grainger Town area. In streets where underuse of upper floors occurs, commercial returns on the building are reduced and the building becomes poorly maintained, creating an impression of decline and dereliction (see Photograph 4.2). A strategy was proposed to rectify this situation with a combination of support from the private sector and grant aid from the public sector (which would ultimately be derived from local tax payments, i.e. a banded council tax based on local property values). To investigate the public accept-ability of such a strategy, a contingent valuation study sought to determine how much citizens of Newcastle would be willing to pay towards the restoration of historic buildings in Grainger Town (Garrod *et al.*, 1996).

Although almost 90% of respondents in the survey recognized the need to renovate the older and more historic buildings in Grainger Town, only 53%

Table 4.3 OLS regression model of willingness to pay bids

Variable	Parameter estimate	t-Value
Intercept term	0.8951	4.92
Respondent shops, eats, drinks and conducts other recreational activities in Grainger Town	0.6887	3.41
Household has two or more cars	0.3449	1.54
Number of children in household	−0.2734	−2.22
Respondent considers need to renovate and regenerate buildings in Grainger Town as a problem in need of urgent and immediate attention	1.0646	5.34
Member of National Trust in household	0.6327	2.64
Member of local history society in household	0.9267	2.08
Respondent is unemployed or otherwise economically non-active (but not retired)	−0.4256	−1.63

Note: $n = 162$, $R^2 = 41.1\%$, R^2(adj.) = 38.4%.

were willing to pay additional council tax to support the initiative. The main reasons for respondents not wishing to contribute were that they felt they already paid enough council tax, or believed the upkeep of the buildings was the responsibility of the owners. Mean WTP for the renovation and restoration of buildings in Grainger Town was £13.76 per household per year (1995 prices), with a median of £10.00. Truncating the distribution by 5% reduced mean WTP to £11.67; whilst a 10% truncation reduced the mean bid to £10.11. In terms of its construct validity (conformity with theoretical economic expectations), 40% of the variation in WTP between households was explained by the model outlined in Table 4.3. This is quite a high level of explanation for a contingent valuation study, and provided strong evidence that respondents' WTP bids were not random responses.

Distributing WTP amounts by the council tax band into which the respondent's property was grouped, and aggregating over the number of properties in Newcastle in these council tax bands, after adjustment, produced an aggregate value for the Grainger Town renovations of £0.95 million per year. Whilst not a huge sum, the Grainger Town strategy is contingent on a 50% leverage of private funding for the renovation of buildings, which would increase available funding considerably. Regeneration will proceed over a number of years and, assuming they are brought back into beneficial economic use, the renovated buildings will have a long project life providing a future stream of discounted benefits.

CONCLUSIONS

The studies reported in this chapter have demonstrated that expressed preference techniques, such as contingent valuation, can be used to establish the non-market benefits of cultural goods and thus suggest means of generating revenue to support their continued provision. While the Durham Cathedral contingent valuation study estimated the magnitude of an entry fee that would maximize revenue for the church authorities, the Warkworth Castle experiment suggested it is not always easy to replicate actual consumer behaviour through expressed preference techniques. These techniques may prove more successful in estimating the potential benefits of restoring and renovating cultural goods, and the final case study illustrated this when local people were asked to value improvements to Grainger Town, an historic area at the heart of the city of Newcastle-upon-Tyne.

Use of such techniques may dismay some commentators who argue that non-market valuation techniques are adopted by policymakers as a means of rationalizing pro-development decisions that will reduce the supply of environmental, or in these cases cultural, goods. Ironically, unless these techniques are correctly applied they can (and often do) suggest that public goods should be provided when the general public's real preferences for the good do not support such a conclusion (see Hoehn and Randall, 1989).

Assuming that the correct quantity of the cultural heritage good has been identified, and this includes a 'public good' element, the major question is how should this element of the cultural heritage commodity be funded? In some cases it may be possible to subsidize the public good attributes of a site through exploiting certain of its other more marketable aspects. This can involve charging users for access to excludable parts of the site, or by sales of literature and information about it. This happens in many historic buildings and sites in the UK.

Many organizations make strenuous efforts to maximize revenue from visitor activities. But for some organizations, such as English Heritage, this use value revenue is only a small proportion of expenditure required to maintain its historical heritage stock. In 1991/92, for example, English Heritage spent some £102.9 million, but only derived £12.7 million (12.3%) of this from income for admissions, membership fees, and sales of souvenirs; the £90.2 million remainder was provided by the government as grant aid. Despite considerable efforts to increase non-grant income, in 1996/97 non-grant income had only increased to 19% of expenditure. Whilst a policy objective of maximizing income from visitor activities is laudable for organizations such as English Heritage, the cultural goods which they provide have numerous public good elements. These public good elements are never likely to be funded from visitor charges alone.

In practice this leaves a large proportion of the public good element of the cultural commodity to be provided through some other mechanism. Ideally the mechanism utilized should result in a Lindahl equilibrium, where each individual contributes in direct proportion to what the cultural good is worth to them. Different individuals will, however, have different preferences and values for different cultural goods, and for the various public good elements of these goods. Inevitably the public good element of different types of cultural goods will need to be funded through taxation, a mechanism which may have a distortionary effect on the economy.

An additional complication is that some cultural heritage goods will also have local public good elements. For example, the external architectural and historic fabric of Grainger Town can be enjoyed free of charge by visitors because excludability is impractical or inefficient. Local residents and businesses contribute towards the maintenance of the area through ownership of the buildings or through local tax payments, part of which are devoted towards the preservation of the fabric of the area.

Visitors contribute indirectly in the sense that the hotels in which they stay pay commercial local taxation rates. However, this amount is often less than the benefit they derive from the local public good. To help maintain local public goods visitors could pay directly through the introduction of local hotel taxes, the proceeds of which would be used for the maintenance of the same aspects of local culture that attracted them to the area. Spatially differentiated taxation aimed at visitors and tourists is adopted in some areas of the world and may go some way towards promoting a more equitable allocation of the costs of local public goods. Of course the amounts which individuals should contribute, and the type and attributes of the cultural goods that should be provided, depend upon the demand for such goods and the benefits that people derive from them. Non-market valuation studies such as those outlined in this chapter provide some useful insights for such decisions.

ACKNOWLEDGEMENT

The photographs of Grainger Town were taken by Sarah Cherrill.

REFERENCES

Bovaird, A.G., M.G. Tricker and R. Stoakes (1984), *Recreation Management and Pricing: The Effect of Charging Policy on Demand at Countryside Recreation Sites*, Aldershot: Gower.

Fishbein, M. and I. Ajzen (1975), *Belief, Attitude, Intention and Behaviour: An Introduction to Theory and Research*, Reading, MA: Addison-Wesley.

Garrod, G.D., K.G. Willis, H. Bjarnadottir and P. Cockbain (1996), The Non-Priced Benefits of Renovating Historic Buildings: A Case Study of Newcastle's Grainger Town. *Cities* 13, 423–30.

Hoehn, J.P. and A. Randall (1989), Too Many Proposals Pass the Cost–Benefit Test. *American Economic Review* 79, 544–51.

Mitchell, R.C. and R.T. Carson (1989), *Using Surveys to Value Public Goods: The Contingent Valuation Method*, Washington, DC: Resources for the Future.

Willis, K.G. (1994), Paying for Heritage: What Price for Durham Cathedral? *Journal of Environmental Planning and Management* 37, 267–78.

Willis, K.G. and N.A. Powe (1998), Contingent Valuation and Real Economic Commitments: A Private Good Experiment. *Journal of Environmental Planning and Management* 41, 611–19.

5. Valuing the impacts of air pollution on Lincoln Cathedral

Marilena Pollicino and David Maddison

INTRODUCTION

Lincoln is a small city of just under 100,000 inhabitants in the east of England. The importance of the city dates back to Roman times, although few physical reminders of that period remain. Without doubt, the most notable feature of the city is its cathedral, dating from shortly after the Norman conquest. The cathedral is built on a chalk cliff and dominates not only the city itself but also much of the surrounding countryside. Indeed, until the construction of the Eiffel Tower, Lincoln Cathedral was, remarkably, the tallest man-made object in the world. Unfortunately, although Lincoln Cathedral is one of the largest and arguably most beautiful cathedrals in the UK, it is nonetheless suffering significant damage caused by air pollution. Much of this air pollution would at one time have been caused by power stations situated along the Trent Valley to the west. Nowadays, however, it seems probable that much of the soiling which is so evident on the exterior of the building is caused by road transport within the city itself. The objective of this study is to evaluate the gross benefits arising from a hypothetical cleaning programme applied to Lincoln Cathedral. These benefits are expressed in monetary terms through the implementation of a contingent valuation method (CVM) survey. In this way the true scale of the problem can be assessed. The survey also probes individuals' attitudinal beliefs with regard to air pollution in general, and its impact on the cathedral in particular, and builds upon earlier work (Yates *et al.*, 1998).

Monetary values for air pollution impacts are obtained in this study using CVM. Respondents were presented with different photographs which show the cathedral as it appears now, as well as how it would appear in the future under two different cleaning programmes. Individuals are informed that these cleaning programmes would impact to a differing degree upon the annual tax bill paid by their household. The individual is then asked which of the hypothesized cleaning programmes they would support. From these data household willingness to pay for the cleaning programmes can be inferred.

This study is only the third in the UK to utilize the CVM technique for the purposes of valuing general changes in the appearance of historical monuments. The first was on Durham Cathedral and posited a hypothetical per visit charge for 'maintenance purposes'. The second was on willingness to pay to renovate the historic Grainger Town area of Newcastle (see Chapter 4 for details on both of these studies). Another CVM study aimed at evaluating the benefits associated with the change in road layout surrounding the Stonehenge site in Wiltshire (see Chapter 7). Only the Lincoln Cathedral study focuses on the impacts of air pollution rather than the more general threats to cultural heritage.

The remainder of the chapter is organized as follows: the next section explains how the present survey was designed. The following two sections examine the demographic characteristics of the respondents to the questionnaire and their attitudinal beliefs respectively. The fifth section analyses the data in terms of whether the responses are consistent with the expressed attitudinal beliefs of the respondents, whether the method suffers design limitations, and the general influence of the socio-economic characteristics of the respondents on their willingness to pay. The sixth section takes these values and aggregates them over all households in Lincolnshire. These benefits are expressed in terms of a charge for the annual depreciation in the appearance of the building. The final section concludes with a discussion of the achievements and limitations of the present study, along with opportunities for future research in this area.

DESIGN AND IMPLEMENTATION OF THE QUESTIONNAIRE FOR LINCOLN CATHEDRAL

The survey instrument for Lincoln Cathedral was divided into a number of sections. Section A contained questions relating to the knowledge and attitudes of the respondents towards air pollution. It also asked respondents about how frequently they visited the cathedral, as well as their reasons for doing so. Section B focused on the valuation questions, and here the questionnaire was divided into a number of differing versions. More specifically, each individual was randomly assigned one of four alternative versions, each of which was characterized by different payment levels. A series of debriefing questions was also included, in order to better understand the motives underlying an individual's willingness to pay or refusal to pay. Section C gathered information on the socio-economic characteristics of the individual. The survey was designed in such a way as to respect the National Oceanic and Atmospheric Administration (NOAA) panel guidelines (Federal Register, 1993).

The survey was issued in Lincoln as well as in different towns of Lincolnshire by means of face-to-face interviews with people in the street. These interviews took place over a period of three months beginning in April 1998. Individuals were not informed in advance about the subject and purpose of the questionnaire until their participation had been secured. The structure and wording of the questionnaire were guided by an earlier pilot study undertaken with the intention of testing the comprehension and acceptability of various statements. The pilot study was conducted by interviewing 60 people in Lincoln. The main survey contained most of the questions present in the pilot, without many substantial changes. The question of how much people would be willing to pay to reduce air pollution impacts on the cathedral was approached by creating a hypothetical scenario in which individuals were confronted with the question of whether to have the cathedral cleaned more frequently, albeit at greater personal cost. This approach was adopted in order to avoid the unwanted inclusion of other values relating to the more general benefits of air pollution. Individuals were informed that the source of air pollution affecting the cathedral was mainly traffic and electricity generation. Photographic materials and detailed descriptions of the damage inflicted upon the cathedral by air pollution were provided in order to show people how different cleaning programmes could produce different effects on the appearance of the buildings. These photographs illustrated the situation midway through two hypothetical cleaning cycles (see Photograph 5.1).

Considerable effort was expended searching archives in order to find suitable photographs to illustrate the changes in appearance of the building associated with the different cleaning cycles. These photographs depict the same features but immediately after cleaning, five years after cleaning and 20 years after cleaning. Hence, they illustrate the situation midway through a 10 and 40-year cleaning cycle respectively. Thus individuals are in effect being asked to value 15 years' accumulation of dirt on the exterior of the cathedral.[1] It is important to emphasize that what is being valued is only a change in the appearance of the cathedral following cleaning, rather than a more inclusive general maintenance programme. The most cleaning can achieve is the removal of the accumulated dirt on the exterior of the building. The consumption of stone and associated loss of detail is not so easily repaired. Accordingly, the hypothetical cleaning programme aims at measuring only a subset of the effects of air pollution on the cathedral. It was also proposed that, out of the many different cleaning techniques that could be applied, the method employed would not cause any significant damage to the stonework. In this way the effect that substandard cleaning techniques might have on individual willingness to pay for the cleaning programme was dealt with. In addition, no reference was made to the scaffolding and other temporary structures that might be erected in the process of cleaning, and the impact these might have on the appearance of the cathedral.

The chosen payment vehicle was an increase in annually paid household taxes required to pay for the shorter cleaning cycle. The idea that the Council

Photograph 5.1   Change in appearance after cleaning of Lincoln Cathedral

might be compelled to raise taxes in order to finance the proposed scenario seems plausible, and until recently the Council did indeed require tax revenues for precisely this purpose. The current scenario involving the 40-year cleaning cycle was held not to require additional taxes.

The respondents' willingness to pay to move from the 40-year cleaning cycle to the 10-year cycle was elicited using the double-bounded dichotomous choice technique. More specifically, each of the respondents was asked if they would be willing to pay a certain amount of money in order to move to the shorter cleaning cycle. Depending upon the response obtained, each individual was then asked whether they would pay a lesser or greater amount. Four different starting points were used in the survey: £5 (followed by £3 or £10), £20 (followed by £15 or £30), £35 (followed by £25 or £50) and £60 (followed by £40 or £100). The use of a yes/no format simplifies the problem confronting the respondent and accordingly is also able to reduce the number of non-responses by making it cognitively easier for respondents to successfully complete the valuation procedure. The pretest revealed that the scenario, even though hypothetical, was considered plausible and easy to understand.

DEMOGRAPHIC PROFILE OF THE RESPONDENTS

In total 328 questionnaires were completed. About 30% of those approached agreed to be interviewed. Of the completed questionnaires, 108 were distributed in some of the small towns surrounding Lincoln, namely Grantham, Louth, Market Rasen and Sleaford whilst 220 were distributed in Lincoln itself. The two sexes were equally well represented: 163 male and 165 females were interviewed. The average age of the interviewees was 43 years.

In terms of educational attainment, 10% of the sample attended only primary school, whilst 35% possessed only O levels or equivalent. 18% had A levels or equivalent, whilst 9% presented professional qualifications or had attended college. 21% of the sample had a first degree or professional equivalent, whilst 6% of the sample had higher degrees. The average age at which people exited full-time education was 19 years. In terms of their occupation, 34% of people interviewed had a professional or managerial job, 38% had a skilled or semi-skilled job, 11% were unskilled and 17% declared themselves to be unemployed, housewives or retired. Average monthly after-tax household income was £1,298. Average household size was 2.7 persons. These demographics compare reasonably well with the demographic characteristics of the East Midlands region as a whole.

Of the people interviewed 5% were members of English Heritage, 16% were members of the National Trust and 12% were members of other environmental or cultural societies and organizations.

The completion rate of the questionnaires was excellent. Just two respondents preferred not to reveal at what age they completed their education. Four respondents did not like to declare their educational level, and 22 respondents did not declare their income. The latter constitutes a refusal rate of just 7%, which is far lower than that reported by most other CVM studies.

ANALYSIS OF ATTITUDES

The first part of the questionnaire was intended to probe the attitudes of respondents with regard to their personal views on air pollution in general and its impact on Lincoln Cathedral in particular. Also included were questions designed to reveal as much as possible about the underlying motives for supporting the cleaning of the cathedral, so as to aid in the interpretation of the values which emerge.

The questionnaire recorded the damages from air pollution which were of major concern to the respondents themselves. These were mentioned spontaneously by the respondents without prompting. Predictably the main concern was the health effects of air pollution (80%), followed by ecosystem impacts (38%). Third, however, was the impact of air pollution upon buildings, a concern for 19% of respondents. This indicates that damage to buildings is a major concern for a large number of people.

A very high percentage of respondents (94%) had visited the cathedral. Given that the sample was drawn exclusively from Lincolnshire this high figure is unsurprising. The survey also discovered that 32% of people interviewed visited the cathedral less than once a year, 29% once or twice a year, and 33% more than twice a year. The most frequently cited reason for visiting the cathedral was just to look at it (90%). Only a small percentage of respondents went to the cathedral for religious reasons or cultural events. This makes clear the importance of the good physical appearance of the cathedral.

A number of attitudinal statements were read to the interviewees, who were then asked whether or not they agreed with each statement. The first of these questions asked individuals whether the cathedral has a value for people even if they never visit it. Respondents overwhelmingly agreed with this statement, indicating that existence values might be an important component of overall values. A large number of individuals are also, at least in principle, prepared to pay something in order to protect the cathedral. The responses given to the final two attitudinal questions appear to contradict one another. A large majority think that the cathedral should be protected at all costs, whilst a similarly large number think that there are more important things to worry about than the cathedral. Evidently individuals do not always stop to think about the implications that open-ended statements such as 'The cathedral should be protected at all costs' might have. This underlines an important difference between the different kinds of information provided by mere statements of support and actual willingness to pay.

STATISTICAL ANALYSIS OF THE WILLINGNESS TO PAY RESULTS

This section presents various statistical analyses of the data generated by the questionnaire. These analyses are all run on a restricted sample of the data. More specifically, the sample excludes 57 respondents who refused to pay anything, saying instead that the Church should pay, visitors should pay, the Council should pay, the polluters should pay or similar. Also excluded are 12 individuals who said that yes, they were willing to pay, but were uncertain about their ability to do so. Individuals who refused to pay anything because they were insolvent, because they did not care, because they did not think the damage caused by air pollution was so very bad or there were more important things to spend money on were of course retained in the sample, along with the receptives (i.e. people who volunteered to pay something).

Table 5.1 records the percentage of respondents accepting each bid level. The table indicates that 10% of individuals questioned would not even pay £3 per annum to switch to the higher frequency cleaning cycle, whereas 8% of individuals would pay at least £100 to affect the change. The table broadly indicates that as the bid level is increased, the number of individuals willing to pay the amount tails off. It is noticeable, however, that the inverse relationship between the bid level and the percentage of individuals who are willing to pay is not at all a smooth one. Part of the reason for this is the influence of starting point bias (see below).

The data are also analysed using regression techniques. More specifically, a regression equation is developed which predicts the probability of an individual accepting a given bid level contingent upon a large number of other covariates. The maximum likelihood technique employed for this purpose accounts for the censored nature of the data and uses the standardized cumulative normal distribution to map the probability of acceptance onto the unit interval. The log-likelihood (LL) function used to determine the parameter values is given by:

$$\begin{aligned}LL = {} & YY \times \log(\Phi(\alpha \times X + \beta + HB)) + YN \times \log(\Phi(\alpha \times X + \beta \times IB) \\ & - \Phi(\alpha \times X + \beta \times HB)) + NY \times \log(\Phi(\alpha \times X + \beta \times LB) \\ & - \Phi(\alpha \times X + \beta \times IB)) + NN \times \log(1 - \Phi(\alpha \times X + \beta \times LB))\end{aligned}$$

where YY takes the value unity if the individual agrees to pay the first and second bid level and zero otherwise, YN takes the value unity if the individual agrees to pay the first but not the second bid level and zero otherwise, and so on. Φ is the cumulative standardized normal distribution, α is a vector of parameters, X is a vector of covariates and β is another parameter. HB, IB and LB are the highest, and intermediate and lowest bid levels respectively. The LL function is maximized over all observations with respect to the parameter values. The maximum likelihood parameter estimates are given in Table 5.2.

Table 5.1   The relationship between bid level and propensity to accept

Bid level	Percentage acceptances
£3	90%
£5	87%
£10	63%
£15	80%
£20	74%
£25	72%
£30	30%
£35	62%
£40	63%
£50	28%
£60	43%
£100	8%

Source: See text.

An important aspect within any CVM study is whether the answers given can be shown to have a basis in the attitudinal beliefs expressed by the respondents as well as by their socio-economic characteristics. Model 1 contains various attitudinal variables as well as a large number of socio-economic variables. It is seen that individuals who are members of the National Trust or English Heritage are willing to pay significantly more than those who are not. Those who said they were concerned about the impact of air pollution on buildings, or those who visited the cathedral more than twice a year, were also willing to pay more, but neither of these variables was significant at the 95% level. Possibly the reason for the insignificance of the latter variable was that the question fails to distinguish between those individuals who visit the cathedral much more regularly, perhaps even on a weekly basis.

Table 5.2   Empirical models showing the probability of payment

	Model 1	Model 2	Model 3
Constant	−2.53280	0.109618	0.188121
	(−2.33894)	(0.205052)	(0.930613)
Respondent lives in Lincoln	0.298280	0.426095	0.415992
	(1.42662)	(2.47176)	(2.44229)
Male	−0.198142	−0.128846	
	(−1.24056)	(−0.864330)	
Age	−0.41E–02	0.25E–03	
	(−0.595727)	(0.041916)	
Monthly after-tax income of the	0.51E–03	0.59E–03	0.61E–03
household/family size	(2.31479)	(2.94611)	(3.07284)
Educational level	−0.60E–02	0.73E–02	
	(−0.237180)	(0.325586)	
Starting point	0.037108	0.031193	0.031040
	(6.72503)	(6.36556)	(6.36930)
Bid level	−0.056876	−0.049159	−0.049128
	(−13.6091)	(−13.1103)	(−13.1154)
English Heritage and/or	0.621450		
National Trust member	(3.06559)		
Concerned about effect of air	0.360338		
pollution on buildings	(1.48229)		
Visits the cathedral more than	0.024477		
twice a year	(0.130689)		
Thinks the Cathedral should be	0.264437		
protected at all costs	(1.89139)		
Would not mind paying to protect	0.822792		
the Cathedral	(4.37481)		
Thinks there are more important	−0.300568		
things to spend money on	(−2.51414)		
LL function	−267.271	−302.704	−303.148
Number of observations	242	242	242

Source: See text. The figures in parentheses are *t*-statistics.

The remaining attitudinal variables were represented by a Likert scale of 1 (strongly disagree) to 5 (strongly agree). Those individuals who thought the cathedral should be protected irrespective of cost were more likely to pay any given amount. Those individuals who thought there were more important things than the appearance of the cathedral were less likely to pay any given amount.

The significance of these variables, however, is not high. Unsurprisingly, the attitudinal variable with the greatest predictive power was how willing the individual himself or herself was on a scale of 1 to 5 to make a payment. A positive answer to this question was generally indicative of the individual agreeing to pay a large sum. In total, therefore, the attitudinal variables are all correctly signed but, with two exceptions, the significance of the variables was only marginal. This might be attributed to the relatively small sample size as well as the large number of attitudinal variables entered in the equation and the possible multicollinearity between them.[2]

Model 1 also includes a test for any anchoring or starting point effect. This effect occurs when the responses given by an individual are not wholly internal to them but are instead conditioned by values provided to the individual. One test for the anchoring effect would be to include three different dummy variables for the four different starting points of the bids. An alternative procedure (and the one adopted here) is to treat the starting point as a continuous variable. This variable is highly significant and, if taken literally, implies the willingness to pay increases with the size of the initial bid level. This indicates that the amounts offered are not wholly internal to the individual. Despite the problem of the starting point bias, the coefficient on the bid variable is negative and highly significant, indicating that higher bids were more likely to be declined. This of course is a theoretical requirement, as is the significance of the variable describing monthly after-tax income of the household divided by family size. Two different measures of educational level were used: age at the time of exit from full-time education and whether the respondent possessed a degree or professional equivalent (not shown). In neither instance was educational level found to be significant.

In Model 2 the attitudinal variables are removed and the equation is left containing only the bid level, the starting point and socio-economic variables. It is seen that, apart from income and the dummy variable for local people, no other socio-economic variable is significant. Finally, Model 3 drops the insignificant variables with little effect on the significance of the retained variables (the Lincoln dummy, monthly household income per capita and the starting point and bid level) or on their coefficients.

DISCUSSION

The main feature of the estimated model of willingness to pay is the existence of a significant anchoring effect. The sign at the starting point of the bid indicates that the higher the starting point, the higher the final amount the individual will agree to pay. This exerts a considerable influence on the estimated willingness to pay, as can be seen from evaluating the expression at different starting points. There is no entirely satisfactory solution to the problem of the starting point bias, and in many research papers it is treated as a random effect (see, for example, Langford *et al.*, 1994). That is to say, whilst some bids are biased upwards the researcher hopes an equal number are biased downwards. In this chapter the following procedure is adopted in an attempt to overcome the starting point bias. It is assumed that the response obtained is a weighted average of the individuals' 'true' willingness to pay and the level of the starting bid (other assumptions are possible). From this it follows that, when the calculated willingness to pay exceeds the level of the starting bid, there exists a downward bias. If, on the other hand, the calculated willingness to pay lies beneath the starting bid, there is an upward bias. This can be represented as follows: $\text{WTPR} = \lambda \times \text{WTPT} + (1 - \lambda) \times \text{SP}$, where WTPR is reported willingness to pay, WTPT is true willingness to pay, SP is the starting point and λ is a parameter between 0 and 1. It is clear from the above equation that $\text{WTPR} = \text{SP} \Rightarrow \text{SP} = \text{WTPT}$. This makes it possible to retrieve 'true' willingness to pay from Model 3 in Table 5.2. A very similar approach to dealing with the problem of starting point bias is adopted by Herriges and Shogren (1996) who, in their study of water quality in Storm Lake, Iowa, assume that reported WTP is a geometric average of true WTP and the starting point.

Median WTP values are obtained by setting the left-hand side of the equation equal to zero and solving for the bid level at the average level of after-tax monthly income per family member for the sample. This is the bid level which 50% of such individuals would accept. In following this procedure one implicitly accepts the possibility that some individuals may have a negative willingness to pay for a higher frequency cleaning cycle. This was prompted by the interviewers encountering several individuals who justified their refusal to pay anything by stating that they positively preferred old things to look old. The adjustment parameter λ is calculated as 0.37.[3] This is extremely low and indicates the extent to which the true willingness to pay figures are revised once the starting point is revealed to the respondent. For example, if a starting point of £5 is proposed to a resident of Lincoln, the measured willingness to pay is just £21.48. If a starting point of £60 is proposed the measured willingness to pay becomes £56.23. It is interesting to note that the value calculated for the adjustment parameter is almost identical to the corresponding value which emerges from the Herriges and Shogren study (0.36). The income elasticity of mean willingness to pay is estimated to be 0.4.

Even after addressing the problem of the starting point bias, it is clear that a significant number of individuals are prepared to commit their households to a significant increase in annual taxes in order to improve the appearance of the cathedral. This is particularly the case when one considers households living within the boundary of the city itself. The mean willingness to pay of people interviewed in Lincoln was £49.77 per household per year, while the mean willingness to pay of those interviewed outside the city was £26.77.

Aggregate willingness to pay of the entire population is determined by multiplying household willingness to pay by the number of households in Lincoln and the number of households in Lincolnshire but residing outside the city respectively (see Table 5.3). Aggregate willingness to pay is found to be £5.5 million for households outside Lincoln and £1.8 million for Lincoln itself. Adding these figures together for the whole of Lincolnshire implies that the annual willingness to pay to move from the 40-year cleaning cycle to the 10 year cleaning cycle is £7.3 million. Dividing the £7.3 million sum by the 15 years of accumulation of dirt which represents the difference between the midpoints of the 10 and 40-year cleaning cycle, one obtains a figure of £0.5 million. This can be taken as an approximate estimate of the value of the damage inflicted on the cathedral by each additional year of air pollution. Naturally, the marginal valuation of the damage done might vary with the actual degree of soiling. Furthermore, insofar as future pollution levels might differ from those experienced over the recent past, the damage done and the value associated with each additional year of exposure to pollution may, in the future, be different.

Table 5.3   Aggregation of mean willingness to pay estimates

Population	Mean WTP per household	Number of households	Total
Residents of Lincoln	£49.77	36,216	£1.8m
Residents of Lincolnshire excluding Lincoln	£26.77	205,454	£5.5m
Total			£7.3m

Source: Own calculations.

CONCLUSIONS

This research has succeeded in demonstrating that individuals living in and around Lincoln hold significant values for preserving the good appearance of Lincoln Cathedral. That these values are so large should not be surprising. They reflect a very significant deterioration in the appearance of a very beautiful and historically very important building. The amounts offered by individuals were shown to be linked to attitudinal beliefs of the individual, and also to obey fundamental economic laws such as price sensitivity and responsiveness to income. These values were obtained by presenting individuals with a choice between cleaning cycles of different duration and asking them whether they were willing to pay the higher charges associated with the shorter cycle. It has not attempted to answer the much more difficult question of how frequently the cathedral should be cleaned given the cost of doing so and the less-than-perfect means available.

The current survey has a number of limitations which it would have been desirable, with hindsight, to change. One of these would be to include a question asking the number of times that the respondent visited the cathedral during the last 12 months. In the present survey the question was posed in a categorical fashion (less that once a year, about once a year, more than once a year). It would, with hindsight, also have been desirable to ask people whether or not they made voluntary contributions towards the upkeep of the cathedral. Many individuals do make voluntary contributions to the cathedral, and this might be an important predictor of whether individuals would support obligatory payments.

The most important step for future research would be to extend the survey to include individuals living outside Lincolnshire. Given the reduction in willingness to pay which is evident even between the residents of the city of Lincoln and those living outside the city, it is probable that those living even further afield would be willing to pay only small amounts. In aggregate, however, the values expressed by those living outside Lincolnshire might amount to a considerably larger sum than the aggregate amount expressed by residents of Lincolnshire.

It is also highly desirable that any future study should test for scope effects and embedding. In the current context scope effects refer to whether individuals' willingness to pay is sensitive to the amount of soiling. Thus, for example, a comparison between a 20-year cleaning cycle and a 40-year cleaning cycle as baseline ought to yield a smaller amount than willingness to pay to move from the 40-year cycle to the 10-year cycle. Testing for scope effects in terms of testing whether willingness to pay changes with the number of buildings cleaned is likely to be less informative since, whilst there are many extremely old buildings in Lincoln, there are none which compare with the cathedral itself. Thus, even in the presence of scope effects the willingness to pay to clean all of Lincoln's historic buildings would not be very different from the willingness to pay to clean the cathedral. Turning to the question of embedding, it is possible that individuals do not have separate values for the general maintenance of the cathedral and just one element of it. This might be explored by attempting to value a more inclusive good (general maintenance), which includes cleaning the building as one aspect. The problem here is that maintenance covers a very diverse set of tasks, and the consequences of neglect are hard to illustrate to people.

The survey also found evidence of starting point bias in the elicitation method employed. This is one of the known drawbacks of the double-bounded dichotomous choice technique. It is of course undesirable that the values expressed for a public good should be anything other than wholly internal to the individual. Even though this was treated it is therefore desirable to check that similar values emerge from the use of an alternative elicitation method not susceptible to the problem of anchoring, such as the simple maximum-willingness-to-pay question.

It is also desirable to examine the sensitivity of the values obtained to the use of different photographs. Whilst there is no particular reason to suppose that the photographs used were in any way unrepresentative, it would be expedient to confirm that this is indeed the case. It is also important that future research should provide an illustration of the cleaning process itself. This would include the use of scaffolding and plastic sheeting to cover the facade of the building. Information on the frequency with which the building would be covered in this way should be provided to the respondents. It is possible, or even likely, that reminding individuals of the disruption caused by frequent cleaning would diminish individuals' willingness to pay for a shorter cleaning cycle.

Finally, individuals proved to be surprisingly well informed regarding the risks associated with the use of substandard cleaning techniques, and on several occasions spontaneously raised the issue. It would be desirable therefore to provide information to individuals on the risks of the different techniques, and to emphasize which technique was going to be employed. This, however, would increase the length of the interviews and mean that interviewing individuals in the street would become increasingly difficult. Until these many uncertainties have been resolved, it would be difficult to justify using these results to inform policy decisions.

ACKNOWLEDGEMENTS

The authors would like to thank Tim Yates, David Pearce, Susana Mourato and Brett Day for helpful comments on an earlier version of this chapter. Any remaining errors are the sole responsibility of the authors. The financial support of the ESRC and the BRE are gratefully acknowledged.

ENDNOTES

1. Individuals were not asked to value an undulating flow of benefits derived from the good appearance of the building, but instead a change in its 'average' appearance. A more complex model would have to show how the benefits change over the course of the two cleaning cycles, with progressive deterioration in the appearance of the cathedral.
2. It might also be because the model treats what are essentially categorical variables as continuous variables in order to save degrees of freedom.
3. The value of λ is calculated as follows. Setting the left-hand side of the equation generated by Model 3 in Table 5.2 equal to zero and solving for the bid level gives:

$$BID = \frac{0.188121 + 0.415992 \times LINCOLN + 0.616097E - 03 \times INCOME/FAMILY}{0.049128} + \frac{0.031040}{0.049128} \times SP$$

where the coefficient of SP represents $(1-\lambda)$.

REFERENCES

Federal Register (1993), *Natural Resource Damage Assessments Under the Oil Pollution Act of 1990*, National Oceanic and Atmospheric Administration.

Herriges, J. and J. Shogren (1996), 'Starting Point Bias in Dichotomous Choice Valuation with Follow-Up Questioning', Journal of Environmental Economics and Management, Vol. 30(1), 112–31.

Langford, I., I. Bateman and D. Langford (1994), *Multilevel Modelling and Contingent Valuation. Part I: Triple Bounded Dichotomous Choice Analysis*, Working Paper GEC94–04, Centre for Social and Economic Research into the Global Environment (CSERGE), University College London and University of East Anglia.

Yates, T., J. Medhurst and M. Pollicino (1998), *National Material Exposure Programme. Part 3: Economic Evaluation of the Effect of Air Pollution on Buildings and Building Materials*, Working Paper BRE CR160/98, Garston, Watford: Building Research Establishment.

6. Preserving cultural heritage in transition economies: a contingent valuation study of Bulgarian monasteries

Susana Mourato, Andreas Kontoleon and Alexi Danchev

INTRODUCTION

Bulgarian Christian–Orthodox monasteries are an important component of the country's cultural, artistic, historical and religious legacy. They are widely regarded as sanctuaries of national consciousness, cultural continuity and tradition, and many possess a broad recreational and economic potential. Currently, there are 164 monasteries in Bulgaria of which the most famous, the Rila Monastery, listed as a World Heritage Site since 1983, attracts thousands of visitors every year. However, the general state of conservation of monasteries is poor; a significant number of sites are in urgent need of repair, restoration and maintenance works. The damage is in many cases irreversible; with every destroyed site, future generations lose an opportunity to be enriched by their cultural history.

The reasons behind the declining state of Bulgarian monasteries can be partly attributed to the non-existence of adequate government support. Currently, the financing structure for monasteries is unclear even for those working in the sector. There is no unique mechanism to finance conservation and repair works. Most financial support is linked to the state budget, either directly or indirectly through the Ministry of Culture, the National Institute of Cultural Monuments, the Directory of Religious Affairs and the regional municipalities (Danchev and Mourato, 1997).[1] The economic rationale for the use of state grants is the theory of public goods. Essentially, there is a presumption that individuals will understate their true willingness to pay for the benefits of a public good because (i) its provision can be jointly enjoyed by everyone and (ii) no individual can be excluded from its benefits.

The institutional restructuring (liberalization, privatization, decentralization) currently taking place in Bulgaria, necessary to meet the challenges of a transition economy, has resulted in public sector down-sizing and harsh budgetary cut-backs (European Bank for Reconstruction and Development, 1997). The consequences of this fiscal tightening for state-dependent non-market public/mixed goods, such as monasteries, are dire since their conservation benefits are not readily perceived by policy makers. Indeed, the share of cultural expenditures in the state budget has been decreasing sharply over recent years, and available funds are currently thought to be largely insufficient to restore deteriorated monasteries and maintain the state of the remaining ones, although no precise estimation of costs actually exists (Danchev and Mourato, 1997).

Claims that governments have an obligation to protect cultural heritage are common, in spite of the fact that hardly any efforts have been made to actually evaluate the total economic benefits of heritage conservation against its costs. This chapter sheds some light on the debate by investigating the nature of public attitudes and preferences towards the conservation of Bulgarian monasteries, subsequently translating them into economic values using the contingent valuation method (Mitchell and Carson, 1989). By demonstrating the existence of considerable social benefits from monasteries conservation, this study may help make a case for public subsidy, informing the process of allocating state resources in a transition society with numerous urgent and competing needs.

BULGARIAN MONASTERIES

Monasticism developed rapidly in Bulgaria after Christianity was adopted as the official religion of the country in 865. Further to their religious role, monasteries also became centres of education, culture and art. Over the centuries, they managed to survive the intense political turmoil endured by the country, remaining as sanctuaries of national consciousness, cultural continuity and tradition.

The distinguishing architecture of Bulgarian monasteries was developed on the basis of the inherited Slavonic vernacular style, eastern Proto-Bulgarian urban planning, the rich Roman and Thracian heritage and contacts with Byzantium and the Middle East. The monasteries are characterized by their picturesque brickwork, a profusion of niches, striking facades, portals full of reliefs with ornaments and figures, limestone and marble cornices, floors made of mosaics and ceramic tiles and, above all, walls covered with powerful icons, magnificent frescoes, mosaics, decorative ceramic plates, woodcarvings, pulpits and thrones (see Photograph 6.1). Some of the icons and frescoes are of monumental proportions and constitute unique masterpieces. Another distin-

*Photograph 6.1   From top to bottom row: Rila, Bachkovo and Trojan
               Monasteries*

guishing feature of Bulgarian monasteries is their almost organic integration
with the surrounding natural environment by means of careful planning of the
grounds, functional arrangement of premises and the feeling of scale, spatial and
facade composition. As depicted in Photograph 6.1, many monasteries are built
in spectacular surroundings, on steep slopes with magnificent views.

In Bulgaria's post-war state, eager to instil in the country's inhabitants a
strong sense of history and pride in national culture, museums, art galleries and

historical old buildings were well supported and subsidized. However, religious monuments didn't do so well; while the most prestigious like the Rila Monastery were protected and considered landmarks of Bulgarian achievement, the majority were allowed to fall into neglect and misuse. Moreover, in recent years, political turmoil and economic difficulties have diverted public attention from cultural issues to more urgent practical matters. Hence, today, a significant proportion of the existing monasteries are in a bad state of conservation and in need of urgent repair works. Some are currently no more than ruins.

METHODOLOGICAL FRAMEWORK

To explain the welfare measures that are empirically estimated through the valuation exercise, consider the following indirect utility function for a representative Bulgarian citizen:

$$V = U(Y, X, Q) \tag{6.1}$$

where Y is income, X a vector of individual characteristics and Q the state of conservation of monasteries. Consider a policy that improves the state of conservation of monasteries from the current state Q_0 to Q_1. The welfare measure to be empirically estimated is then given by:

$$V(Y - \text{WTP}, X, Q_1) = V(Y, X, Q_0) \tag{6.2}$$

where WTP is the maximum amount a consumer would be willing to pay to secure the welfare gain from a move from the current monasteries conservation state (Q_0) to a state with better conserved monasteries (Q_1). This corresponds to a Hicksian compensating variation measure.

The empirical estimation of the benefits arising from the conservation of Christian–Orthodox monasteries in Bulgaria was pursued within the context of a contingent valuation (CV) survey. The choice of the CV method (CVM) was made on the basis that it is unique in evaluating both use and non-use values of non-market goods. Estimating the latter is of fundamental importance in the case of religious cultural heritage, where arguably non-use benefits may constitute a significant proportion of total value.

The simplest way of empirically estimating the WTP welfare measure is by using an *ordinary least-squares regression* (OLS), assuming that observed willingness to pay equates to true willingness to pay as:

$$\text{WTP}_i = \beta' x_i + \varepsilon_i \quad \varepsilon_i \sim \text{N}(0, \sigma_\varepsilon^2) \tag{6.3}$$

where WTP is the observed hypothetical willingness to pay, x_i is a vector of individual attributes, β is a vector of unknown parameters, and ε_i is the error term, assumed to be normally distributed with zero mean and constant variance, that reflects unobserved taste components. This specification assumes linearity in parameters.

However, the dependent variable—WTP for monasteries preservation—is censored at zero. That is, all reported WTP values are larger than or equal to zero since it is not possible to bid negative amounts. The presence of censoring in the range of the WTP variable may lead to seriously biased OLS estimates of the parameters of interest (Greene, 1997).[2] The *censored regression or Tobit model* (Tobin, 1958) is commonly used to estimate relationships where the dependent variable is censored. The model recognizes the fact that there are two underlying choices in observed WTP behaviour: a participation and a payment decision. The model assumes that both decisions are determined by the same relationship, including the error structure. In other words, the characteristics that make a person decide to pay for cultural heritage protection equally determine the choice of how much to pay.

The general formulation of this model is given by:

$$\text{WTP}_i = \Pi \ (\text{WTP}_i^* > 0)\text{WTP}_i^* \tag{6.4}$$

where Π is an indicator function that takes the value 1 when the expression in parentheses is satisfied and 0 otherwise. WTP_i^* denotes the latent true willingness to pay—that can be potentially negative if the proposed change in cultural goods is welfare reducing—while WTP_i is its observed counterpart which is censored at 0.

The censored regression model is estimated by maximum likelihood. Identifying the zero WTP subsample by '0' and the positive WTP subsample by '+', the log-likelihood for the model can be written as:

$$\log L = \sum_0 \log\left[1 - \Phi\left(\beta' \, x_i \, / \, \sigma_\varepsilon\right)\right] + \sum_+ \log\left[f\left(\text{WTP}_i\right)\right] \tag{6.5}$$

where Φ denotes the distribution function of the standard normal and f is the normal density function. The first part of the log-likelihood corresponds to the probability of observing a limit observation (i.e. zero WTP); the second part corresponds to the classical regression for the non-limit observations (i.e. positive WTP).

The marginal effect of a particular regressor in this model is given by:

$$\partial E(\text{WTP}_i|x_i)/\partial x_i = \Phi(\beta x_i/\sigma_\varepsilon) \, \beta \tag{6.6}$$

McDonald and Moffitt (1980) suggested a decomposition of this marginal effect that is very informative in the WTP framework:

$$\partial E(\text{WTP}_i|x_i)/\partial x_i = E(\text{WTP}_i^*|\text{WTP}_i^* > 0)\, \partial \text{prob}(\text{WTP}_i^* > 0)/\partial \mathrm{d}x_i$$
$$+ \text{prob}(\text{WTP}_i^* > 0)\, \partial E(\text{WTP}_i^*|\text{WTP}_i^* > 0)/\partial x_i. \qquad (6.7)$$

Thus, a change in any regressor x_i has two effects: (i) an impact on the probability of a positive bid (times the conditional mean of that bid); and (ii) a change in the conditional mean of the WTP, in the positive part of the distribution. Both effects are of interest in the CVM framework.

Another potential source of bias in the estimation arises from the presence of self-selection in the sample. To test for possible selectivity bias in the data, *Heckman's selectivity model* (Heckman, 1979) can be employed. In contrast to the Tobit model, the Heckman model assumes that the participation and payment decisions are determined by a different set of variables, that need not be mutually exclusive. The model assumes that the observed positive WTP is not randomly sampled from the population of interest, but from a subgroup of that population (those who choose to participate) associated with some unobserved selection rule. The Heckman model can be defined as:

$$\text{WTP}_i = \Pi(Z_i^* > 0)\text{WTP}_i^* \quad Z_i^* = \alpha'w_i + u_i. \qquad (6.8)$$

In the specification above, WTP is only observed when individuals decide to participate in the market. In the participation equation, w_i is a vector of individual attributes and α a vector of unknown parameters. Z_i^* is not observed; its observed dichotomous counterpart is Z_i that takes the value 1 if an individual participates ($Z_i^* > 0$) and 0 otherwise ($Z_i^* \leq 0$). The error terms u_i and ε_i are assumed to have a bivariate normal distribution with zero means and correlation ρ. Respondents select themselves into the sample of payers on the basis of the participation equation.

The parameters of the Heckman model can be estimated by a two-step procedure (Heckman, 1979).

(i) First, the parameters of the participation equation are estimated using a probit model. Then, for each observation the inverse Mills ratio, λ_i, is computed, as:

$$\lambda_i = \phi(\alpha'w_i/\sigma_\mu)/\Phi(\alpha'w_i/\sigma_\mu). \qquad (6.9)$$

(ii) Second, the parameters of the payment equation are estimated by applying OLS to a 'selectivity-corrected' regression of WTP on x_i and the computed inverse Mills ratio. The respective coefficients β and $\theta = \rho\sigma_\varepsilon$ are estimated. The standard errors also need to be adjusted.

SURVEY INSTRUMENT

Following the pre-test stages, the final survey took place in January 1997. A random sample of 483 people, representative of the Bulgarian population, was personally interviewed in 17 sampling points across Bulgaria.[3] First, textual and visual information were provided describing the current state of conservation of Bulgarian monasteries. Then, a management programme to protect all monasteries and start conservation works where needed was described. Photographs were used to illustrate the effects of restoration of buildings and frescos. The programme would be financed through increased taxes. Following the description of the conservation programme and its provision mechanism, respondents were asked for their maximum willingness to pay for the programme. The questionnaire also included extensive sections with attitudinal and demographic questions. The survey instrument worked well in the field, with only 9% of the respondents finding the questions difficult to understand.

Best-practice guidelines for CV studies set out by the NOAA panel (Arrow *et al.*, 1993) favour a dichotomous choice approach to elicit welfare measures. Nonetheless, an open-ended valuation format was adopted in this study after the pilot phase showed respondents did not find the valuation task cognitively unattainable, did not link the hypothetical payment with the likely costs of a restoration programme and could answer the WTP questions without needing external guidance. Furthermore, dichotomous choice elicitation seems to generate significantly higher estimates of WTP than open-ended designs due to the so-called 'yea-saying' phenomenon (Mitchell and Carson, 1989). Hence,

Table 6.1   Sample descriptive statistics

Variable	Mean	S.D.
Male (%)	0.48	0.50
Age (years)	45	17
Family size	3	1.2
Education		
Primary (%)	0.23	0.42
Lower secondary (%)	0.53	0.50
Upper secondary (%)	0.05	0.23
University (%)	0.19	0.39
Income (BGL)	23,910	13,087
In full-time employment (%)	0.52	0.50
No car (%)	0.52	0.50

Note: S.D., standard deviation; BGL, Bulgarian Leva.

the choice of an open-ended format actually conforms to another recommendation from the NOAA panel that supports the choice of the most conservative welfare estimate.

Descriptive statistics are given in Table 6.1. It is interesting to note the relatively high education level of Bulgarians, with about a fifth of the sample having a university degree. This finding is common across Eastern Europe. The average gross monthly household income is about BGL24,000 (which corresponds to US$48, using a December 1996 exchange rate of BGL500=US$1). The survey also showed a high concentration of respondents in the highest and lowest income ranges, reflecting existing disparities in income distribution.

RESULTS AND DISCUSSION

Uses and Attitudes

In the light of current social and economic difficulties in Bulgaria, the survey explored in some depth public attitudes towards cultural heritage conservation in general and monasteries in particular.

The overwhelming majority of Bulgarians have visited at least one monastery at some point in their lives. The survey showed that 96% of the sample had visited at least one monastery and nearly 40% had visited more than five. Unsurprisingly, the most popular monasteries are the most prestigious such as the Rila, Bachkovo or Trojan Monasteries. Only 12% of the visits were motivated by religious purposes, 20% were mainly for recreation and relaxation while a majority of 68% visit monasteries because of an interest in Bulgarian history and cultural heritage. Paradoxically, actual personal knowledge of the role of monasteries in the country's history and culture ranged from average to poor for 70% of respondents.

Bulgarian monasteries are publicly perceived as being in need of repair works, with less than 10% of respondents considering them to be in a good overall state of conservation. Notwithstanding the fact that most of the population can be classified as users, the most worrying consequences of the degradation of monasteries were found to correspond to losses in non-use values. More than 60% of respondents identified the loss of Bulgaria's cultural and artistic heritage as their major concern, while an additional 30% mentioned losses for future generations. The decreased recreational value of the sites was the foremost concern of only 2% of the sample. Moreover, only 13% disagreed with the statement that 'monasteries have a value even for those people who do not visit them'. These indicators constitute strong evidence of the existence of significant values not directly linked to actual use and confirm the idea that

Bulgarians venerate their monasteries as an emblematic icon of the nation's culture (Danchev and Mourato, 1997).

Decomposing the total sample into subgroups with respect to visitation patterns (people who have visited less than five monasteries versus people who have visited five or more) revealed additional information about the nature of preferences towards monasteries preservation. Comparative results are depicted in Table 6.2. Confirming prior expectations, the subsample that had visited a greater number of different monasteries (57% of the total sample), irrespective of the frequency of these visits, displayed a relatively higher interest in cultural heritage and monasteries conservation in general, a more accurate perception of the current state of conservation of monasteries, a greater knowledge of their historical and national significance and were more willing to contribute monetarily for their conservation.

Monasteries have to compete for public funds with many other cultural concerns, and indeed with many other types of public issues such as health and education. The survey showed that monasteries, followed by churches, were considered to be the built cultural assets in most need of financial support. Indeed, nearly 60% of the sample said they wouldn't mind paying something for monasteries preservation given their importance (while a fifth of the sample disagreed). However, unsurprisingly, cultural heritage protection does not rank highly when compared to other public concerns; it was considered only seventh out of a list of social issues, coming after crime prevention, increased employment, improved health services and environmental protection. Hence, while the attitudinal results of the survey support the existence of positive benefits from increased monasteries preservation, they also suggest that such values may be low and unevenly distributed across the population, maybe concentrated on the wealthiest strata.

The questionnaire also sought to obtain some information about the cultural habits of the Bulgarian population by asking about several cultural activities undergone in the previous year. Bulgarians seem to be very culturally oriented, with a third of the sample reporting trips to the theatre, opera, classical music concerts, museums and/or art galleries. Bulgaria has a richness of cultural possibilities that, in parallel with the generally high education levels, may explain the surprisingly high figures found in cultural heritage indicators. In addition, half of the respondents followed a TV series about monasteries.

Willingness to Pay

Inspection of the data showed that a large proportion of respondents, about 40%, were not willing to pay anything for the preservation of Bulgarian monasteries. This is hardly surprising and conforms to the results from the attitudinal section of the questionnaire, which had uncovered a low priority attributed to

Table 6.2   Attitudes and visits

Attitudinal variables	Subsample I: less than five monasteries	Subsample II: more than five monasteries
Interest in cultural heritage (5—very interested; 1—not interested at all)	3	4
Importance of monasteries conservation (5—very important; 1—not important at all)	4	5
Perceived state of monasteries conservation (5—excellent; 1—very bad)	3	2
Personal knowledge of monasteries' historical role (5—very good; 1—very poor)	2	3
'I feel a sense of responsibility over the preservation of our cultural heritage' (5—definitely agree;1—definitely disagree)	3	4
'Monasteries have a value even for people who don't visit them' (5—definitely agree;1—definitely disagree)	4	5
'I don't mind giving up money to protect monasteries' (5—definitely agree;1—definitely disagree)	4	5
Cultural activities index: trip to museum, theatre, opera, classical concert, seen TV programme on monasteries (0—none; 1—all)	0.2	0.4
Reasons for visiting monasteries: Religion	13.2%	10.5%
History and culture	46%	62%
Percentage of sample	43%	57%

the protection of cultural heritage vis-à-vis other areas of public expenditure. Those who were willing to pay a positive amount for monasteries preservation were prepared to pay on average BGL3,203 (US$6.4) per household per year. Averaging over the whole sample yields a mean WTP of BGL1,943 (US$3.9) and a median of BGL500 (US$1).[4] Figure 6.1 depicts the WTP distribution.

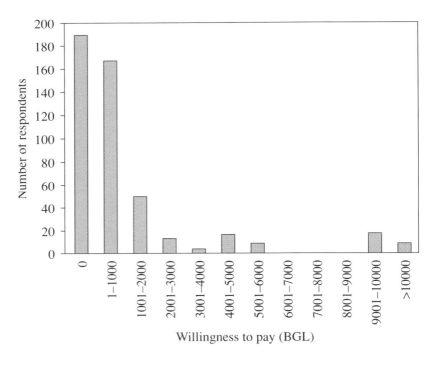

Figure 6.1   Distribution of willingness to pay

But not all null responses are necessarily valid representations of people's preferences. Some people may decide not to participate due to objection, lack of understanding or disinterest in some aspect of the questionnaire or the scenario presented.[5]

In order to identify possible invalid answers, the survey included a number of follow-up questions to the valuation section that purported to investigate the motivations behind null WTP responses. Respondents were asked to choose the main reason why they were not willing to pay for the preservation of Bulgarian monasteries, out of a list of various possible motivations. The motivations classified as invalid reflected free-riding behaviour ('the Government should pay', 'those who visit should pay' or 'the Church should pay'), objection to the payment vehicle ('I pay too much tax already'), a disbelief in the proposed conservation programme ('the authorities are incapable of implementing the plan') or lack of time or information ('I did not have enough time or information to decide'). Reasons that reflected a 'true' zero WTP included 'I am not really concerned about this issue', 'monasteries in Bulgaria are fine and don't need any more money spent on them', 'I would like to pay but I can't afford it' and 'we should wait until the Bulgarian economy gets stronger'.

Following these criteria, about 15% of null WTP responses were classified as an invalid expression of preferences for monasteries preservation. Overall, this amounts to less than 6% of all answers. Considering valid answers alone yields a mean WTP per household per year of BGL2,062 (US$4.1) and a median of BGL500 (US$1). Table 6.3 presents summary statistics of the willingness to pay for the preservation of Bulgarian monasteries.

Table 6.3   Willingness to pay statistics

Variable	N (%)	Mean WTP in BGL (s.d.)
Full sample	483	1,943 (6,294)
WTP>0	293 (60.7%)	3,203 (7,832)
WTP=0	190 (39.3%)	–
Valid answers	162 (33.5%)	–
Invalid answers	28 (5.8%)	–
Total valid answers	455 (94.2%)	2,062 (6,466)

Note: s.d., standard deviation.

In order to examine the impact of selected regressors on willingness to pay, the various econometric specifications described above were estimated. Table 6.4 describes the variables used in the estimation. These include socio-economic characteristics (sex, age, education, income), behavioural variables (number of monasteries visited), perceptions (perceived state of conservation of monasteries), attitudes towards heritage conservation (sense of responsibility over heritage preservation, bequest values, priority of monasteries conservation), attitudes towards the proposed programme, a cultural index and a generosity proxy.

Table 6.5 contains the results of the econometric estimations. A probit model was used to analyse the determinants of the probability of stating a protest bid (first column). As expected, those who perceived monasteries to be in a good state of conservation, objected to various aspects of the conservation programme or found the questionnaire boring are more likely to protest.

The second column of Table 6.5 presents the results of the Tobit regression. This specification assumes that participation and payment are determined by the

Table 6.4 Variables description

Variable name	Description
WTP	Annual household WTP in Bulgarian Leva (in taxes)
ONE	Constant
SEX	Dummy variable: 1—male; 0—female
AGE	Interval midpoints from seven age groups
EDUCATION	4—university; 3—upper secondary; 2—lower secondary; 1—primary
INCOME	Interval midpoints from 12 income groups
STATE	'What do you think is the general state of conservation of Bulgarian monasteries?' 1—very bad to 5—excellent
MONASTERIES PRIORITY	'When considering public spending in cultural heritage, how much of a priority is monasteries conservation?' 1—low priority to 5—high priority
BEQUEST	'What is the most worrying consequence of monasteries degradation?' Dummy variable: 1—the next generation won't see them; 0—other reasons
NUMBER	Number of monasteries visited
RESPONSIBILITY	'I feel a sense of responsibility over the preservation of our cultural heritage' 1—definitely disagree to 5–definitely agree
CULTURAL INDEX	Index variable reflecting number of cultural activities taken in the past year (theatre, classical concert, museum, opera, TV series on monasteries): 0—none to 1—all five activities
PROGRAMME INDEX	Index variable reflecting attitudes towards the proposed programme (perceived public support, tax payment vehicle, capability of relevant institutions, fulfilment of objectives): 0—negative attitude to 1—positive attitude
CHARITY	Dummy variable: 1—made a charitable donation in the past year; 0—otherwise
BORING	Dummy variable: 1—thought the questionnaire was boring; 0—otherwise

same model. The signs and significance of the key variables confirm prior expectations and the findings from the attitudinal analysis. Income and age are found to be significant determinants of WTP, with the value of conservation varying positively with income and inversely with age. Attitudes and perceptions also have a strong influence over WTP, with those who feel a sense of

Table 6.5   Econometric models

	Probit (protests) (1)	Tobit (2)	Probit (participation) (3)	Selection (two-stage) (4)
CONSTANT	−1.73586*** (0.73602)	−12187.6*** (3444.34)	−1.67563*** (0.45232)	−9794.3* (5305.24)
SEX	0.54360** (0.26018)	1426.23 (923.477)	0.25640* (0.14655)	1137.26 (1046.32)
AGE	−0.00312 (0.00819)	−67.3017** (30.5648)	−0.00418 (0.00463)	−71.1934** (34.2309)
EDUCATION	−0.11396 (0.14813)	569.033 (501.621)	0.13869* (0.07829)	493.427 (602.337)
INCOME	0.000002 (0.00001)	0.14028*** (0.03841)	0.000008 (0.000006)	0.17145*** (0.04459)
STATE	0.27827** (0.13638)	−658.357 (487.841)	−0.02339 (0.07676)	−864.337* (537.213)
MONASTERIES PRIORITY	–	641.204 (473.61)	–	1070.72** (494.817)
BEQUEST	–	648.854 (1035.25)	–	2121.2** (1127.78)
NUMBER	–	106.083** (53.3504)	–	83.6474* (51.7241)
RESPONSIBILITY	–	1237.69*** (410.202)	0.23051*** (0.06080)	848.977 (595.735)
CULTURAL INDEX	−0.42982 (0.55595)	3351.94* (1991.74)	0.56678* (0.33189)	3503.06 (2234.77)
PROGRAMME INDEX	−0.23152** (0.10966)	426.993 (459.852)	0.18687 (0.06967)	–
CHARITY	–	1728.8* (981.413)	0.68524*** (0.16954)	–
BORING	1.13473*** (0.38637)	–	–	–
LAMBDA/SIGMA	–	8124.55 (366.26)	–	3977.35 (3009.23)

Table 6.5   continued

	Probit (protests) (1)	Tobit (2)	Probit (participation) (3)	Selection (two-stage) (4)
RHO	–	–	–	0.49
E(WTP)	–	0.64	–	–
P(+)	–	0.36	–	–
R^2	–	–	–	0.16
CHI^2 (d.f.)	29.03(8)	76.86(12)	78.72(9)	42.96(10)
LOG-LIKELIHOOD	–62.4492	–2717.991	–205.8675	–2624.15
N	411	377	386	254

Notes:
Dependent variable: WTP; standard errors in parentheses.
*** Significant at the 1% level; ** significant at the 5% level; * significant at the 10% level.
McDonald and Moffitt decomposition: E(WTP) is the effect on the payment decision and P(+) is the effect on participation; d.f. = degrees of freedom.

responsibility over heritage preservation willing to pay more. As expected, those who visited a larger number of monasteries attributed a higher value to preservation (which implies that use values are significant). People scoring more highly on the index of cultural activities also have a higher WTP, and having donated money to charity is also seen to have a positive impact on WTP (charitable giving can be interpreted as a proxy for 'generosity' traits).

The results of the McDonald and Moffitt decomposition of the marginal effect in the Tobit model, for an equi-marginal change in all dependent variables when initially set at their mean values, are shown in the last half of the table as E(WTP) and P(+). About 34% of the effect is in the probability of submitting a positive bid (P(+)), with the remaining 66% being in the size of the WTP amount, conditional on participation (E(WTP)). Hence, interpreting the Tobit marginal effects as simply reflecting the impact of an explanatory variable on the magnitude of WTP would lead to a non-trivial over-estimation of the corresponding elasticity.

Given the high percentage of respondents reporting zero WTP (39%), it was important to investigate whether some form of sample selection generated the positive bids. Columns (3) and (4) in Table 6.5 correspond to the two-step Heckman selectivity model. The coefficient of *lambda*[6] was found to be statistically insignificant at the 10% level, which implies that self-selection bias is not a serious problem in the data (the estimated correlation coefficient is

0.52). Nevertheless, the results obtained from this specification are quite informative as they allow the participation and payment decisions to be modelled
separately. Column (3) shows that participation seems to be driven mainly by:
education (the higher the level of education the higher the probability of par-
ticipating); interest in cultural activities (the more culturally active people are,
the more likely they are to participate in the programme); generosity attributes,
as measured by charitable giving (those who donate to charitable causes are
also more likely to pay for monasteries conservation); and a sense of responsibility over heritage preservation (which impacts positively on participation).
These results all conform to prior expectations.

In turn, the decision of how much to pay (column (4)) is mainly driven by:
income (which has a strong positive impact on WTP); age (which is negatively
correlated with WTP); number of monasteries visited (with a positive influence
on WTP); perceived state of monasteries conservation (the better the perceived
conservation state the lower the WTP); and two attitudinal variables (both those
with bequest concerns and those who think monasteries should have high
priority amongst heritage investments are willing to pay more).

In the Tobit specification, the different motivations behind participation and
payment choices do not become apparent. This constitutes a limitation to the
applicability of the results from this model, as untangling the determinants of
both decisions may have important implications in terms of policy. For example,
the model estimates from columns (3) and (4) show that an increase in income
may not lead to a significant increase in the number of those willing to participate in a heritage conservation programme. In order to increase participation,
education campaigns and efforts to raise cultural awareness may be more
effective. On the other hand, the results imply an income elasticity of WTP
above 1, which embodies a potential for increase in aggregate WTP as a result
of economic growth.

Hence, notwithstanding the moderate sample size (483), the empirical econometric models successfully identified the major determinants of the three
choices of interest: the protest decision, the participation decision and the
payment decision.

POLICY IMPLICATIONS

This chapter has presented and discussed the results of a contingent valuation
survey of Bulgarian monasteries including World Heritage Sites such as the
Rila Monastery. The findings suggest that, on average, Bulgarians attribute a
significantly positive value (about 0.1% per capita GNP) to the conservation and
restoration of their Christian–Orthodox monasteries. The implication is that

damages to these cultural goods are undesirable and the public would be willing to pay positive amounts to avoid them or to slow the rate at which they occur, despite the country's difficult economic and political situation. Non-use values were found to be important determinants of WTP.

Results also show that nearly 40% of respondents reported a zero WTP, the majority of which correspond to genuine zero values. This large proportion of people stating zero values seems to be a recurring feature of cultural heritage valuation studies (as indeed of many environmental valuation studies). Hence, the welfare of a significant proportion of the population seems to be unaffected by changes in these cultural assets.

The elicited values perform well in terms of standard statistical validity testing. The econometric models show that the positive estimated values are driven by the more educated and wealthier segments of the population, typically those with more diverse and intense cultural interests. In particular, education, cultural interests, a sense of responsibility over heritage protection and generosity are found to be significant determinants of the decision to pay for monasteries protection; while income, age, use of monasteries, perceived state of conservation and a positive attitude towards conservation are the main factors affecting the size of the payment.

This study helps to make a case for public subsidy, demonstrating the existence of considerable social benefits. However, in a country such as Bulgaria, the presumptive case for state provision is eroded by the risks of state finance, not least the likelihood that heritage may be seen as a 'luxury' item in times of hardship for public revenues. Additionally, state finance may lead to some state control, and centralized bureaucrats may not be the best judges of how optimally to exploit cultural heritage for the benefit of the nation as a whole. Long-term sustainability thus implies the need to look at alternative market-based financing mechanisms to appropriate benefits and increase the effectiveness of efforts to protect monasteries (Pearce and Mourato, 1998).

The findings reported in this chapter have important implications in the range and design of alternative financing mechanisms that can be used to appropriate the estimated benefits of monasteries conservation. Any mechanism should bear in mind the heterogeneous distribution of benefits across the population and, particularly, the fact that a significant proportion of the public is not willing to pay for the protection of monasteries. As such, using general tax increases may not be an adequate way of achieving conservation objectives and may have undesirable distributional impacts.

Charging for 'use' of monasteries is the clearest way to capture economic value, given their mixed good characteristics. In recent years many countries have experimented with the introduction of self-financing or partial self-financing entry and view charge systems for cultural goods. The obvious problem with market pricing is that it may defeat the wider objective of securing the widest possible appreciation of monasteries because optimal pricing deters people from the site. In particular, the idea of charging for religious heritage may seem objectionable, although the survey showed that only 12% of people visit monasteries for religious purposes.

Nevertheless, these problems can be overcome to some extent. First, fees can be charged for optional complementary services such as car parks, museums and souvenir shops. This would allow everyone to enjoy the monasteries, while capturing some of the willingness to pay of the wealthiest visitors. Second, some discrimination in prices is possible. The most familiar is the charging of different prices to national and foreign visitors. This 'two-tier' pricing is already current practice in some monasteries. For example, the Rila Monastery Museum discriminates prices between Bulgarians and foreign tourists.

While the potential for generating visitor revenues may be quite substantial in the case of the most famous monasteries, user values alone may not be enough to deliver sustainability for the large majority of less-known monasteries. A charitable organization, specializing in the financing of heritage conservation, using public and corporate donations, could be a way of supporting monasteries conservation in Bulgaria. Of course donations are voluntary, thus subject to free-riding. However, they are compatible with situations where the benefits are concentrated in certain segments of the population that, once identified, could be the focus of specially targeted appeals.[7]

A final possibility is state or local lotteries. Provided they conform to underlying cultural values, they can be extremely powerful sources of finance. In 1997, for example, the Heritage Lottery Fund in the UK awarded more than 600 grants to heritage projects, worth £405 million, which constitutes an enormous boost to the heritage sector (Heritage Lottery Fund, 1997).

Future research is needed to investigate the sensitivity of the value of heritage conservation to changes in the pricing and provision mechanisms. Alternative stated preference techniques such as the contingent ranking method show promise in this respect by allowing several conservation programmes, with varying scopes or characteristics, to be valued simultaneously, explicitly accounting for trade-offs between programmes.

ACKNOWLEDGEMENTS

The research underlying this study was funded by the European Union PECO 1994 Programme. Susana Mourato gratefully acknowledges a grant provided by the Portuguese Junta Nacional de Investigação Científica e Tecnológica (JNICT) through the PRAXIS XXI Programme. The authors are also indebted to David Pearce.

ENDNOTES

1. Other sources of revenue are contributions from national and international non-governmental organizations, charitable donations from individuals and corporations, visitor expenditures and revenues from the monasteries' own economic activities, such as agriculture (Danchev and Mourato, 1997).
2. OLS estimates can be shown to underestimate the impact of the regressors x_i.
3. The survey was implemented by a professional survey company with previous experience of administering CV questionnaires.
4. These values may seem low in absolute terms; however, they correspond to about 0.1% per capita GNP, which is in the same order of magnitude as for other cultural heritage studies (Pearce and Mourato, 1998).
5. Indeed, invalid answers may also occur amongst positive WTP observations. For example, respondents may be valuing a good that is different from the one intended by the researchers.
6. The coefficient of *lambda* (the inverse Mills ratio) indicates whether the sample selection specification used to model the data is statistically significant, i.e. whether selectivity on positive willingness to pay is significant.
7. The best example of such a charity is probably the UK's National Trust, a registered charity, founded in 1895 to preserve places of historic interest or natural beauty permanently for the benefit of the nation. The Trust is the largest conservation charity in Europe, protecting through ownership some 244,564 hectares and 575 miles of coastline. 251 properties were opened to the public in 1997, attracting 11.7m paying visitors. Associated with this are some 20,000 vernacular buildings, 183 houses of historic interest, 160 gardens, 73 landscape and deer parks, 1,000 scheduled ancient monuments and over 40,000 sites of archaeological interest. In 1997 the National Trust had 2.5m members.

REFERENCES

Arrow, K., R. Solow, P. Portney, E. Leamer, R. Radner and H. Schuman (1993) "Report of the NOAA Panel on Contingent Valuation", *Federal Register* 58 (10), 4602–14.

Danchev, A. and S. Mourato (1997) "Bulgaria in Transition: Economy and Heritage", In *The Measurement and Achievement of Sustainable Development in Eastern Europe*, Report to DGXII.

European Bank for Reconstruction and Development (1997) *Transition Report 1997: Enterprise Performance and Growth.*

Greene, W.H. (1997) *Econometric Analysis*, 3rd edition, Macmillan, New York.

Heckman, J.J. (1979) "Sample Selection Bias as a Specification Error", *Econometrica* 47, 153–61.

Heritage Lottery Fund (1997) *Annual Report and Accounts 1996–1997*, National Heritage Fund and National Heritage Memorial Fund, London.

McDonald, J.F. and R.A. Moffitt (1980) "The Uses of the Tobit Analysis", *Review of Economics and Statistics* 62, 318–21.

Mitchell, R. and R. Carson (1989) *Using Surveys to Value Public Goods: The Contingent Valuation Method*, John Hopkins Press, Baltimore, MD.

Pearce, D.W. and S. Mourato. (1998) "The Economics of Cultural Heritage: World Bank Support to Cultural Heritage Preservation in the MNA Region", Report to the World Bank, Washington, DC.

Tobin, J. (1958) "Estimation of Relationships for Limited Dependent Variables", *Econometrica* 26, 24–36.

7. Valuing different road options for Stonehenge

David Maddison and Susana Mourato

INTRODUCTION

Stonehenge is one of the best known and archaeologically most important monuments in the world. It was constructed between 5,000 and 3,500 years ago and is composed of a circle of stones arranged in a pattern whose true significance remains a mystery. Apart from the stone circle, the surrounding area, much of which is owned by the National Trust,[1] contains over 450 archaeological monuments such as Bronze Age barrows and the Cursus, which is variously interpreted as an ancient racecourse or a processional way. Stonehenge is managed by English Heritage[2] and is one of the 16 UK sites designated by the United Nations as a World Heritage Site. Last year, 700,000 people paid to get into Stonehenge.

Despite the undisputed importance of the site, Stonehenge suffers considerable intrusion in the form of two roads that pass close by on either side. The A303 passes to the south of the stone circle about 150 m away whilst the A344 passes to the north of the stone circle about 50 m away. This road layout is shown in Figure 7.1. Both roads are quite busy (the A303 particularly so) and visitors to the site can hear the traffic whilst walking around the stones. Even though the whole of the National Trust area is open to the public, these roads prevent visitors from wandering over the site. The situation of Stonehenge was described by a recent public enquiry as a 'national disgrace'.

Prompted in part by the growing congestion on the single carriageway A303 and the unsatisfactory nature of the current road layout a variety of proposals have, at various times, been made to change the existing layout. The road option favoured by heritage conservation organizations such as English Heritage and the National Trust consisted of closing the A344 and building an on-line cut-and-cover 2-km dual carriageway tunnel for the A303, as it passes through the Stonehenge bowl. The 2-km tunnel was considered to possess certain 'heritage' benefits for the Stonehenge landscape: the road would be invisible from the stones, eliminating any noise, visual intrusion and land severance effects. In parallel, a possible welfare-reducing impact of the tunnel would derive from drivers not being able to see Stonehenge while driving along the A303. While the external benefits are thought to outweigh the external costs, both positive and negative impacts need to be considered. The construction and maintenance costs of building this tunnel were estimated to be about £125m.

Current means of road appraisal in the UK do not place monetary values on environmental impacts such as cultural values, visual intrusion and noise. Given the extreme sensitivity of the Stonehenge site, it is clear that any attempt to conduct a 'conventional' cost–benefit analysis of the alternative proposals, comparing just time savings and accidents with the costs of construction, would overlook the main reason why people wish to change the current road scheme. Of course environmental considerations are not ignored completely by current practices; in the present procedure, non-monetary impacts are identified and weights attached to them. Unfortunately these weights are difficult to interpret and provide only an institutional view of what the general public might think about whether particular environmental improvements provide value for money.

In preparation for the 1998 UK roads review, English Heritage commissioned a contingent valuation study to determine the monetary value of the 'heritage benefits' of the 2-km tunnel option, *over and above* all other benefits normally identified in roads appraisal.[3] The monetization of heritage benefits would enable the 'full' benefit–cost ratio to be computed for that road option. This chapter presents the results of the contingent valuation study undertaken to value the heritage benefits of a 2-km tunnel for Stonehenge, relative to the current scenario. Both use and non-use values were measured. The results indicate that, despite the fact that cultural heritage concerns are not considered to be a priority for the majority of the population, the benefits that UK citizens derive from improvements in the Stonehenge landscape justify the construction of the tunnel.

PREVIOUS LITERATURE

To our knowledge, this is the first study in the UK that has attempted to value the environmental impact of changes in road layout using contingent valuation techniques. In Sweden, a number of valuation studies have been undertaken with regard to the environmental impacts of the construction of new roads (Grudemo, 1998). These studies focus exclusively on the environmental impacts of new roads (i.e. excluding time savings and accidents) and are in this respect similar to the Stonehenge study. However, these attempts are at most exploratory in nature, consisting of a referendum asking how many people support and how many do not support a particular project, with a valuation question added at the end.

Although there are now a small number of studies dealing with the economic value of cultural assets, this literature was found to be of only limited relevance to the Stonehenge study. This is because existing studies tend to consider impacts on the object itself (e.g. a poor state of physical repair, damage caused by air pollution, etc.). The value of the landscape surrounding the monument as a highly complementary good is an issue that has not yet been addressed. Values associated with the appearance of large and diverse tracts of terrain have, on the other hand, been estimated, but these studies tend to refer to changes in agricultural practices so this literature cannot be held up as evidence that individuals might be willing to pay to prevent visual intrusion caused by roads around Stonehenge.

Construction of the 2-km tunnel would permit visitors unrestricted access to all of the archaeologically important area surrounding Stonehenge, whereas at the moment the area is 'severed' by the A303 and A344. The only contingent valuation study used to assess the environmental benefits of re-routing traffic through a tunnel was done by Soguel (1994a). The stated purpose of this tunnel was to reduce community severance caused by surface traffic in Neuchatel. However, since it is presumably difficult to disentangle the community severance effect from other benefits of such a tunnel, in the form of the reduced visual intrusion of traffic, noise, odour and air pollution, the benefits which emerge are likely to be almost identical to the list of benefits from building a tunnel under Stonehenge. Nonetheless, the issues have been addressed in the context of an urban and residential area rather than in the context of open countryside. Alternative road options for Stonehenge also offer the possibility of a change in ambient noise levels at the site of the stone circle. There have been a small number of studies using the contingent valuation technique to value changes in ambient traffic noise levels (e.g. Soguel, 1994b) but, once more, these are invariably in the context of urban areas.

Hence, the Stonehenge study presents a significant number of new challenges that distinguish it from existing heritage or environmental valuation studies.

THEORETICAL FRAMEWORK

A contingent valuation survey (Mitchell and Carson, 1989) was used to elicit the benefits associated with the 2-km tunnel relative to the current situation. The survey elicited respondents' maximum willingness to pay to secure the construction of the tunnel. This amount corresponds to the Hicksian compensation variation for the proposed improvement (Just *et al.*, 1982):

$$U(Y - \text{WTP}_A, Q_1) = U(Y, Q_0) \qquad (7.1)$$

where U represents the indirect utility function of a representative individual, Y is the income level, Q_0 is the current environmental quality of the site, Q_1 is the environmental quality of the site with the new road option and WTP_A is the maximum amount the individual would be willing to pay to secure the change, i.e. the welfare measure of interest. For purposes of empirical estimation, it is common to specify the WTP welfare measure so described as:

$$WTP_i = X_i\beta + \varepsilon_i \qquad (7.2)$$

where X_i represents a vector of explanatory variables, β is a vector of parameters and ε_i corresponds to unobserved differences in taste. The parameters of interest can then be estimated by maximum likelihood (Cameron, 1988).

An underlying assumption of the above specification is that the tunnel is welfare-enhancing, i.e. Q_1 is 'better' than Q_0 and WTP>0. However, as noted above, some people may actually experience a disbenefit due to the fact that the stone circle would cease to be visible from the roads if the tunnel were constructed. This situation can be represented by:

$$U(Y - WTP_B, Q_0) = U(Y, Q_1) \qquad (7.3)$$

where Q_0 is perceived as being 'better' than Q_1 and WTP_B is the maximum that an individual would be willing to pay to avoid the change. WTP_B is, in this sense, an equivalent variation measure of welfare change (Just *et al.*, 1982).

In the survey, both the external heritage benefits and the external heritage costs of the proposed road change were explicitly taken into consideration. The former consists mainly of aesthetic improvements, noise reduction and re-unification of the landscape from the point of view of those visiting the stone circle, and a range of benefits not related to any particular use of the site such as existence, bequest and option values arising from the improvement of the landscape. The latter includes the loss of view from the road accruing to those driving along the A303. A respondent's observed WTP will reflect the *net* welfare impact of the proposed tunnel. To the best of our knowledge, this is the first valuation study to explicitly allow for both welfare-enhancing and welfare-reducing impacts from a particular policy affecting cultural assets.[4]

SURVEY DESIGN AND IMPLEMENTATION

The final survey was implemented in March 1998 after extensive pre-testing that included a focus group, stakeholder interviews and two pilot surveys. A professional market research company with prior experience in contingent valuation surveys administered the questionnaire face-to-face. The final survey comprised a national sample of about 500 households, interviewed off-site in various locations around the country, and a sample of 300 UK visitors interviewed on-site while visiting Stonehenge. The south-west region of Britain (in which Stonehenge is located) was deliberately over-sampled on the prior assumption that willingness to pay values might be higher in this region. The samples were divided into two, with half of the respondents receiving a standard contingent valuation treatment and half receiving an alternative treatment (see endnote 4).

The contingent valuation scenario illustrated the changes that would occur if the A344 were closed down and an on-line 2-km tunnel built for the A303 (see Figure 7.1). The scenario was presented by means of a verbal description (reproduced in Table 7.1) reinforced by means of maps and photographs (Photograph 7.1). Computer-enhanced colour photographs illustrated the current and counterfactual situations. By using the same set of photographs and manipulating the images by computer in order to change the road layout, the influence of differences between photographs—such as a clear blue sky versus an overcast sky—is eliminated. Respondents were also reminded that if the A303 was put through a 2-km tunnel, drivers would no longer be able to see the stone circle

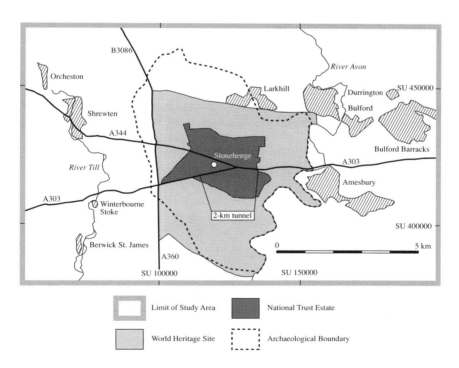

Figure 7.1   Tunnel scenario

Picture Card A: The current scenario

Photograph 7.1   Photographs used in interviews

Picture Card D: Closure of the A344 and a 2km tunnel for an enlarged A303

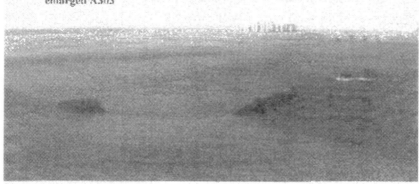

whilst driving past. Note that the method of constructing the 2-km tunnel was not referred to in the survey. It is conceivable that this might have had an impact upon the values that were attached to this road option, i.e. some individuals might have preferred a bored tunnel to a 'cut-and-cover' solution or vice versa.

Table 7.1   Verbal description of the 2-km tunnel option

(SHOW PICTURE OF CURRENT SCENARIO) 'This picture shows the current situation with Stonehenge in between two roads: the A344 and the A303. Traffic noise can clearly be heard whilst standing next to the stone circle. The roads prevent visitors from wandering over most of the surrounding National Trust area.'

(SHOW PICTURE OF 2-KM TUNNEL OPTION) 'This picture shows what the site would look like if the A344 was dismantled and the A303 became a dual carriageway. But with this option a 2-km (1-mile) tunnel would be built for the A303 as it goes past Stonehenge. The A303 would then be invisible from Stonehenge and it would be impossible to hear the traffic whilst standing next to the stones. Visitors would be able to walk over the entire National Trust area.'

After presenting the alternative scenarios, respondents were asked to identify their most preferred road option, independently of any financial considerations. The objective here was to sort respondents into two groups: those who prefer the current scenario to the 2-km tunnel and those who prefer the 2-km tunnel to the current scenario. As noted above, this avoids the presumption that all individuals receive a net benefit from the tunnel and gives explicit consideration to those whose welfare losses from not being able to see the stones from the road outweigh the heritage benefits.

Respondents were then invited to state their maximum willingness to pay in order to secure their most preferred road option. The chosen payment vehicle was an increase in tax, necessary to pay for the construction of the new roads.[5] The exact form of the tax was not specified to avoid individuals rejecting the scenario on the basis of one or other tax being unfair. Given that the tax was intended to represent the cost of the work being done, it was presented neither as a one-off payment nor as a per annum payment, but rather as an amount of money to be paid over the duration of the construction work. This was assumed to be two years.[6]

A ladder of monetary values was then introduced and respondents were asked to identify with a tick the amounts they were sure they would pay to secure their most preferred road option, leave a blank space for the amounts they were unsure whether they would pay or not and identify with a cross the amounts they were sure they would not pay. The range of values over which individuals were uncertain was therefore identified. An illustrative payment ladder is contained in the Appendix. Follow-up questions were used to identify the motivations behind positive and zero willingness to pay answers.

In order to exclude values arising from consideration of time savings or reduced accidents, the following protocol was adopted. First, no mention was made of the extent of any time savings or reduced risks of an accident associated with the proposed tunnel. Second, respondents were specifically told which impacts were to be considered: visual intrusion; noise experienced on site; landscape severance; loss of view from the road. Finally, individuals were asked whether any assessment of accident costs or time savings was present in their willingness to pay response. If so, then their response was discarded from the subsequent analysis.

The survey also included extensive sections on attitudinal beliefs, current use of the site and the demographic characteristics of the respondents and their households.

ATTITUDINAL RESPONSES

This section summarizes some of the findings from the attitudinal questions contained in the questionnaire, focusing in particular on preferences for the various road options. The questions were designed to reveal as much as possible about the underlying motives for supporting cultural heritage conservation so as to aid in the interpretation of the valuation responses and, at the same time, make respondents explore their personal thoughts on cultural heritage issues as a preparation for responding to the valuation question.

More than 53% of the national sample had never visited Stonehenge. After being presented with a visual and textual description of the current setting of Stonehenge, all respondents (independently of whether they had visited Stonehenge before or not) were asked to what extent, if any, they thought the nearby roads affected the setting of Stonehenge. Table 7.2 presents the results.

Table 7.2   Extent to which nearby roads affect the setting of Stonehenge

| | Site is improved | | | Site is much worse | |
	1	2	3	4	5
Off-site	2%	15%	49%	18%	16%
On-site	<1%	12%	40%	26%	22%

A significant number of respondents (about 48% on-site and 34% off-site) considered the site to be disfigured. This seems to suggest that changes in the road layout will be perceived as beneficial for a substantial proportion of the population. At the same time, however, just under half of the sample is indifferent towards the current Stonehenge road layout and between 13% and 17% actually think the roads improve the setting of the stones. Hence, there is also an indication that a number of respondents may not be willing to pay anything to change the current situation, and may indeed prefer the status quo over any proposed tunnel option.

Overall, 46% of respondents in the national sample had never travelled along the stretch of the A303 which passes Stonehenge, and 32% travelled less than once a year. Only 3% travelled more than once a week. Those who had travelled along the A303 stretch were asked whether they would miss seeing the stone circle if the A303 was put through a tunnel. The results, given in Table 7.3, show that, at least for some, there is a 'cost' attached to the construction of the tunnel in the form of lost views from the road, although it does not necessarily follow that all these individuals will obtain a *net* disbenefit from the tunnel, as the external benefits may well outweigh the costs.

Table 7.3   Attitudes towards not being able to see Stonehenge from the road

| | Miss a lot | | | | Not miss at all |
	1	2	3	4	5
Off-site	11%	17%	18%	15%	39%
On-site	16%	27%	24%	13%	20%

The balance between external benefits and costs became clearer when individuals were asked to select their most preferred road option, independently of any financial ramifications. Slightly less than half of the off-site sample (46%) selected the 2-km tunnel option while the remainder (54%) wanted to retain the current scenario. On-site, these figures are reversed with 42% of individuals favouring the retention of the current scenario and 58% opting for the tunnel. Thus, the sample seems to be split between finding the tunnel option welfare-enhancing and welfare-reducing. It remains to analyse how deeply these views are held. Preference strength can be assessed when attitudes are translated into monetary values.

ECONOMETRIC ANALYSIS

In total, 357 individuals were successfully interviewed using the contingent valuation questionnaire. Of these, 129 individuals were interviewed on-site whilst the remainder were interviewed in their homes throughout the regions of the UK. Respondents were asked to state their WTP, by means of a payment ladder, either to obtain the tunnel or to preserve the status quo, depending upon their preferences. In what follows the sample is in effect re-weighted in order that it is representative of the entire UK, rather than being biased towards the south-west region.

Econometrically, the information provided by the payment ladder can be treated as interval data (Cameron and Huppert, 1989). This is because the last tick in the ladder means that an individual is willing to pay at least that amount and anything up to the next amount left blank (see the Appendix for an example of a payment ladder). For example, when an individual ticks £3 and leaves blank the next highest amount (which is £5 in the payment ladder shown in the Appendix), this indicates that he/she is certain he/she would pay an amount between £3 and £4.99.[7]

The econometric model used assumes that for each group willingness to pay is distributed log-normally, partly on the basis that negative willingness to pay is ruled out (individuals who would experience a welfare loss being dealt with separately) and that the willingness to pay values are found to be highly skewed. The following log-likelihood function was employed to analyse the data:

$$LL = d_1 \times \log[\Phi((\log Z_1 - \beta X)/\sigma)] + d_2 \times \log[\Phi((\log Z_2 - \beta X)/\sigma)]$$
$$- \Phi((\log Z_1 - \beta X)/\sigma)] + ... + d_{24} \times \log[\Phi((\log Z_{24} - \beta X)/\sigma)]$$
$$- \Phi((\log Z_{23} - \beta X)/\sigma)] + d_{25} \times \log[1 - \Phi((Z_{24} - \beta X)/\sigma)]$$

where d_i is a dummy variable which takes the value unity when interval i on the payment ladder is selected and zero otherwise; Φ is the cumulative standardized normal distribution; Z_i is the bid level corresponding to the upper bound of payment interval i; β is a vector of parameters to be estimated; X is a vector of variables and σ is the standard deviation parameter also to be estimated. Note that 25 payment intervals were specified on the payment card. This likelihood function is maximized over all observations with respect to both the vector β and σ.

The results from estimating the log-normal specification for each of the two groups of respondents are depicted in Table 7.4. 'Protest' or otherwise invalid bids were dropped from the data set. A variable was included to represent the responses of off-site individuals living in the south-west region of the UK in which Stonehenge is located. This variable turns out to be insignificant, which probably reflects the national rather than regional importance of the Stonehenge site. The estimation is based on the total pooled sample (on and off-site interviews) as the table shows, somewhat surprisingly, there is no statistically significant difference between the valuations of the two groups. There is, however, a small but significant difference in the probability that an individual questioned on-site will prefer the 2-km tunnel option, as shown by Table 7.5.

Table 7.4   Results of the econometric analysis of willingness to pay

Variable	Proposed tunnel scenario		Current scenario	
	Model I	Model II	Model I	Model II
Constant	0.635663	0.70186	–5.96846	–5.08615
	(2.11564)	(4.21769)	(1.89995)	(2.08615)
On-site dummy	0.021132	–	1.57937	–
	(0.54250)		(1.09971)	
South-west dummy	0.289022	–	1.78852	–
	(0.648613)		(0.939027)	
σ	1.91007	1.92073	3.56632	3.64967
	(11.6144)	(11.6214)	(1.82000)	(1.88823)
Log L	–382.105	–382.331	–85.9637	–87.202
No. of observations	144	144	126	126

Note: Figures in parentheses are t-statistics.

Table 7.5   Probit analysis of the probability of supporting the 2-km tunnel option

	Proposed tunnel scenario	
Variable	Model I	Model II
Constant	–0.141573	–0.099107
	(1.38301)	(1.19189)
On-site dummy	0.347037	0.304571
	(2.29610)	(2.19353)
South-west dummy	0.125296	–
	(0.713006)	
Log L	–244.771	–245.025
No. of observations	357	357

Note: Figures in parentheses are t-statistics.

Using the parameter estimates from Table 7.4, mean willingness to pay is estimated to be £12.80 and £4.80 for the 2-km tunnel scenario and the current scenario respectively.[8] The striking feature of these numbers is the illustration that, even though the number of individuals preferring one scenario to the other is very similar, the mean willingness to pay of the group preferring the 2-km tunnel massively outweighs the mean willingness to pay of the group preferring the current scenario. This is indicative of the presence of much stronger preferences amongst those who prefer the tunnel, as compared to the supporters of the status quo. Arguably, the latter group may be near their indifference point between the two options.

Follow-up questions revealed the main reasons for wanting to pay to secure the construction of the tunnel: to protect Stonehenge for future generations; because Stonehenge was a national landmark; because the roads spoiled the appearance of Stonehenge.[9] Conversely, the main reason for wanting to pay to retain things as they currently are was missing the sight of Stonehenge from the road, or not liking to drive through long tunnels.

Many of the zero bids for the construction of the 2-km tunnel were due to an inability to pay higher taxes. As regards the maintenance of the current scenario, most zero bids also turned out to be legitimate. People said that, whilst they did prefer the current scenario, they didn't care strongly enough about it to pay, didn't feel able to afford anything or had more important things to spend their money on. Indeed, whereas only 37 out of the 144 valid bids registered for the tunnel scenario were between £0.00 and £0.50, as many as 112 out of 126 valid bids registered for the current scenario fell into the same payment interval. Predictably, the main reason for rejecting zero bids for this latter group was a rejection of the payment vehicle; some individuals did not see why they had to pay to retain the current scenario when no construction works were being undertaken.

Table 7.6 presents the full external heritage benefit estimates. The elicited WTP referred to a tax per year for *each* of the next two years, raised to cover the costs of construction. The present values are computed using a 6% discount rate. The benefits to the two different groups, those who prefer the 2-km tunnel option and those who prefer the current scenario, are dealt with separately. The second column reports the mean willingness to pay per household, when the protest bids are excluded. The third column takes the present value over two years using a 6% discount rate. The fourth column reports the level of support for each of the options among the general population.[10] The final column multiplies the present value by the probability of support and the 23.1m households in the UK. The final row indicates that the net heritage benefit from the construction of the 2-km tunnel would be £149m. If the median values are used instead, then aggregate willingness to pay falls to almost exactly zero.[11]

Table 7.6   The value of the 2-km tunnel to UK residents

	Mean bid per household	Present value bid	Probability of support	Aggregate value
For the tunnel	£12.80	£24.90	0.46	£265m
For the current scenario	£4.80	£9.30	0.54	£116m
Difference				£149m

Note: The probability of support is taken from the off-site sample.

CONCLUSIONS

This chapter has taken a valuation-based approach to examining the heritage benefits of an alternative road layout for the Stonehenge site: building an on-line 2-km tunnel for the A303. The heritage benefits of the proposed tunnel refer to changes in the levels of visual intrusion, noise and land severance relative to the current scenario. Specifically excluded are values relating to the effect on time savings and reduced accident rates, although future researchers might well prefer to value the entire set of benefits and disbenefits associated with the construction of a new road.

To our knowledge, this is the first occasion on which valuation-type approaches have been used to measure the environmental benefits and disbenefits associated with changes in road infrastructure in the UK. This made the study more challenging because a new range of issues had to be addressed without the benefit of any guidance from existing studies.

In standard valuation studies, the sole change to be evaluated is declared more or less universally to be either good or bad, and the only task is to measure the size of the impact. In contrast, this study estimated *both* the environmental benefits and the environmental costs associated with the 2-km tunnel (the latter in the form of individuals who would miss the view of the stones from the road).

The main findings of the study can be summarized as follows. Significant numbers of individuals derive satisfaction from viewing Stonehenge as they drive past and would miss the view if it were taken from them. This justifies the structure of the questionnaire, whereby individuals are, if they wish, able to post a positive bid to retain the current scenario with its 'excellent view from the road'. There was also strong but not unanimous support for the view that the roads adversely affected the Stonehenge site. There is no contradiction or inconsistency in the same individual expressing both the idea that the view from the road is pleasant and that on-site the traffic has an adverse effect on people's enjoyment. It is simply to say that individuals are confronted with two different and mutually exclusive goods: the view from the road and the view from the site.

The heritage benefits arising from the construction of the tunnel are £149m using this approach. Hence, heritage benefits alone justify the building of the tunnel as they exceed present value maintenance and construction costs. They also exceed the value of time savings and reduced accidents associated with any of the road options. Although these are clearly very large sums, a significant number of people regard Stonehenge as the most important site of cultural heritage in the UK. Many more were unwilling to disagree with the statement.

Finally, the large net heritage benefit associated with the construction of the tunnel is at variance with the bare majority in favour of its construction. This may be due to the fact that many individuals, rather than strongly opposing the construction of the tunnel, do not in reality care which option goes ahead. It is also interesting to note that if the values used are median willingness to pay, then the aggregate benefit of the tunnel is almost exactly zero. This indicates that, if an approach is taken whereby the decision is based upon majority voting, then the 2-km tunnel option is not supportable, at least on the grounds of any supposed heritage benefits.

POSTSCRIPT

Since this study was finished, the UK Government has announced its intention to go ahead and construct a 2-km tunnel for the Stonehenge site.

ACKNOWLEDGEMENTS

The research underlying this study was funded by English Heritage. The authors are indebted to David Pearce, Geoffrey Wainwright, Carrick James, Marilena Pollicino and Andreas Kontoleon for helpful comments and contributions.

APPENDIX

Example of completed willingness to pay ladder

£/year	✓ or ✗
Nothing	✓
50p	✓
£1	✓
£2	✓
£3	✓
£5	
£7	
£10	✗
£12	✗
£15	✗
£17	✗
£20	✗
£25	✗
£30	✗
£40	✗
£50	✗
£60	✗
£70	✗
£80	✗
£90	✗
£100	✗
£150	✗
£200	✗
Over £200	✗

ENDNOTES

1. The National Trust is the largest conservation charity in Europe. It was founded in the UK in 1895 to preserve places of historic interest or natural beauty permanently for the benefit of the nation. The Trust protects through ownership some 244,564 hectares and 575 miles of coastline. Associated with this are some 20,000 vernacular buildings, 183 houses of historic interest, 160 gardens, 73 landscape and deer parks, 1,000 scheduled ancient monuments and over 40,000 sites of archaeological interest.

2. English Heritage is a national body created in the UK in 1984 and charged with the protection of the historic environment and with promoting public understanding and enjoyment of it. English Heritage is the UK Government's official adviser on all matters concerning heritage conservation, provides substantial funding for archaeology, conservation areas and the repair of historic buildings, and is responsible for some 400 historic properties in the nation's care.

3. The study also estimated the heritage benefits associated with a number of other road options vis-à-vis the current situation, using contingent ranking techniques. The alternative schemes included an on-line dual carriageway option, a 500-m tunnel option and options to divert the A303 further north or south of the stone circle. The results of this study can be found in Mourato and Maddison (1999).

4. A common feature in contingent valuation studies dealing with cultural assets is the relatively large proportion of zero values (Pearce and Mourato, 1998). Many of these zeros may possibly be masking underlying negative values, implying that the proposed change may be welfare-reducing for a number of individuals. However, this possibility is typically not taken into consideration.

5. There is of course no precedent for indicating to individuals how much of the tax they pay is spent on particular road projects. However, the idea that the government is compelled to raise taxes in order to finance road infrastructure developments was found to be highly plausible.

6. In one instance, the payment vehicle proposed by the survey might not have been entirely credible to the respondents. This is where individuals who prefer the current scenario against the 2-km tunnel were asked to pay to retain the current road layout. Individuals might well feel that they already have the right to the existing road layout and should not be asked to pay for it again. In mitigation, protests against the use of this payment vehicle can be identified and eliminated from further analysis. A more credible payment vehicle might be a toll on the existing road, but clearly any toll is an effective payment mechanism only for those who travel upon the road, not for everybody. Furthermore, the institution of road tolling would raise additional problems of acceptability.

7. Note that the range of uncertainty identified in the payment ladder can also be taken into consideration by an interval data approach. For example, if an individual places a tick next to £3 and a cross next to £10, this means that he/she might pay anything from £3 to £9.99. For the purposes of this chapter, only values which individuals were certain they would pay were considered, following a desire to arrive at conservative estimates.

8. The formula for calculating the median value is:

$$\text{Median} = \exp(\mu)$$

whilst the formula for calculating the mean value is:

$$\text{Mean} = \exp(\mu) \times \exp(\sigma^2/2)$$

where the natural logarithm of the variable in question is normally distributed with mean μ and standard deviation σ.

9. Those who said that the amount they were offering was for the protection of all similar sites and not just Stonehenge, or that the bid was motivated by the desire to obtain time savings or a reduction in the number of accidents en route, were classified as invalid answers and removed from the subsequent analysis.

10. It would be more appropriate to use different values for on-site and off-site probabilities of support since these differ. But given that the willingness to pay for each option is the same and that the number of households visiting Stonehenge each year is very small in relation to the number of households in the UK, these calculations suffice.
11. The median voter is in fact located at the 7th percentile of the willingness to pay distribution for those wishing to retain the current scenario.

REFERENCES

Cameron, T. (1988) 'A New Paradigm for Valuing Non-Market Goods Using Referendum Data: Maximum Likelihood Estimation by Censored Logistic Regression', *Journal of Environmental Economics and Management* 15, 355–79.

Cameron, T.A. and D.D. Huppert, (1989) 'OLS versus ML Estimation of Non-Market Resource Values with Payment Card Interval Data', *Journal of Environmental Economics and Management* 17, 230–46.

Grudemo, S. (1998) 'Encroachment Costs of New Roads: A Summary of the Results of CVM and For or Against Studies', Swedish National Road and Transport Research Institute, Linkoping, Sweden.

Just, R.E., D.L. Hueth, and A. Schmitz, (1982) *Applied Welfare Economics and Public Policy*, Prentice-Hall, Englewood Cliffs, NJ.

Mitchell, R. and Carson, R. (1989) *Using Surveys to Value Public Goods: The Contingent Valuation Method*, John Hopkins Press, Baltimore, MD.

Mourato, S. and D. Maddison, (1999) 'Valuing Different Road Options for the A303: A Contingent Ranking Analysis', CSERGE Working Paper (forthcoming).

Pearce, D.W. and S. Mourato, (1998) 'The Economics of Cultural Heritage: World Bank Support to Cultural Heritage Preservation in the MNA Region', Report to the World Bank, Washington, DC.

Soguel, N. (1994a) 'Costing the Traffic Barrier Effect: A Contingent Valuation Survey', IRER, University of Neuchatel.

Soguel, N. (1994b) 'Measuring Benefits from Traffic Noise Reduction using a Contingent Market', Working Paper GEC94–03, Centre for Social and Economic Research on the Global Environment (CSERGE), University College London and University of East Anglia.

8. The contribution of aboriginal rock paintings to wilderness recreation values in North America

Peter Boxall, Jeffrey Englin and Wiktor Adamowicz

INTRODUCTION

Most countries in the world comprise many cultures. Thus, valuing cultural heritage could include individuals of one culture in a country valuing aspects or artifacts of another culture in that same country. This situation occurs in North America, where the native aboriginal peoples have existed for several centuries with European settlers and immigrants. The impact of aboriginal culture on these Europeans and other immigrants over time has had a profound influence on the emerging cultural mosaic of North America. This chapter focuses on the values that non-aboriginal individuals have for some historical elements of this aboriginal culture.

We examine the influence of aboriginal rock paintings on visitation levels to wilderness areas in the Precambrian Shield region in central Canada. The region contains about 400 paintings on extensive rock faces found along water courses (Rajnovich, 1994), and some of these rock faces are located in popular canoeing areas (e.g. Quetico Provincial Park; Dewdney and Kidd, 1962). Many locations of these pictographs are noted in the popular and semi-popular wilderness literature (e.g. Beymer, 1989).

Anthropological scholars call these paintings pictographs because they represent picture writing and not necessarily works of art. These drawings were and may continue to be used to communicate among individual travellers or with the spirit world by the aboriginal peoples. Anthropologists believe some of the pictographs in the Shield region are 2000 years old (Rajnovich, 1994). Thus, there has been concern regarding their documentation and preservation for historical and cultural reasons. Of particular concern is their degradation through weathering and changing water levels. Vandalism, however, has also been a concern to wilderness management authorities and others.

Pictographs and other artifacts are still being discovered as a result of proposed hydroelectric developments in parts of the Canadian Shield, and new pictographs are catalogued periodically. Many older pictographs have been covered by mosses and lichens, and remain undetected. Thus, the remote areas of this region of Canada may hold many more of these artifacts than are currently documented.

Pictographs in the Shield still have spiritual and cultural significance to aboriginal peoples, which is evidenced by the discovery of recent offerings of tobacco, clothing and prayer sticks on ledges below the paintings (personal observation; Dewdney and Kidd, 1962). However, as this chapter will demonstrate, they are also sought by wilderness recreationists who consider them an enjoyable feature of a wilderness experience. Ecotourism operators who use them to attract clients interested in cultural experiences also promote pictographs. The discovery of pictographs may increase visitation levels to wilderness areas, and may generate recreation and tourism benefits.

In this chapter we report results from a survey of wilderness canoeists, in which the hypothetical presence of pictographs in a park in the Canadian province of Manitoba was presented. This park does not currently have any documented pictographs, but more remote wilderness areas surrounding the park do. The influence of hypothetical pictographs on the number of visits to the park is assessed in a contingent behaviour analysis. The results confirm that pictographs generate considerable recreation benefits to non-aboriginal peoples.

METHODOLOGY

The Study Area

Nopiming Provincial Park is a 1440-km^2 area situated in the Precambrian Shield, about 145 km east of Winnipeg (Figure 8.1). It contains numerous rock outcrops that can rise as much as 36 m above the surrounding countryside and are a dominant feature in the park. These rock outcrops and faces are similar to those in other areas on which pictographs are found. Our study team conducted back-country surveys to search for pictographs and other features and none were found. However, this fieldwork allowed us to identify places that were very similar to those in other wilderness areas where pictographs are found.

Nopiming Park is poorly drained and contains sedge meadows, bogs, rivers and many lakes of differing sizes. The river systems consist of many small rapids and waterfalls that are attractive to wilderness users interested in canoeing and kayaking. This terrain does not permit overnight wilderness hiking, and as a result much of the park is only accessible by canoes, kayaks or boats that can be carried overland. This accessibility is further reduced because there is only one unpaved road that runs through the park. The canoe routes, however,

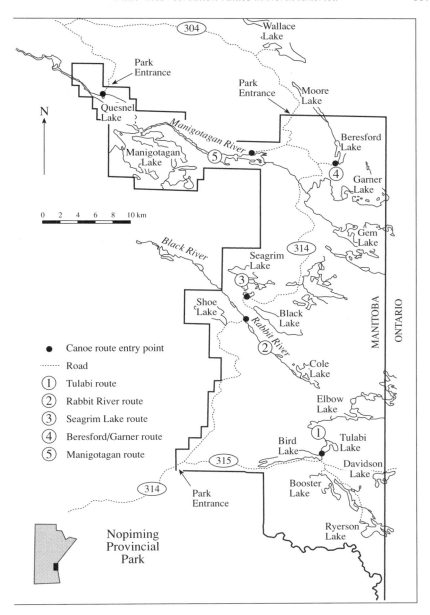

Figure 8.1   A map of Nopiming Provincial Park, Manitoba

Note: Our fieldwork suggested that rock faces along the canoe routes marked 3 and 5 would be suitable places for pictographs.

provide opportunities for wilderness experiences that cater for a wide range of individuals with varying skills and experience.

While there is no entry fee for use of the wilderness, there is a registration system that visitors are encouraged (but not required) to use. Because overnight wilderness trips involve canoes, kayaks and, to a lesser extent, motor boats, six provincial government registration stations were located at boat launches and other less developed route entry points. In 1993 the existing registration system was modified to enhance participation in the registration system and provide a more accurate assessment of use (Watson *et al.*, 1994). Eleven new registration stations were established throughout the park, making a total of 17.

All group leaders who registered for a wilderness trip from May to September in 1993 and 1994 comprised the sample, and were sent a mail survey. A total of 661 registrations were completed: 389 in 1993 and 272 in 1994. On average these groups consisted of 4.03 people. The original sample of 661 registrants was reduced to 587 by eliminating multiple trips by the same individual, and incomplete addresses. The sample included individuals from five Canadian provinces and three American states.

The Questionnaire

The questionnaire collected socioeconomic characteristics of the group leaders, their self-rated levels of canoeing expertise, knowledge and past use of parks in the Shield and specific wilderness areas in Nopiming, and preferences towards various management and environmental features. Socioeconomic characteristics included age, gender, household income and level of education. Canoeing expertise was measured by asking a respondent to rate themselves as novice, beginner, intermediate or advanced. Preferences for management and environmental features were assessed by respondents. Respondents were asked to rate 16 social, physical and management items on how enjoyable each would be on a water-based wilderness trip using a 5-point Likert scale. The questionnaire also collected information on the number of trips that each respondent took to the park during the period examined. This information constitutes the revealed preference (RP) data used in the analysis described below, rather than the trip information gathered in the voluntary registration procedure.

One section of the questionnaire contained a stated preference experiment involving the hypothetical presence of pictographs in the park. This experiment consisted of three contingent behaviour scenarios, only one of which will be analysed in this chapter. The first scenario involved presenting a pictograph (see Photograph 8.1) to individuals at a canoe route, which we knew the individual had not visited in the past four years. The individuals were asked if they would have switched their actual route taken to see the pictograph if they knew it was present. The second scenario repeated this with a vandalized

Photograph 8.1   A photograph of the pictograph used in the contingent behaviour scenario

pictograph. The analysis of these scenarios is not addressed in this chapter, but is reported in Boxall *et al.* (1998).

The third scenario asked the respondent to report if they would have taken more trips to the park than they actually did to view the undamaged pictograph shown in Photograph 8.1. In this case the question was asked as follows:

Would you have made an additonal trip to Nopiming in 1993 or 1994 (the year of your actual trip) to see a pictograph like the one shown in photograph E?

Yes ———— No ———— If yes, how many trips?

Note that this question examines the intention of a respondent to change their behaviour in response to the presence of a pictograph. This change can be compared to the actual trip level in which pictographs are absent from the RP information gathered from the questionnaire. Thus, we had two pieces of information from each respondent, their actual number of trips to the park and a hypothetical number of trips from the contingent behaviour scenario.

The initial mailing to the 587 group leaders took place in March 1995. After two weeks a reminder postcard was sent to those who had not responded, and after five weeks a replacement questionnaire was sent to non-respondents. This resulted in the return of 431 completed questionnaires which, adjusting for undeliverable questionnaires, represented a response rate of 81%.

Econometric Estimation

In order to examine the influence of pictographs on recreation values, we used the pooled RP and contingent behaviour (CB) count data model described by Englin and Cameron (1996). The count specification was preferred because of the non-negative integer nature of trips. In our analysis the CB information was used to enhance the RP data estimation in a joint estimation. In this case we had two observations of trip counts (one RP and one CB) from each respondent, and the only difference between them was the presence of pictographs. Only these two trip counts were available for each respondent, and thus the more complex panel specifications described by Englin and Cameron (1996) were not possible to implement.

The pooled model we estimated was:

$$E[\text{TRIPS}_i] = \exp(\tau_0 + \tau_1\text{CB}_i + \beta_0\text{TCOST}_i + \beta_1(\text{CB}_i \times \text{TCOST}_i)) + \gamma_i\text{S}_i \tag{8.1}$$

where TRIPS_i refers to the number of trips taken to Nopiming Park reported by group leader i in the questionnaire, CB_i is a dummy variable which equals 0 for the actual trip count and 1 for the trip count in the presence of the pictograph, TCOST_i refers to the travel costs from i's home to the park, S_i is a vector of individual socioeconomic and other characteristics, and the τ's, β's and the γ_i vector represent the parameters to be estimated.

The group leader's name identified the group and each group was treated as an 'individual' in the econometric analysis. This required the assumption that all individuals in a group come from the same origin as the group leader, and have the group leader's socioeconomic characteristics.[1] The use of group leaders' residences to represent those of all others in their group is common in the recreation demand literature (e.g. Hellerstein, 1991). Thus, although the model estimated was based on group trips, a trip record was considered as one from an individual weighted by the number of people accompanying the leader of the group.

The following formula identifies the travel cost calculation used:

$$\text{TCOST} = \$0.22 \times \text{DIST} + \text{TIME} \times \text{GRPSIZE} \times 1/4 \times (\text{INC}/2080) \tag{8.2}$$

In this formula DIST represents the round-trip distance in kilometres between a group leader's origin and Nopiming Park. The out-of-pocket expenses for the vehicle were estimated at $0.22/km (in Canadian dollars). TIME is the number of hours required to drive the round-trip distance, assuming an average speed of 80 km per hour. The opportunity cost of travel time was estimated at one-fourth of the wage. Note that the wage rate involved income earned over 2080 hours per year, and that the entire value of time term is weighted by the size of the group. Group size for each record was approximated by the average size of groups over the sample (4.03 people).

The estimation sample consisted of information from 350 respondents. This sample was smaller than the 431 questionnaires received due to item non-response. The variables used to characterize individual influences on trip frequency (i.e. the vector S_i) are shown in Table 8.1. The sample is primarily male, intermediate in terms of canoeing expertise and middle aged. Other individual characteristics, such as education or income, were collinear with these variables or exhibited higher item non-response in the survey and were not utilized in this analysis.

Table 8.1. Characteristics of individuals in the sample of backcountry canoeists from Nopiming Provincial Park, Manitoba

Characteristic	
Gender (% female)	17.4
Expertise	
Beginner (%)	16.8
Intermediate (%)	67.2
Advanced (%)	16.0
Age (mean in years)	36.7
Travel costs (group mean in dollars)	141.7
Mean number of trips with no pictograph (RP)	4.16
Mean number of trips with pictograph (CB)	4.87

The initial specification used to estimate the parameters was a Poisson count model. Because the information did not include any individuals who did not visit the park, the Poisson distribution involved truncation at 0 so that only those who took one or more trips were permitted in the analysis. However, an undesirable feature of Poisson count models is the assumption of the equality of the conditional mean and variance. This assumption is especially problematic in empirical research, because conditional variances are typically greater than conditional means in socioeconomic data, leading to an effect called overdispersion. Overdispersion, if present, allows consistently estimated means of parameter estimates, but causes the standard errors of these estimates to be biased downward, resulting in erroneous tests of their statistical significance (Cameron and Trivedi, 1986). Thus, the negative binomial model was also used. This model allows for overdispersion by compounding the Poisson distribution with a gamma distribution (Hausman *et al.*, 1984).

Choosing between the two specifications involves examination of the α parameter, which appears in the calculation of the conditional variance of the dependent variable (Grogger and Carson, 1988). If this parameter is greater than 0, the variance is greater than the mean. As α approaches 0, however, the negative binomial model degenerates to the Poisson. Thus, testing for $\alpha = 0$ provides a case for selecting the negative binomial over the Poisson, and indirectly the presence of overdispersion.

RESULTS

In this sample of wilderness users, finding pictographs on the rock outcrops along canoe routes was one of the highest rated factors influencing the enjoyment of a backcountry trip (Table 8.2). Seeing moose was the only factor rated higher by the individuals in our sample. We do not have information on how many of these individuals have previously experienced pictographs in wilderness settings, but from the survey we do know that about 25% of them had visited other wilderness parks in the region in which pictographs are found (Watson *et al.* 1998). This information allowed us to hypothesize that the presence of pictographs would affect trip behaviour and thus generate economic welfare effects.

Table 8.2   The highest rated factors affecting enjoyment of a backcountry or wilderness area by a sample of backcountry canoeists from Nopiming Provincial Park, Manitoba

Factor	Mean score
Seeing moose along canoe routes	4.84
Finding aboriginal rock paintings on rock outcrops	4.50
Being in area not accessible by motor boats	4.29
Presence of white water along the route	3.91
Short and easy portages	3.86
Meeting other paddlers on the route	3.81

Note: Mean score calculated using a 5-point Likert scale, where 1 was not enjoyable and 5 was most enjoyable.

The final results of the maximum likelihood estimation of parameters for the pooled RP–CB data are shown in Table 8.3. Other variables were tried in the models but were statistically insignificant. For the first negative binomial specification all variables, except the interaction between the CB constant and TCOST, are statistically significant at the 5% level or better. The CB–TCOST interaction term was removed in the second model due to its insignificance. The parameter for α is significantly different from zero. This result suggests overdispersion in the data and that the negative binomial model was the correct model to use.

Table 8.3   Parameter estimates from truncated count data models applied to trip data for Nopiming Provincial Park, Manitoba

Variable	Negative binomial 1		Negative binomial 2	
	Coefficient	Standard error	Coefficient	Standard error
INTERCEPT	1.21450	0.09277	1.21210	0.09007
TRAVEL COST	−0.00101	0.00023	−0.00099	0.00018
CB CONSTANT	0.21021	0.08864	0.21485	0.07107
BEGINNER	−0.47549	0.10156	−0.47549	0.10155
GENDER	0.37619	0.08755	0.37626	0.08754
CB × TRAVEL COST	0.00003	0.00035		
α	1.20590	0.15748	1.20590	0.15748
Log likelihood	−1650.02		−1650.02	

For the negative binomial model the parameter on TCOST is negative as expected, suggesting that the farther away one lives from Nopiming, the fewer trips are taken to the park. Similarly, being a BEGINNER in terms of canoeing expertise has a negative influence on the number of trips. The parameter on the CB dummy is positive and significant at the 5% level, suggesting that if all things were equal, the pictograph (if present) would generate an increase in the number of trips taken to the park. Finally, being female would have a positive influence on the number of trips.

We assessed the welfare implications of the presence of pictographs using the negative binomial model. An issue with this calculation was the fact that we estimated demand conditional on taking a positive quantity of trips, while the unconditional demand curve (including 0 trips) is really of primary interest. It is conventional in the literature to use the truncated model to approximate the untruncated one (e.g. Yen and Adamowicz, 1993). This results in a logarithmic function where consumer surplus per trip is equal to the negative inverse of the travel cost parameter $(-1/\beta_0)$.

This consumer surplus calculation using the negative binomial travel cost parameter generated a value of $1007.20 per trip per group. Dividing this by the average group size of 4.03 individuals results in a consumer surplus estimate of $249.93 per trip. This estimate is reasonably close to the consumer surplus estimates for trips to Nopiming reported in another study. Englin *et al.* (1998) used the registration data for these same individual group leaders and generated consumer surplus estimates ranging from $117.89 to $293.23 per trip. In that study the estimation also used count models, but trips to and prices of substitute wilderness areas were formally incorporated into the model. In the present study it was not possible to include these features, which may have an effect on the estimated welfare measures.

Examining the value of pictographs requires accounting for the presence of the pictograph on the increase in trips. This can be done in two ways. The first involves information from the trips reported in the questionnaire by those respondents in the estimation sample (Table 8.1). In this case the presence of the pictograph would generate on average an increase in the number of trips taken by 0.71 per individual. Multiplying this by the value of each trip per individual ($249.93) yields a value of the pictograph of $177.45 per person.

The second method uses the negative binomial model to predict the number of trips with and without pictographs.[2] For the average person in the data (i.e. a person with the mean characteristics of all independent variables reported in Table 8.1), this yields estimates of 2.88 without pictographs and 3.57 with pictographs. In this case the presence of the pictograph would generate an increase of 0.69 trips per person and a resulting consumer surplus estimate of $172.92 per person. This approach can be extended to examination of the value of pictographs for beginners and non-beginners. For beginners a pictograph would generate an additional 0.46 trips, and for others 0.75 trips. The resulting values of pictographs are, therefore, lower for beginners ($116.45/person) than non-beginners ($187.35 per person).

DISCUSSION

This research indicates that aboriginal rock art is a valued aspect of wilderness recreation in Canadian Shield waterways. Our results point to the possibility of increased trips to areas to see rock paintings if recreationists knew their locations. The specialized wilderness recreation literature describes the locations of pictographs and other aboriginal cultural artifacts (e.g. Beymer, 1989), and there is other literature available that describes the form and spiritual functions of pictographs (e.g. Rajnovich, 1994). For the less advanced canoeist, information about pictographs and where to see them outside tourist-oriented parks is difficult to find. Our findings suggest that the presence of pictographs would

Photograph 8.2 Two examples of vandalized pictographs found by the authors during fieldwork in the regions of the Canadian Shield during 1994

generate greater benefits for intermediate and advanced canoeists than for beginners. This could, in fact, be the result of the availability of literature to this more advanced recreation group.

Providing this information more widely to individuals with a range of abilities, however, suggests a management conundrum. With increasing visitation to view rock art comes the potential for intrusion into areas of spiritual and cultural significance for aboriginal peoples.[3] In many such places the locations of pictographs are purposely not advertised to reduce the potential for conflict between non-aboriginal individuals who wish to see them and aboriginal peoples who view the area as culturally and spiritually significant. Furthermore, with increased visitation comes the potential for vandalism of the pictographs. Steinbring and Elias (1968), Dewdney and Kidd (1962) and others describe pictographs that have been shot at by hunters and where vandals have spray-painted their names or initials over them. Two such examples that we encountered during our fieldwork in other parks in the Shield are shown in Photograph 8.2. This illustrates that pressure does exist between the value of pictographs to recreationists, the importance of them to aboriginal cultures and the risks of vandalism.

Wilderness managers might be interested in forecasting demand to view pictographs, not only to estimate their benefits, but also to provide information on the potential for their defacement. Harrison (1976) points to vandalism decreasing the values of things people seek to see or experience. We demonstrated this in another paper, where the values of vandalized pictographs were far less than pristine ones (Boxall *et al.*, 1998). It would be instructive to relate the potential for vandalizing such artifacts to the abilities or knowledge of recreationists.

ACKNOWLEDGEMENTS

We acknowledge the Canada–Manitoba Partnership Agreement in Forestry, the Northern Ontario Development Agreement and the Canadian Forest Service for funding this research. We also thank David Watson for leading the fieldwork and data collection aspects of this research programme.

ENDNOTES

1. This assumption was examined, where possible, by comparing the addresses of group members with that of the leader. In virtually every case where we had the addresses, the town or city of residence was similar. An individual-level model would require the addresses of every group member. This information would be very difficult to gather in a voluntary self-registration system at entry points due to the high response burden.
2. Since the use of count models imposes a semi-logarithmic functional form, the predicted number of trips is calculated by:

$$E[\text{TRIPS}] = \exp(\tau_0 + \tau_1 \text{CB} + \beta_0 \text{TCOST} + \gamma_1 \text{BEGINNER} + \gamma_2 \text{GENDER})$$

where the parameters represent those in model 2 from Table 8.3 and the values of the variables represent the sample means from Table 8.1.
3. Some might argue that, given the age of some pictographs they may not have spiritual significance for aboriginal peoples today. However, in conducting fieldwork for this project, we found tobacco offerings on ledges beneath pictographs in Woodland Caribou Provincial Park. This area is remote and about 100 kms from the nearest aboriginal settlement, suggesting the rock face still has significance to local aboriginal peoples.

REFERENCES

Beymer, R. 1989. *A Paddler's Guide to Quetico Provincial Park*. W.A. Fisher, Virginia, MN.

Boxall, P.C., J. Englin and W.L. Adamowicz. 1998. Valuing undiscovered attributes: a combined revealed–stated preference analysis of North American aboriginal artifacts. Paper presented at the First World Congress of Environmental and Resource Economists, June 25–27, 1998, Venice, Italy.

Cameron, A.C. and P.K. Trivedi. 1986. Econometric models based on count data: comparisons and application of some estimators and tests. *Journal of Applied Econometrics* 1:29–53.

Dewdney, S. and K. Kidd. 1962. *Indian Rock Paintings of the Great Lakes*. University of Toronto Press, Toronto.

Englin, J. and T.A. Cameron. 1996. Augmenting travel cost models with contingent behavior data. *Environmental and Resource Economics* 7:133–47.

Englin, J., P.C. Boxall and D.O. Watson. 1998. Modeling recreation demand in a Poisson system of equations: an analysis of the impact of international exchange rates. *American Journal of Agricultural Economics* 80:255–63.

Grogger, J.T. and R.T. Carson. 1988. Models for truncated counts. *Journal of Applied Econometrics* 6:225–38.

Harrison, A. 1976. Problems: vandalism and depreciative behavior. Chapter 24, in G.W. Sharpe (editor), *Interpreting the Environment*. John Wiley, New York.

Hausman, J., B. Hall and Z. Griliches. 1984. Econometric models for count data with an application to the patents–R&D relationship. *Econometrica* 52:909–38.

Hellerstein, D.M. 1991. Using count data models in travel cost analysis with aggregate data. *American Journal of Agricultural Economics* 73:860–6.

Rajnovich, G. 1994. *Reading Rock Art: Interpreting the Indian Rock Paintings of the Canadian Shield*. Natural Heritage/Natural History Inc., Toronto, Ontario.

Steinbring, J. and D. Elias. 1968. A key pictograph from the Bloodvein River, Manitoba. *American Antiquity* 33:499–501.

Watson, D.O., L. Peters, P.C. Boxall, J. Englin and K. Chakraborty. 1994. The economic value of canoeing in Nopiming Park in relation to forest and park management. A report of the 1993 field season: Volume I. Canada–Manitoba Partnership Agreement in Forestry, Canadian Forest Service, Edmonton, Alberta.

Watson, D.O., P.C. Boxall and B. McFarlane. 1998. Characteristics and management preferences of wilderness users in eastern Manitoba. Unpublished Manuscript, Canadian Forest Service, Edmonton, Alberta.

Yen, S.T. and W.L. Adamowicz. 1993. Statistical properties of welfare measures from count-data models of recreation demand. *Review of Agricultural Economics* 15:203–15.

9. Economic benefits to foreigners visiting Morocco accruing from the rehabilitation of the Fes Medina

Richard T. Carson, Robert C. Mitchell and Michael B. Conaway

INTRODUCTION

This chapter describes a study for the World Bank which measured some of the economic benefits from a proposed project to preserve and restore the Fes Medina, a World Heritage Site. This study focused on the benefits to foreigners visiting Fes and to foreigners visiting Morocco but not visiting Fes. The economic benefits were measured using three contingent valuation survey instruments which were developed for this study and administered in Fes, Casablanca, and Tangier. The design, development, and administration of these survey instruments are described, and the data analyses for the two groups of foreign visitors are presented separately. The Turnbull lower bound on the sample mean for the Fes visitors was $69.59; the related aggregate estimate for the 161,149 estimated adult visitors to Fes who stayed overnight in a Fes hotel was $11,233,148. Similarly, the Turnbull lower bound on the sample mean for visitors to Morocco who did not visit Fes was $30.92; the related aggregate estimate for the estimated 1,516,169 adult visitors who stayed overnight in a Moroccan hotel but did not visit Fes was $46,879,945.

Description of Morocco and the Fes Medina

The Kingdom of Morocco (Morocco), known locally as Al-Mamlakah Al-Maghribiyah or by the shorter name Al-Maghrib, lies on the northwestern coast of Africa, bordering the North Atlantic Ocean and the Mediterranean Sea, and across the Strait of Gibraltar from Spain. With an area of some 446,550 km^2, it is slightly larger than California. It borders Algeria and Western Sahara and has a coastline of some 1835 km.

The population of Morocco is around 30 million and growing at about 2% per year. Approximately 99% of the population is Arab or Berber; about 99%

of the population is Muslim. Arabic and Berber dialects are the common languages; the official language is Arabic but French is often spoken in business, government, and diplomacy. About 50% of those aged 15 and over are literate.

The city of Fes is the oldest of Morocco's four imperial cities. Its founder, Idris I, established it around 789. By the 11th century, under the Almoravids, Fes had become a major Islamic city. Although it reached its zenith as a center of learning and commerce under the Marinids in the mid-14th century, it has continued to serve as an important religious center for Morocco and the Islamic world.

A notable feature of the city today is that its medina retains a great deal of its ancient cultural and economic integrity. The oldest portion of the Fes Medina, Fes el-Bali (the name means old city) is the home of more than 100,000 inhabitants whose 12,000 or more traditional houses are still partially surrounded by the ancient battlements. Its numerous narrow, twisting streets are lined by hundreds of small shops and workshops where traditional crafts are pursued; these streets are crowded with people and the animals that carry goods to shops and workplaces. It contains the oldest mosque in northern Africa, a famous Islamic university founded in 859, and numerous other culturally important buildings and fountains. The Fes el-Jedid, while called the new city, actually dates back to the 13th century. It contains the Royal Palace and the adjoining Great Mosque as well as the old Jewish quarter.

Today the Fes Medina's cultural heritage is a world-renowned attraction for tourists. According to one tourist guide:

> The medina of Fes el-Bali is one of the largest living medieval cities in the world and the most interesting in Morocco. With the exception of Marrakesh, Cairo and Damascus, there is nothing remotely comparable anywhere else in the Arab world. (Simonis and Crowther, 1995: 216)

It is also in jeopardy. According to this same guide:

> [T]he old city especially, some experts have warned, is slowly falling apart. . . . in the long term it will need huge investment if its unique beauty is to be preserved. (Simonis and Crowther, 1995: 216)

The cultural importance of the Fes Medina was recognized in 1980 by UNESCO, which named it as the first place in Morocco to be listed as a World Heritage City.[1] A more complete account of the history and the current culture of the Fes Medina can be found in Escher and Wirth (1992).

Description of Proposed World Bank Project in Fes

The ties between economic development and cultural tourism have long been recognized (McNulty, 1986) and have been factored into several World Bank projects (Goodland and Webb, 1989). UNESCO, the United Nations organization with responsibility for preserving the international environmental and cultural heritage, turned to the World Bank because of the Bank's expertise in project evaluation and experience in community and municipal development, in the hope that some cultural heritage preservation and restoration projects, when viewed in a holistic manner, would be eligible for Bank funding.[2] Recently, in collaboration with UNESCO, and in partnership with the J. Paul Getty Foundation, the World Bank launched a major initiative directed at preserving and restoring cultural heritage and developing methods of measuring the benefits of cultural heritage projects (World Commission on Culture and Development, 1996).

Specific focus of this study
In March 1997, as part of the studies undertaken to develop a strategy for the rehabilitation of the non-monumental built environment in the Fes Medina, the Harvard Graduate School of Design and Morocco's Agence Pour La Dedensification et la Rehabilitation de la Medina de Fes published a report (March, 1997) proposing a comprehensive strategy for the rehabilitation of the Fes Medina. A brief summary of Fes history and the rehabilitation project may be found in Darles and Lagrange (1996). The proposed rehabilitation strategy seeks to halt the Medina's structural and economic decline by an array of interventions, carefully designed to retain both its historic character and economic vitality. Based on this strategy, components for immediate action were detailed and the project plans were sent to the World Bank for possible funding. This paper reports on work we undertook to quantify some of the economic benefits that would likely accrue to foreign visitors to Morocco if the Fez rehabilitation project were successfully completed.

Sources of economic benefits
Economic benefits accruing from the project involving the Fes Medina being considered by the World Bank can be divided into five categories (see Table 9.1), depending upon the beneficiary.

Table 9.1   Categories of economic benefits

Category	Beneficiary source
1	Fes residents
2	Other Moroccans
3	Foreign visitors to Fes
4	Other foreign visitors to Morocco
5	Foreigners not visiting Morocco

The environmental assessment report by the Harvard Graduate School of Design and Agence Pour La Dedensification et la Rehabilitation de la Medina de Fes (June, 1997) considers the benefits that will accrue to Fes residents (category 1). In this chapter, we do not consider any of the potential benefits to Moroccans (categories 1 and 2), but rather concentrate on attempting to quantify to various degrees the potential benefits in categories 3 and 4 likely to accrue to foreign visitors to Morocco and/or Fes if the project is undertaken. A complete comprehensive benefit–cost analysis should include all five of these benefit categories, rarely done in practice because of the expense and difficulty of measuring all sources of benefits and the widely held belief that benefits of most projects outside the immediate area or country are likely to be negligible. While this may be true in general, it is unlikely to be the situation where substantial cultural or environmental resources are at issue. In this particular instance the project involves a rapidly deteriorating UNESCO World Heritage Site which has long been a major tourist destination. In such instances it has long been known (Dixon and Sherman, 1990) that a substantial fraction of the benefits of an improvement project may accrue not to local residents but rather to foreign visitors to the site. These benefits are often measured using either contingent valuation or travel cost approaches (Freeman, 1993). Most of the effort in this study was directed toward quantifying benefits that fall into category 3.

Since World War II, many factors in the developed world, including rising incomes, declining transportation costs, increasing urbanization, increasing population, increasing education, and increasing leisure time, have promoted the demand for tourism (Jud and Hyman, 1974). In econometric analyses of tourism demand, the income of tourists and the relative prices found in desti-nation countries have been found to be important determinants. Other factors include marketing, transportation costs, exchange rates, political unrest, economic recession, and international events such as the Olympics (Crouch, 1995; Lee *et al.*, 1996). The effects of the determinants of tourism demand are likely to vary by country-of-origin and country-of-destination, making it necessary to examine particular sites. Crouch (1995) notes the importance of differentiated, unique tourism destinations, and how they are likely to have more inelastic demand curves than those of more generic tourist destinations. Historic cities have become increasingly popular destinations, and the desig-nation of World Heritage Sites has drawn further attention to already popular attractions (Ashworth and Tunbridge, 1990; Drost, 1996).

Less frequently measured are the potential benefits accruing to other foreign visitors to the country (category 4) and to those not living in or visiting the country where the project is being considered (category 5). Benefits may accrue to agents in these two categories due to passive use considerations (Krutilla, 1967; Carson *et al.*, 1999). These considerations include an appreciation for the existence of the cultural resources in Fes or a possible desire to visit Fes in the future. One would expect economic benefits from such considerations on a per-agent basis to be greater for category 4 beneficiaries than category 5 beneficiaries. In both categories one would expect to see per-agent estimates of economic value which are lower than category 3 beneficiaries. However, due to the much larger number of agents in these categories, even very low per-agent benefits may translate into large aggregate contributions to the total benefit estimate. This effect, inherent in the nature of public goods, raises important issues about the choice of the order in which goods are valued (Hoehn and Randall, 1989; Carson *et al.*, 1998). This issue is of less importance to the consideration of category 3 benefits since these are benefits to private agents who made the decision to visit Fes.

In this chapter, we look at category 3 benefits and category 4 benefits measured using several different contingent valuation (CV) surveys administered in Fes, Casablanca, and Tangier. In a report to the World Bank on the larger study (Carson *et al.*, 1997) of which these CV surveys were a part, we also attempt to develop a crude estimate of the possible magnitude of category 5 benefits in Europe using a Delphi approach which asked CV researchers to provide their best professional guess of the likely results of undertaking a CV survey in Europe.

METHODOLOGY OF CV STUDY

Sampling Design for Moroccan Surveys

We designed a multi-stage sample of 600 adult visitors to represent all English and French-speaking visitors to Morocco during June–July, 1997, including tourists and those visiting for business or other purposes. The overall sample size of 600 respondents and the use of at most two languages was determined by time and budget constraints. The two languages chosen were French and English, as an examination of the 1996 visitor information showed that visitors from countries speaking these languages comprised the two largest proportions of visitors to Fes during our study months of June and July, 38.5% and 15.4%.

In order to be sure of an adequate representation of visitors to Fes, the group of primary interest in this study, we allotted 400 out of the total 600 budgeted interviews to be completed in Fes. One hundred and twenty of the remaining 200 interviews were allotted to Casablanca and 80 to Tangier, on the basis of their respective visitor flows. Some of the Casablanca and Tangier sample had been or were planning to visit Fes during their current visit; others were not. The former group plus the interviews conducted in Fes constitute our Fes visitor sample. The latter group constitutes our non-Fes visitor sample.

We used a three-stage sampling design: first, from a list of the other major Moroccan cities we randomly selected two other cities (Casablanca and Tangier); second, in each of the three cities, we sampled hotels from a list of that city's one-star and higher hotels; third, we sampled a target number of guests to interview in each hotel from the guests identified by the hotel as French, American, British or Canadian in nationality. In practice, the low occupancy rates during the slow tourist season in June and July in Fes required us to increase the size of our hotel sample somewhat. The target number of interviews for each hotel was determined by the hotel's size, as measured by number of rooms and modified, as necessary, by its actual room occupancy when the interviews were conducted. Additional details on sampling are contained in Appendix B of the Carson *et al.* (1997) report.

Development of Fes CV Instruments

We used three interview forms in this study: Form 1 was used for the interviews conducted in Fes; Form 2 was used for the Casablanca–Tangier interviews of visitors who had or intended to visit Fes during this trip; Form 3 was used for those visitors in the same two cities who did not intend to visit Fes this trip. Each of the three forms contained the same basic scenario, with modifications as necessary for the different locations and experiences of the respondents. Whether a respondent in Casablanca or Tangier received Form 2 or 3 depended on the respondent's answers to a short series of screener questions about the visitor's itinerary. Each of the three forms has an English and French version, for a total of six versions. The three questionnaire forms were finalized in English and then translated into French.[3] Each of the six location–language versions was administered to equivalent subsamples (subsamples a–f), each of which received a different payment amount (price-point) in the willingness-to-pay (WTP) question. This design makes possible the use of the pattern of answers to the WTP question to trace the demand curve.

In designing the survey instruments for this study, we relied on the principles for CV survey design we have developed and used successfully in other CV surveys. [Carson *et al.* (1997) contains a copy of each form and language variant.] Our goal was to design instruments that could easily be administered in person in a short period of time and would be clearly understood by the respondents with sufficient information so that the respondents would understand the nature of the choice without being overwhelmed or bored by unnecessary detail. We place a great deal of emphasis in our design on avoiding demand effects where the respondent would feel that a certain type of answer is expected. Whenever we were unsure about the possible effect of a design feature, we chose the option that seemed likely to underestimate, rather than overestimate, the respondent's willingness to pay.

Below we present an overview of Form 1, the instrument used in Fes, and comment, where appropriate, on the Form 2 and Form 3 variants. We will consider each of the instrument's four sections in turn, and identify the questions that play a role in our estimation equations by the acronyms used for our analysis.

Section 1

The first section consists of 16 questions,[4] which obtain information about the person's visit to Morocco and to Fes. They include questions about the reason for visiting Morocco (Q. 4 HCITY[5]) and the amount of knowledge they had before visiting Fes (Q. 6 KNOW). Many of the earlier questions ask about the respondents' travel experiences in Morocco, including questions (Q. 12) about visits to other cities such as Marrakesh (MARK), Meknes, and Rabat (RABAT), which are potential substitutes for Fes. Questions 13 to 15 measure the visitors' attitudes about how interesting they found the Fes Medina (Q. 13), how strongly they would recommend it to friends (Q. 14 FTRIP), and whether they would like to visit it again some time in the future (Q. 15 RTRIP).

Section 2

The material in this section contains the Fes scenario, that consists of a short narrative supplemented by show cards featuring colored photographs of the Medina. The purpose of this text, which was the same for each form, is to provide each respondent with a standardized set of information about the character and condition of the Fes Medina today. The text describes the Fes Medina and its cultural importance, and explains that the condition of the Fes Medina is deteriorating, due to insufficient resources for rehabilitation. The text concludes by saying that, without a major rehabilitation effort, the Medina will continue to decline. Three photographs on show cards visually document the story told in the text; they help maintain respondents' interest and attention to the narrative. Table 9.2 presents the scenario's entire text and a description of the show card displayed during the reading of each part of the text.

Section 3

The third section of the instrument describes the conditions of the WTP choice presented to the respondents. It presents a plan to rehabilitate the Fes Medina, which is described as having been developed by "the Moroccan Government in collaboration with experts from international agencies". The respondent is told the plan would accomplish three things: improve the Medina's appearance and repair and clean up buildings, streets, sewers, public spaces, and monuments; preserve the Medina's traditional character and cultural heritage for future generations; ensure that the Medina will continue to be a productive and vibrant living city.

Table 9.2   Description of the scenario used in all forms of the Fes rehabilitation survey

Text read by the interviewer	Description of show card
As you may know, the Fes Medina is one of the largest living medieval cities in the world. Because of its uniqueness it was one of the first cities in the world to be named by UNESCO as a World Heritage City.	
HAND R. THE PHOTO CARD I. This photograph is an aerial view of the Fes Medina. Founded around 800 A.D., the 12,000 traditional houses in this part of Fes are now the home of more than 100,000 people. The Medina is the setting for numerous historic mosques, palaces, monuments, gardens, and fountains.	This card contained a single color aerial photograph of the Medina. At the top it was titled "The Fes Medina". At the bottom a caption read: "The Fes Medina was founded
Of special importance is that it continues to be a living city with numerous markets and many workshops where traditional crafts are practiced. The largest of the two parts of the Medina, the Fes el-Bali, is still surrounded by the ancient wall. Visitors enter its maze of twisting alleys through the traditional gates.	around the year 800 A.D. It is one of the largest living medieval cities in the world. In 1980 it was the first place in Morocco to be listed as a UNESCO World Heritage City".
HAND R. PHOTO CARD II. Over the years many of the Medina's buildings have deteriorated because of over-crowding and inadequate city services. Photo A shows a recently repaired house.	This card contains four color photographs (reproduced by color xerox from original photographs downloaded from the Harvard
Unfortunately government resources are too limited to keep up with the need for rehabilitation. [PAUSE] As a result, many houses continue to deteriorate and every year, as shown in photo B, some collapse before they can be restored.	Design School Fes Project Office's digital photograph files). Each pair was chosen to show a representative well-maintained and
The Medina has hundreds of streets. Photograph C gives an example of a well-maintained street, [PAUSE] Because funds for maintenance and city services are inadequate, many streets, like the one in photograph D, are badly paved and dilapidated.	not well-maintained features. The captions read: "A House", "B Ruin of House", "C Residential Street", and "D Residential Street".
HAND R. PHOTO CARD III. Despite the efforts of local authorities, some of its important public buildings have become run down, such as the building in photograph F. Many public spaces urgently need refurbishing, to keep them from further deterioration. Only a few of its numerous fountains now flow with water.	This card contains four photographs, paired in the same manner as before. The captions read: "E Public Building", "F Public Building", "G Fountain", and "H Fountain
There is concern that unless a major effort is undertaken, the old Fes Medina will continue to decline and may soon lose its historical character, perhaps forever.	Repair".
TAKE PHOTO CARDS BACK.	

125

These prospective accomplishments represent the public goods that the proposed rehabilitation plan will provide. The respondent is then told "the rehabilitation plan will be expensive and cannot be implemented without additional sources of support". We use this wording to help overcome any belief respondents might have that the Moroccan Government, UNESCO, or some other agency might pay the full cost.

The choice portion of the interview contains a number of specific features that we describe below and summarize in Table 9.3.

Payment vehicles and choice mechanisms   The respondent is then told that "one way to help pay for it" would be for visitors to pay a special fee. Because CV surveys should offer respondents a choice that is as plausible as possible, so that they take the choice seriously, we used two types of fees (which constitute the payment vehicle) for different portions of our sample. Table 9.3 summarizes these differences. We asked the Fes visitors (Forms 1 and 2) what decision they, as consumers, would have taken about including Fes in their itinerary if they had to pay a Fes preservation fee of a specified amount (see below) when they registered at their Fes hotel. This way of framing the issue reminds respondents that they have substitutes, other historical Moroccan cities that are already in their itinerary or which could be in their itinerary. It forces them to consider whether Fes would still be worth visiting if the cost of the visit was increased by the stated amount. Further, the use of a mandatory Fes hotel visitor fee as the payment mechanism carries with it the implication that it is not a marginal change in the characteristics of the Fes Medina being valued, but rather the preservation/restoration plan versus the disappearance of the Fes Medina as an integral whole under the current status quo situation.

In all versions, the interviewers showed respondents a Card C which briefly summarized the choice presented to them. For example, Card C for Form 1 read as follows:

1. Still come to Fes even though the preservation fee would add to the cost of my visit.

Or

2. Not include Fes in my itinerary for this trip and use the money for other purposes.

Since this type of choice would not be meaningful for the non-visitors to Fes (Form 3), we asked them about a departure fee that all foreign visitors would have to pay when they left the country. Here we presented the choice in terms of whether or not they would favor the imposition of such a departure fee at a specified amount if not paying it would lead to the "likely deterioration of the

Table 9.3 Characteristics of the choice for preserving the Fes Medina by form

Component	Form 1	Form 2	Form 3
Payment vehicle	Special "cultural heritage preservation fee" to be paid when registering at hotel during each visit to Fes	Special "cultural heritage preservation fee" to be paid when registering at hotel during each visit to Fes	Special "Fes preservation departure fee" on all visitors when they leave Morocco
Choice mechanism	Personal decision whether to still come to Fes if the fee adds a specified amount per adult to cost of visit OR not to include Fes in trip itinerary	Personal decision whether to still come to Fes if the fee adds a specified amount per adult to cost of visit OR not to include Fes in trip itinerary	Whether to favor departure fee of specified amount that would increase the cost of each visit to Morocco OR oppose fee and accept the likely deterioration of the Fes Medina
Fiduciary mechanism	Special fund solely for the preservation of Fes	Special fund solely for the preservation of Fes	Special fund solely for the preservation of Fes
Elicitation mechanism/number of price points	Binary/choice 6	Binary/choice 6	Binary/choice 6
Stated price amounts in dirhams	50, 100, 250, 500, 1000, 2000	50, 100, 250, 500, 1000, 2000	25, 50, 125, 250, 500, 1000
French franc equivalent	29, 59, 147, 294, 588, 1176	29, 59, 147, 294, 588, 1176	15, 30, 74, 147, 294, 588
Dollar equivalent	5, 10, 25, 50, 100, 200	5, 10, 25, 50, 100, 200	2.50, 5, 12.50, 25, 50, 100

Fes Medina". This type of choice is similar to the referendum-type choice whether to tax oneself that we and others have found effective in CV studies conducted elsewhere. We did not pose the question in an explicit referendum format in this study, because it would not have been meaningful to the respondents since they are not Moroccan citizens.

Anecdotal evidence from the field director indicates that the respondents paid attention to the interview and found the payment choice plausible. She reports that a majority of the respondents became so involved in the subject matter of the interview that they wanted to continue to discuss the Medina after the conclusion of the interview. Those who chose not to pay typically took the time to explain their choice. One woman even presented 100 dirhams (the amount she was asked about) to the interviewer because she thought she had to pay the amount at the end of the interview.

Fiduciary mechanism   We included the strong assurance that the fee "would go into a special fund for the preservation of the Fes Medina and could *not* be used for any other purpose" in an attempt to overcome anticipated skepticism about whether the money would in fact be used for that purpose. In our experience, such skepticism is common in the US, and we expected that it would be at least as common among our respondents in Morocco. If respondents are skeptical, they are likely to choose not to pay for the program, biasing the results downward.

Elicitation mechanism   We used a binary, discrete-choice elicitation question that identified a specific cost (one of six price-points randomly assigned to respondents) in dirhams. Fes visitors (Forms 1 and 2) were asked whether they would have visited Fes during the present trip if they had to pay the stated amount. Foreign tourists, who did not plan on visiting Fes during this trip, were asked whether all visitors to Morocco should have to pay a fee of the specified amount for Fes (Form 3).

Price points   In this study, we randomly assigned each respondent to one of six price-point subsamples that varied between 25 and 2000 dirhams. Table 9.3 shows the amounts. We chose the six amounts to bracket the anticipated range of median willingness to pay and to give us information about the tails of the WTP distribution. Time limitations prevented us from pretesting the distribution, so we were forced to rely on our best judgment about the end points and intervals. We assumed those visitors who were visiting Fes would be willing to pay more than those who were not visiting Fes. We stopped the upper ranges for these two groups at the equivalents of $200 and $100, $200 for the hotel fees for the Fes visitors and $100 for the departure fees for the non-Fes visitors, because these amounts were likely to be the highest plausible amounts the government might contemplate charging for hotel and departure fees.

The price was stated in dirhams, the Moroccan currency. The interviewer also gave its approximate equivalent in other currencies of likely relevance to the respondent. English-speaking respondents were told the equivalent in US dollars and British pounds; French-speaking respondents were told the equivalent in French francs.

The survey scenario consisted of the rehabilitation plan and the means by which it would be financed in a straightforward way, intended to minimize demand effects. When the choice question was reached, we encouraged the respondent to give "your frank opinion" to help legitimize answers (such as choosing not to pay the amount) that some respondents might consider socially undesirable. The wording of the choice in Forms 1 and 2 calls explicit attention to the tradeoff between paying the amount or not including Fes in the respondent's itinerary. The possibility that the respondent might want to "use the money for other purposes" was also invoked.

Section 4

The last section consists of a small number of questions that measure background information that we used to create some important dummy variables for the regression analysis we describe below. Questions 18–20 ask whether the respondent is traveling alone (ALONE) or with family members. Questions 21 and 22 measure age; question 28, gender. In question 23, we asked where the respondent currently lives; from the answer we created a dummy variable (FRANCE/SPAIN) that indicates respondents who live in France or Spain, the two European countries closest to Morocco. Questions 24–26 concern the respondent's education; from these questions we created a simple indicator variable, UGO, which measures whether the respondent has attended university for one or more years.

Measuring income is usually complicated, and asking about income must be handled very carefully in surveys. The major complication comes from the need to measure family income from all sources before taxes; it is not just the salary of the primary wage earner. In an international survey such as this one, asking for family income is even more complicated because several aspects of income which are usually taken into account in the question's wording—currency, income distribution, and the tax structure—vary by country. The compromise we devised is a question that asks respondents to place themselves in their country's income distribution:

Q. 27 What percent of the people in your country have a higher annual income than you? Just your best guess: would you say only one percent have a higher income than you, or ten percent, or twenty percent, or thirty percent, or forty percent, or would you say half or more of the people in your country have a higher income than you?

This formulation also has the merit of reducing the tendency of the income question to evoke sensitivity about revealing income. We do not have information about whether answers to this question tended to overstate or understate the respondents' income. In our analysis we use a dummy variable derived from answers to this question, TINC, which indicates those reporting income in the top 20% in their country.

Field Work

Interviewing began in Fes on June 16, 1997 and continued until July 3 under the direction of Dr. Naima Lahbil Tagemouati, a Moroccan economist with extensive experience in conducting surveys in Morocco. The Casablanca and Tangier interviews were conducted between July 15 and July 25. Three principal interviewers (two men and one woman) worked on the project, all Moroccan nationals with extensive experience working with tourists and fluent in one or both of the two languages in which we conducted the interviews.[6] Permission from the management at the selected hotels was secured to conduct interviews with their guests. Virtually all the interviews, which lasted between 10 and 20 minutes, were conducted in the respondents' hotels at times and places that were convenient to them.

In order to help avoid response-selection bias, we trained the interviewers to limit their explanations of the interview's purpose to scripted responses that did not reveal its true purpose. For example, if a prospective respondent asked about the study's purpose, the script provided to the interviewer stated the following:

> The purpose of this study is to learn what people like you think about your experiences here in Morocco and about some possible future changes in the Fes Medina.

We took a number of steps to avoid interviewer bias. Interviewers were trained to administer the instrument in a neutral fashion and to avoid communicating their preferences non-verbally. We designed the protocol for the practice interviews to give the interviewers experience with respondents who were not willing to pay for the Fes rehabilitation plan. During the interviewer training, we emphasized that our goal was to find out what people really felt about the topics covered in the interview, and emphasized that there were no right or wrong answers to our questions. This statement is also part of the brief introduction the interviewers read to every respondent:

Thank you very much for agreeing to take part in this study. Please understand that there are no right or wrong answers to any of the things I will ask you about. We just want to know what you really think.

If I do not read any part of the questionnaire clearly enough, please let me know right away.

Relatively few visitors who were approached for an interview refused to cooperate. We estimate that the response rate (those who took the interview divided by the total number of people approached for an interview) was approximately 90% in Fes. The non-cooperation rate was highest among older visitors to Fes traveling with group tours whose schedules did not leave the visitors with much free time.

RESULTS

Fes Visitor Estimates

The survey administered to Fes visitors described the plan to improve conditions in the Fes Medina that should result in the preservation of the historic part of the city. The payment mechanism used in the survey was an adult visitor registration fee which would be included in the hotel bill. Two largely identical versions of the survey were administered: the first to foreign visitors staying in hotels in Fes and the second to foreign visitors to Morocco sampled in hotels outside of Fes who either had already visited Fes or intended to visit Fes on this trip to Morocco. The second version of the survey instrument was administered in Casablanca and Tangier. English and French versions of the questionnaire were available, and bilingual interviewers were used. After dropping a small number ($N = 11$) of substantially incomplete observations, we obtained a usable sample of 471 observations.[7]

Survey respondents were randomly assigned to one of six monetary amounts in dirhams, the Moroccan currency. In US dollar equivalents, the amounts used are approximately $5, $10, $25, $50, $100, and $200. Respondents who indicated they would visit Fes despite the hotel tax are treated as *for*, and those who indicated they would not or did not know are treated as *not-for*. The distribution of responses is displayed in Table 9.4. The percentage for the Fes visitation fee systematically declines from 83.1% at $5 to 27.8% at $200.[8] A χ^2 (df = 5) statistic of 84.53 suggests a significant relationship at $p < 0.001$.

In order to obtain median and mean WTP estimates from the data in Table 9.4, one must either assume a parametric distribution for the underlying latent distribution or estimate bounds on the statistics of interest non-parametrically. A non-parametric technique proposed by Turnbull (1976) was applied to the data in Table 9.4. This technique is now often used in CV surveys (Carson *et al.*, 1994; Haab and McConnell, 1997). This model has a log-likelihood of −280.81. The Turnbull technique imposes the restriction from economic theory that the percentage willing to pay does not increase as the monetary amount asked about is increased. That restriction is not violated by the raw data displayed in Table 9.4.

Table 9.4   For/not-for responses at each visitation fee amount

Amount ($US)	% Not-for	% For	N (row)
$5	16.87	83.13	83
$10	25.00	75.00	84
$25	45.00	55.00	80
$50	57.89	42.11	76
$100	69.74	30.26	76
$200	72.22	27.78	72

Effectively the Turnbull technique estimates the probability mass that falls into each of the intervals defined by the monetary amounts used in the survey. From Table 9.4 it is possible to determine that median WTP lies between $25 and $50, because 55% of the sample is willing to pay more than $25 while 42% of the sample is willing to pay more than $50. By allocating all of the probability mass at the lower end of each interval, a lower bound on the sample mean is defined. This lower bound on the sample mean is $69.59 and has a 95% confidence interval of [$57.60–$81.58].[9]

Parametric distributions may also be fit to the data. Two parametric distributions commonly fit when the data must be positive are the log-normal and the Weibull. Table 9.5 displays the fit of these two distributions with the standard errors of the location and scale parameters given in parentheses. In both cases the parameters are fit with good statistical precision; both distributions are reasonably close in a statistical sense to the non-parametric fit in Table 9.4. The log-normal distribution yields an estimated median WTP of $38.28 with a 95% confidence interval of [$29.32–$50.79], while the Weibull yields an estimated median WTP of $42.67 with a 95% confidence interval of [$31.47–$53.87].[10]

To examine the construct validity of the CV results, common practice (Mitchell and Carson, 1989) is to estimate an equation, often referred to as a valuation function, which predicts a respondent's answers to the binary discrete choice WTP question as a function of the amount the respondent was asked and variables thought to be related to the respondent's income and preference for the particular good being valued.

Table 9.5   Parametric models

Distribution	Location	Scale	Log-likelihood
Log-normal	3.6450 (0.1368)	2.1252 (0.2465)	−281.854
Weibull	4.4690 (0.1490)	1.9314 (0.2202)	−283.060

With respect to income, we have two possible variables. The first, TINC, is created from a set of two questions, INCCODE and INCPRCT, which ask respondents for their income relative to other people in their home country in a set of categories (INCCODE) or a numerical response (INCPRCT). Anyone reporting income in the top 20% in their home country was given a value of 1 for TINC, while all others were given a value of 0. Those who refused to respond to INCCODE or INCPRCT were classified as zeros. Because some of these respondents are likely to be ones, the effect of TINC on WTP is likely to be biased downward. The other variable, THOTEL, is an indicator variable for staying in a four or five-star hotel at the time of the interview. Because trip costs can be influenced by the number of people in the traveler's party and the payment mechanism is a per adult fee, we also define a variable ALONE which equals 1 if the respondent is traveling alone and 0 otherwise. From several indicators of education in the survey, we define the dummy variable UGO for having attended a university. This variable is likely to be correlated both with income and also with preferences for cultural amenities.

Several variables may relate to the respondent's taste for visiting the Fes Medina. The first of these is an indicator variable FRANCE/SPAIN for being a resident of France or Spain. Both of these two countries are in close proximity to Morocco, so a visit to Fes is likely to be somewhat less exotic for visitors from Spain and France than for visitors from other countries. A second variable looks at the reason for the visit to Morocco. Here we use two of the seven possible responses, wanting to visit historic cities, which is an obvious reason for wanting to visit Fes, and business.[11] Choosing either of these two reasons will result in the respondent being coded as a 1 on HBCITY, while the other possible responses which do not relate to wanting to visit Fes—beaches, natural beauty, wanting to visit modern cities, wanting to visit the countryside, or others—are coded as 0 on HBCITY. There are two key questions asked before the WTP question that relate directly to preferences regarding Fes. A variable from one of these, RTRIP, is coded 1 if the respondent indicates that they would like to return to Fes, and 0 otherwise. The other, FTRIP, is coded 1 if the respondent

Case studies

indicates that a Fes visit would be recommended to a friend, and 0 otherwise. Respondents in the Fes subsample who had not yet been to Fes were not asked the RTRIP and FTRIP questions; for these respondents, FTRIP and RTRIP were coded 0. Since some of these respondents may have been coded 1 had these questions been asked, coding them as 0 may have biased the RTRIP and FTRIP coefficients downward. We also recorded the other major Moroccan locations that foreign visitors might go to. The major competitor sites among the imperial cities are Marrakesh and Rabat. Marrakesh is fairly distant from Fes, while Rabat is fairly close. (There were so few reported/intended visits to the fourth imperial city, Meknes, that statistically reliable estimates of the effect of this city could not be obtained.) The last variable we used was BEFORE, defined as equal to 1 if the respondent was interviewed before visiting Fes and 0 if interviewed after visiting Fes.

The estimated valuation function displayed in Table 9.6 is a probit equation using the log of the monetary amount asked about (see Table 9.4), LAMT, and is equivalent to the log-normal specification reported in Table 9.5 with the addition of covariates. This model has a log-likelihood value of −242.771 and a pseudo-R^2 of 0.262, which indicates valuation function has achieved a relatively good fit for cross-sectional survey data. Further, all of the variables for which there was a clear *a priori* expectation on sign—LAMT, TINC, THOTEL, ALONE, UGO, HBCITY, RTRIP, FTRIP—have the expected sign and generally are quite significant. The parameter estimate for the FRANCE/SPAIN indicator variable suggests visitors from these two countries are willing to pay less than visitors from other countries. Given the close proximity of these two countries to Morocco, this is not surprising. A Marrakesh visit appears to be complementary to a Fes visit, while a Rabat visit appears to be a substitute. Since Fes and Rabat are in close proximity, raising the hotel cost in Fes would make visiting only Rabat more attractive, and visiting both Fes and Rabat less so. Being asked about the Fes project before visiting Fes (BEFORE) is negatively related to the respondent's WTP. One possible explanation for this result is that actually seeing the situation in Fes makes one more willing to pay to see the Medina rehabilitated.

There were several variables such as age and sex that were found to have almost no effect on predicted WTP. This was also true of an indicator variable for whether one had already finished a tour of the Fes Medina (as opposed to being in Fes and having not started or being part way through a Fes Medina visit). The number of days in the Fes visit also had no influence on WTP, although this is perhaps not surprising given that the payment vehicle required a payment per visit to Fes, not per day spent in Fes. A variable for previous visits to Morocco is positively and significantly related to WTP when included in an equation with only LAMT; but this variable becomes insignificant when the more directly related variables, RTRIP and FTRIP, are included.

Table 9.6   Valuation function for foreign visitors to Fes

Variable	Parameter estimate	Standard error	p-Value	Variable mean
Intercept	1.2653	0.3218	0.001	–
LAMT	–0.5461	0.0576	0.001	3.4252
TINC	0.4048	0.1490	0.007	0.3312
THOTEL	0.3467	0.1679	0.039	0.7686
ALONE	–0.2728	0.1471	0.064	0.6348
UGO	0.3791	0.1436	0.008	0.6879
FRANCE/SPAIN	–0.3596	0.1598	0.024	0.6348

Aggregate Estimates for Foreign Visitors to Fes

An aggregate estimate of the annual benefits to foreign visitors to Fes can be obtained by multiplying the desired statistic from the previous section by the number of foreign visitors to Fes. The Moroccan Ministry of Tourism office in Fes estimates that 168,672 visitors from outside North Africa stayed overnight in hotels in Fes during 1996. The payment mechanism in our CV survey pertained only to adults, so we need to reduce this estimate by the percentage who are under 18 years old. From our survey, we obtain an estimate of the fraction of visitors who are under 18 of 4.3%. Applying this correction factor yields an estimate of 161,419 adult visitors to Fes who stayed overnight in hotels; this is the number we will use in the annual benefit estimate presented here. Multiplying the estimated number of adult visitors, 161,419, by the Turnbull lower bound on mean WTP yields an annual aggregate estimate of $11,233,148 with a 95% confidence interval of [$9,297,734–$13,168,562], assuming that sources of uncertainty other than that associated with the sample estimate of the Turnbull lower bound on mean WTP are ignored.

The other sources of uncertainty should be noted. First, the number of visitors in 1997 and future years is likely to be a random variable and could be larger or smaller than that in 1996. If conditions in the Fes Medina were substantially improved, one might well expect visitation to Fes to increase as long as conditions for tourism in Morocco remained favorable. Second, there is uncertainty that stems from deviations of our sample from that of the ideal random sample of foreign visitors to Morocco. In particular, it should be noted that our survey was administered only during the months of June and July. From statistics taken from the Moroccan Ministry of Tourism office in Fes, we know that foreign visitors during this time period are much more likely to be French and less likely to be German than during the rest of the year. We also know that by having the survey only available in English and French, some foreign visitors not fluent in either of these two languages were systematically excluded from the sample. We suspect that this factor leads to a small downward bias in the estimates as the valuation function in Table 9.6 suggests that visitors from France and Spain are willing to pay less than those from other countries, who are less likely to make casual trips to Morocco. Two other factors are likely to bias the aggregate estimate downward: some foreigners visit Fes but do not spend the night in Fes; some foreign visitors, principally backpackers, do not stay in regular hotels. Their WTP for the project is not included in the aggregate estimate.

Estimates for Non-Fes Foreign Visitors to Morocco

The analysis of the foreign visitors to Morocco who did not also visit Fes is similar to that performed for Fes visitors. Here, however, the usable sample size is much smaller ($N = 126$) since two-thirds of the interviews were conducted in Fes and over 35% of the respondents interviewed in Casablanca or Tangier intended to visit or had already visited Fes. The specific attitude questions that were only relevant to people who were visiting Fes were not included in the questionnaire for non-Fes visitors, giving us few potential covariates with which to predict WTP.

Survey respondents were randomly assigned to one of six monetary amounts displayed in terms of the Moroccan currency, dirhams. In US dollar terms, the amounts used are approximately $2.50, $5, $12.50, $25, $50, and $100. The main reason for reducing the amounts relative to those used in the Fes visitor survey was that a departure fee of $200 earmarked for the Fes project seemed unreasonable. The distribution of responses is displayed in Table 9.7. The percentage *for* the Fes visitation fee systematically declines from 80.95% at $2.50 to 10% at $100. A χ^2 (df=5) statistic of 30.24 suggests a significant relationship at $p < 0.001$.

Table 9.7   For/not-for responses for non-Fes visitors

Amount ($US)	% Not-for	% For	N (row)
$2.50	19.05	80.95	21
$5.00	27.27	72.73	22
$12.50	30.00	70.00	20
$25.00	38.10	61.90	21
$50.00	63.64	36.36	22
$100.00	90.00	10.00	20

For the data in Table 9.7, the log-likelihood for the Turnbull model is −70.211. The median falls in the interval [$12.50–$25.00] and the Turnbull lower bound on mean WTP is $30.92 with a 95% confidence interval of [$22.10–$39.75].

In Table 9.8, we report the results of fitting two parametric distributions, the log-normal and the Weibull. The log-normal median is $22.40 [$13.83–$39.88]; the Weibull median is $25.01 with a 95% confidence interval of [$14.43–$35.59].[12]

Table 9.8   Parametric estimates for non-Fes visitors

Distribution	Location	Scale	Log-likelihood
Log-normal	3.1089 (0.2469)	2.0064 (0.4036)	−72.852
Weibull	3.7782 (0.2332)	1.5254 (0.3071)	−71.876

Because the respondents who do not visit Fes on this trip are not asked attitudinal variables directly related to Fes, we define two new dummy variables: PMVISIT takes a value of 1 if the respondent has previously visited Morocco and IMPERIAL takes a value of 1 if the respondent will visit one of the other imperial cities, Marrakesh, Meknes, or Rabat, this trip. The result of fitting a valuation function to these two variables, along with the log of the amount asked (LAMT) and the indicator variable for being in the top 20% of the income distribution in one's home country (TINC), is displayed in Table 9.9. The log-likelihood is −64.625 and the pseudo-R^2 is 0.253, again a relatively good fit for cross-sectional survey data.

Table 9.9   Valuation function for non-Fes visitors

Variable	Parameter estimate	Standard error	*p*-Value	Variable mean
Intercept	1.0950	0.3359	0.001	–
LAMT	−0.5596	0.1097	0.001	2.7851
TINC	0.7228	0.2810	0.010	0.3333
PMVISIT	0.4845	0.2635	0.066	0.4444
IMPERIAL	0.3796	0.2695	0.159	0.4603

We also looked at the other variables we had tried in the valuation function for the Fes visitors. The BHCITY variable used in Table 9.6 was positive and significant when LAMT was the only other variable included, but not when the other covariates in Table 9.9 were included. The FRANCE/SPAIN indicator variable was negative and marginally significant in an equation with only LAMT. A dummy variable for staying in five-star hotels was positive and highly significant without the TINC variable. Unfortunately, only about 10% of our sample were staying in three-star hotels; no respondents were staying in less than three-star hotels. This makes it impossible to estimate the effects of having a sample skewed toward high-end accommodations. This issue is discussed in the next section.

Aggregate Estimate for Non-Fes Foreign Visitors to Morocco

The World Tourism Organization estimates that in 1996 there were 1,876,070 foreign tourists arriving in Morocco from outside North Africa who stayed in hotels and similar establishments. Reducing this estimate by the number of foreign visitors staying in hotels who visit Fes (168,672) yields an estimate of 1,707,398. This estimate in turn needs to be further reduced by our survey estimate of the percentage of children among foreign visitors not going to Fes, 11.2%. Making this reduction yields an estimate of 1,516,169.

This estimated number of foreign visitors multiplied by the Turnbull estimate of the lower bound on mean WTP yields a benefit estimate of $46,879,945 with a 95% confidence interval of [$33,507,335–$60,267,718].

This estimate comes with a number of important qualifications. The first and perhaps most important is that the sample of non-Fes foreign visitors interviewed in Casablanca and Tangier were almost exclusively staying in four and five-star hotels. Ideally one should either reduce the number of visitors to reflect only the number of foreign visitors staying in upper-end accommodations or reduce the estimated WTP to reflect the fact that those staying in lower-end accommodations are willing to pay less due to income and other factors.

Other issues with respect to this sample of non-Fes foreign visitors are similar to those involving foreign visitors to Fes. First, sampling was only done in July; that may be atypical relative to looking at all the visitors to Morocco in a single year. Second, the availability of the survey instrument only in English and French would have systematically excluded potential respondents not fluent in either of these two languages. Finally, even though Casablanca and Tangier were randomly selected from among international entry points, on a per day basis, tourists found in these two cities may be atypical of foreigners who visit Morocco but not Fes. There are two other factors that should be noted with respect to the estimate of the relevant population size. First, the World Tourism Organization estimates that there are 178,000 foreign tourists who arrive on cruise ships but do not stay overnight in Morocco. Second, we do not include in our estimate tourists who do not stay in hotels or similar establishments, or Moroccan nationals residing abroad. To the extent that these people have positive WTP for the Fes project, the aggregate WTP estimate is too low.

Probably the most important factor in determining the aggregate estimate for the non-Fes foreign visitors is the number of years over which individual

WTP should be aggregated. The key issue is whether there is effectively *additional* competition for the amount of value for the Fes project held by foreign visitors to Morocco. Over one year the answer is likely to be *no*. Over a longer time period, other similar rehabilitation projects are likely to be put forth by the Moroccan Government and/or international organizations. Thus aggregation of our point estimate over many years would likely substantially overestimate total benefits, the situation examined in Hoehn and Randall (1989). One very conservative way to largely avoid this issue is to use only the first year's aggregate estimate as the total aggregate estimate over the time period of interest. Using the one-year estimate $46,879,945 as the total aggregate estimate for non-Fes visitors will likely provide a conservative estimate despite the oversampling of visitors in four and five-star hotels.

ENDNOTES

1. The *Convention Concerning the Protection of World Cultural and Natural Heritage* (*the Convention*), adopted by UNESCO in 1972, provides for the *World Heritage List* of natural or cultural sites that are part of the national and international heritage. Currently the *World Heritage List* consists of 582 sites of which six, including the Fes Medina, are in Morocco.
2. In this regard, the World Bank has viewed projects with significant cultural resources in a manner similar to projects with significant environmental resources (Serageldin and Taboroff, 1994; World Bank, 1994).
3. The initial translation into French was made by a consultant to the Harvard Design School. This translation was modified for use in the field by Dr. Tagemouati.
4. The first section of Form 3 consisted of only six questions because the other questions were not relevant to visitors who were not visiting Fes.
5. All the variables in the WTP equations are dummy variables. In this case HCITY is a dummy variable where HCITY = 1 if the visitor's most important reason for visiting Morocco was to enjoy the historic cities.
6. In addition to the three main interviewers, Dr. Tagemouati conducted some of the interviews herself and a few of the Casablanca interviews were conducted by two additional interviewers.
7. In five of the 11 cases dropped, the main WTP question was unanswered as were other key questions. In the other six cases dropped, a substantial number of questions were unanswered or answered with *don't know*. Typically, these cases also had *don't know* for the answer to the WTP question.
8. From the perspective of completely mapping out the latent WTP distribution, it might have been desirable to have placed the highest design point at an amount larger than $200. However, as noted earlier, higher amounts would not have been plausible as a fee on hotel visitors. The implications of not being able to ask higher amounts are that non-parametric estimates of the lower bound on the mean are likely to be more biased in a downward direction than without this constraint and that parametric estimates are more dependent upon the functional form assumed over the right tail of the WTP distribution than would otherwise be the case.
9. The upper bound on the sample mean is not a useful statistic in this case since all that is known is that 27.8% are willing to pay more than the highest amount asked, $200.
10. It is also possible to obtain an estimated mean WTP using the parameters of these two distributions. The log-normal distribution, which is quite sensitive to assumptions about the shape of the right tail of the distribution, yields an estimate of $366. The estimated mean

WTP from the Weibull distribution is $164. A Weibull distribution fit with two additional parameters to allow more flexibility in the left and right tails yields an estimate of $131.
11.   The Fes project is designed in part to enhance commercial opportunities in the Medina.
12.   The log-normal estimate of mean WTP is $167.62; the Weibull estimate of mean WTP is $59.20. A Weibull model with an extra parameter in each of the tails yields a mean WTP estimate of $43.28.

REFERENCES

Ashworth, G.J. and J.E. Tunbridge (1990), *The Tourist-Historic City* (New York: Belhaven Press).
Carson, R., N.E. Flores and W.M. Hanemann (1998), 'Sequencing and Valuing Public Goods', *Journal of Environmental Economics and Management*, 36, 314–23.
Carson, R.T., L. Wilks and D. Imber (1994), "Valuing the Preservation of Australia's Kakadu Conservation Zone", *Oxford Economic Papers*, 46, S727–49.
Carson, R.T., R.C. Mitchell, M.B. Conaway and S. Navrud (1997), "Non-Moroccan Values for the Rehabilitation of the Fes Medina", report to the World Bank.
Carson, R.T., N.E. Flores and R.C. Mitchell (1999), "The Theory and Measurement of Passive Use Value", in I. Bateman and K. Willis, eds., *Valuing Environmental Preferences: Theory and Practice of the Contingent Valuation Method in the US, EC and Developing Countries* (New York: Oxford University Press).
Crouch, G.I. (1995), "A Meta-Analysis of Tourism Demand", *Annals of Tourism Research*, 22, 103–18.
Darles, G. and N. Lagrange (1996), "The Medina of Fez: Crafting a Future for the Past", *The UNESCO Courier*, October 1996, 36–9.
Dixon, J. and R. Sherman (1990), *Economics of Protected Areas: A New Look at Benefits and Costs* (Washington: Island Press).
Drost, A. (1996), "Developing Sustainable Tourism for World Heritage Sites", *Annals of Tourism Research*, 23, 479–92.
Escher, A. and E. Wirth (1992), *Die Medina von Fes. Geographische Beitrage zur Persistenz und Dynamik, Verfall und Erneuerung einer traditionellen islamischen Stadt in handlungstheoretishcer Sicht*, Erlanger Geographische Arbeiten, Heft 35 (Erlangen: Selbstverlag der Frankische Geographischen Gesellschaft).
Freeman, A.M. (1993), *The Measurement of Environmental and Resource Values: Theory and Methods* (Washington: Resources for the Future).
Goodland, R. and M. Webb (1989), "The Management of Cultural Properties in World Bank Assisted-Projects", Technical Paper No. 62 (Washington: World Bank).
Haab, T. and K.E. McConnell (1997), "Referendum Models and Negative Willingness to Pay: Alternative Solutions", *Journal of Environmental Economics and Management*, 30, 251–70.
Harvard Graduate School of Design and Agence Pour La Dedensification et la Rehabilitation de la Medina de Fes (1997), *Project de Rehabilitation de la Ville Historique de Fes: Dynamique Fonciere et Rehabilitation de L'Habitat*, Rapport Provisoire.
Harvard Graduate School of Design and Agence Pour La Dedensification et la Rehabilitation de la Medina de Fes (1997), *Rehabilitation of the Fez Medina: Environmental Assessment*.
Hoehn, J.P. and A. Randall (1989), "Too Many Proposals Pass the Benefit–Cost Test", *American Economic Review*, 79, 544–51.

Jud, D.G., and J. Hyman (1974), "International Demand for Latin American Tourism", *Growth and Change*, 5, 25–31.

Krutilla, J. (1967), "Conservation Reconsidered", *American Economic Review*, 57, 787–96.

Lee, C., V. Turgut and T.W. Blaine (1996), "Determinants of Inbound Tourist Expenditures", *Annals of Tourism Research*, 23, 527–42.

McNulty (1986), "Cultural Tourism: New Opportunities for Wedding Conservation to Economic Development", in *Conservation and Tourism* (London: Heritage Trust).

Mitchell, R.C. and R.T. Carson (1989), *Using Surveys to Value Public Goods: The Contingent Valuation Method* (Baltimore: Johns Hopkins University Press).

Serageldin, I. and J. Taboroff, eds. (1994), *Culture and Development in Africa* (Washington: World Bank).

Simonis, D. and G. Crowther (1995), *Lonely Planet Morocco (Lonely Planet Travel Survival Kit)* (Oakland: Lonely Planet).

Turnbull, B.W. (1976), "The Empirical Distribution Function with Arbitrarily Grouped, Censored, and Truncated Data", *Journal of the Royal Statistical Association*, *B*38, 290–5.

World Bank (1994), "Cultural Heritage in Environmental Assessment", *Environmental Assessment Sourcebook Update* No. 8, September.

World Commission on Culture and Development (1996), *Our Creative Diversity* (Paris: UNESCO).

10. Component and temporal value reliability in cultural goods: the case of Roman Imperial remains near Naples

Patrizia Riganti and Kenneth G. Willis

INTRODUCTION

Cultural goods have both use and non-use value. People consume cultural goods as visitors to cultural and historic sites, and may be willing to pay along with non-users to ensure their continued existence and availability for future generations. Cultural goods such as a prominent archaeological site often comprise many elements[1] that are partly complements but are also substitutes in consumption. In preserving archaeological sites it is important to derive some notion of the value that the general public places on the different elements of archaeological sites to enable the sites to be managed more efficiently. This study explores whether values derived through the contingent valuation (CV) method for different components of an archaeological park in Italy are consistent, and whether the general public's values for the archaeological park remain reliable over time.

The study is based upon one of the most important Roman sites in Italy: Campi Flegrei,[2] an archaeological park west of Naples. Campi Flegrei is an important area of Roman remains which, because the sea level is now higher than that in ancient Roman times, lies partly under the sea where some remains are still located, uncatalogued and unresearched. When compared to Pompeii this site is not as well preserved, as the integrity of the ancient Roman remains has been fragmented by the urban development which has taken place through centuries. However, the glorious past can be perceived when looking at the importance of the remains, which reflects the fact that Campi Flegrei was chosen, during the first century A.D., as the royal summer residence of the Roman Emperors. The reason for this prestigious settlement was mainly due to the unique features of its landscape. The geomorphologic characteristics show the signs of an intense volcanic activity, which has moulded the natural scenery, sometimes smoothly, other times with powerful and sudden interventions, such as the overnight appearance of Monte Nuovo volcano in 1538. The archaeological site currently imposes a constraint on the urban expansion of Naples, and coastal urban development in the area.

COMPONENT AND TEMPORAL VALUE RELIABILITY

The reliability and accuracy of CV estimates have received considerable attention in the literature following the conference organized by Cambridge Economics, Inc., in Washington, DC in April 1992, and the subsequent National Oceanic and Atmospheric Administration (NOAA) report in which good practice guidelines for the conduct of dichotomous choice (DC) CV surveys to elicit non-use values were outlined. On temporal reliability, the NOAA report stated that "a clear and substantial time trend in responses would cast doubt on the 'reliability' of the finding".[3] On component reliability it stressed the need to avoid embedding bias, and that constancy or near constancy of the willingness-to-pay (WTP) does not appear consistent with diminishing marginal utility. Subsequent research has focused on a number of issues, principally the embedding issue and scope effects, and the temporal stability of values over the short term.[4]

The accuracy and validity of CV estimates can be judged following the taxonomy suggested by Mitchell and Carson (1989) in terms of content validity (the appropriate framing of the study, and questions asked in relation to the good being valued); criterion validity (the comparison of CV estimates with actual market or simulated market experiments); and construct validity (the correspondence or *convergence* between a CV measure and other (e.g. travel cost or hedonic price) measures of the same good, and the extent to which the findings of the CV study are consistent with *theoretical* expectations).

The ultimate test of CV methods is criterion validity: how accurate are CV methods in predicting what actually happens in the real world; that is, how good are CV methods at predicting quantities demanded at various prices. However, the accuracy of non-use or passive use values can only be assessed in terms of content validity, and theoretical expectations in construct validity. This study uses statistical significance tests of theoretical expectations to assess whether mean WTP values are significantly different for the whole of an archaeological good compared with its components; whether mean values of components are significantly different from each other; and whether there is temporal stability in mean WTP values over a short time period (two years).

HYPOTHESIS TESTS

The component and temporal stability in CV can be formulated into a number of hypotheses:

$$H_1: \quad WTP(ws) > WTP(ps)$$
$$H_2: \quad WTP(ws_{95}) = WTP(ws_{97})$$

where H_1 implies no embedding effect, i.e. WTP for the whole site (WTP(ws)) exceeds WTP for part of the site (WTP(ps)), and H_2 assumes no significant differences of WTP estimates between 1995 and 1997 over time for the whole site (ws). Both tests have been implemented in the literature,[5] but this chapter discusses the results when combining them to assess welfare estimates of temporal reliability for distinct components of total economic value, in a scenario where passive values appear to be predominant.

The test follows the procedure outlined by Downing and Ozuna (1996) and extended by Carson *et al.* (1997). First, the welfare benefits and their confidence intervals are estimated for each sample. Second, a dummy variable approach is used to determine if the CV choice functions, obtained by two comparable samples independently drawn at two different points in time, are statistically transferable across time. Then, the results obtained in the first and second steps are compared and conclusions are inferred. As a result, five different benefit functions, WTP1 to WTP5, and their estimates, are checked. Temporal stability, and benefit function transferability, are regarded as established if the parameter estimates of the two functions for the different time periods are not statistically significantly different. We then compare the differences of the welfare measure which, in cases where confidence intervals overlap, can be considered statistically similar. We assume that this three-step test gives sufficient confidence in assessing the reliability of the welfare estimates over time.

COMPONENT ELEMENTS AND NON-USE VALUES OF CAMPI FLEGREI

Inside the wider territory of Campi Flegrei, the area of Bagnoli stands out for the different nature of its more recent development. At the beginning of this century, contrary to its natural vocation and historical heritage, this area was chosen as the site for a large industrial plant. Iron and steel industries were located here in an effort to produce jobs for this otherwise chronically depressed economic area. However, at the beginning of the 1990s, following an EC (European Community) directive, the plant was closed. In fact, the industrial plant brought negative externalities to the whole area of Campi Flegrei, affecting the unique features of its landscape, and emphasizing the need for sustainable development in the area. In 1995, at the time the first CV survey was implemented, no decision had yet been taken about future development strategies for this site. During the period of the second survey, in 1997, a detailed plan for the Bagnoli element of Campi Flegrei had been proposed to the Local Planning Authority. However, the overall condition of the site has not changed since the closure of the industrial activity in the area.

Archaeological sites such as Campi Flegrei comprise numerous components. This makes them particularly suitable for methodological investigations into issues such as embedding. Moreover, people readily perceive differences in scope of archaeological commodities and, when such goods are accurately described and presented, are also able to distinguish among their main attributes and values. When confronted with the task of assessing use or non-use values for cultural goods, people seem quite confident, and this is probably due to the nature of the good itself. Issues regarding *unrestricted* or *restricted access* (*use and option values*) to these goods, as well as the importance of their existence *in situ* (*intrinsic, existence value*), or their *benefit to future generations* (*bequest value*) are quite easily understood by respondents, as most respondents have visited similar sites, and therefore experienced the consequences on their utility of not gaining access, according to the relevance that this good has for them. For those who had never experienced a cultural good having characteristics similar to the one being valued, it is however possible to acquire enough information during the survey process itself. Since most people live inside an urban context, the main attributes of a cultural good, whatever the educational level, can be generally appreciated.

Both CV surveys employed in this study were designed to estimate the WTP for the benefits associated with the conservation of the cultural heritage of Campi Flegrei as a whole, and to identify values associated with subsets of this larger complex good. In both CV surveys the WTP instrument moved from valuing the larger good (Campi Flegrei) down to WTP for the smaller one (Bagnoli). Among the objectives of both surveys was the attempt to separate the benefits associated with bequest value and with option value from the larger set of total economic benefits, whilst checking the results for consistency with economic theory according to "within subject tests" (internal tests) across WTPs from the same sample of respondents. In this sense the CV surveys may be regarded as a weak rather than a strong test on component validity. A strong test would require that independent samples were used to value WTP for Campi Flegrei as a whole compared to Bagnoli, and for use compared to bequest value, etc. Sampling the same respondent for WTP for Campi Flegrei and WTP for Bagnoli is more likely to result in WTP(ws) > WTP(ps). However, in another CV study, the same CV results for the whole of Campi Flegrei presented here have been compared with those of two smaller independent CV surveys of other parts of the archaeological park, namely the Castle of Baia and the Park of Cuma (Fusco Girard *et al.*, 1998). In that analysis the "within subject test" on the independent samples was passed at the 5% level of confidence. This allows us to suggest that an accurate CV design is capable of minimizing embedding effects. Moreover, the replication of the first survey after a two-year interval allows us to assess the reliability of the results over time, and to assess the use of CV estimates in policy making with regard to Campi Flegrei.

DATA SOURCES

The first face-to-face survey was administrated in March 1995, and was followed by a second face-to-face survey conducted during July 1997. The two surveys used an almost[6] identical questionnaire, with a referendum approach aimed at eliciting five different WTPs for a conservation programme of the whole Campi Flegrei and one of its parts, Bagnoli.

The survey elicited the maximum monthly amount people would be willing to pay in order to preserve the cultural heritage located in Campi Flegrei. To test the sensitivity to scope of this estimate of total economic benefit, an attempt was made to elicit WTPs for some of its components, such as the benefits associated with bequest values and option values of smaller parts of the Campi Flegrei.

The relationship between Campi Flegrei and Bagnoli can be regarded as both a complement (because Bagnoli complements the wider area of Campi Flegrei) and as a substitute (because future management of the site could preserve some areas at the expense of others). In the CV interviews, WTP responses for both the conservation of Campi Flegrei and of Bagnoli were elicited.

To investigate the components of bequest benefits, respondents were also asked to express their WTPs for the conservation of different components of Campi Flegrei, to access the value of remains if these were limited to future generations only. This is equivalent to subtracting use values from current users, but still providing bequest values. Locals are quite familiar with this state of affairs, as some recently discovered sites have never been open to the public, and probably will not be open for quite a long time. Within the wider territory of "Campi Flegrei", a number of archaeological sites will not be accessible until full restoration is complete. For many of these sites restoration is a lengthy process and might take decades to complete.

Pilot and final surveys were all conducted in person. The range of discrete response bids employed in the final survey was identified from the open-ended responses in the pilot studies. The highest bid (Lit. 150,000/month, approx. £30) was a likely choke price, while the lowest (Lit. 5,000/month, approx.

£1.60) was considered an amount that every respondent might be willing to pay. A total of nine bids was employed.

The first survey was carried out by eight interviewers who conducted 448 interviews over 20 days in March 1995; canvassing both on-site and off-site respondents in the greater urban area of the City of Naples. Although the purpose of the study was not linked with damage assessment, the design of the survey fulfils almost all the guidelines contained in the NOAA panel. Great care was taken in describing the environmental good being valued; before posing the WTP questions respondents were reminded that "any money spent on the project cannot be spent elsewhere", as well as the possible substitutes for the good. Finally, follow-up questions were asked in order to understand the reasons for the stated answers. The respondents were shown a booklet containing maps of the site and pictures of the most significant archaeological remains.

The follow-up survey was carried out by 16 interviewers in July 1997. This study collected 497 interviews in a double-bounded format, which retested the previous single-bounded CV format of the 1995 study, together with an additional 350 interviews in a contingent ranking format. Among the other objectives of the 1997 CV study was an analysis of the effect that different formats can have on WTP estimates, particularly when focusing on complex nested goods. Although the 1997 survey can be considered an "improved version" of the one implemented in 1995, the differences were not so dissimilar as to invalidate our purpose. The two dichotomous choice samples can be regarded as comparable, being quota samples of the Neapolitan population, collected both on and off-site. However, the analysis presented in this chapter disregards the differences and the possible biases introduced by the follow-up WTP questions.[7]

THEORETICAL EXPECTATIONS

A dichotomous choice CV approach is used to test five hypotheses, all of which appear logical in terms of economic theory:

$$
\begin{aligned}
H_3 &: \quad WTP_{(TEV(CF))} > WTP_{(TEV(NAS))} \\
H_4 &: \quad WTP_{(TEV(CF))} > WTP_{(BV(CF))} \\
H_5 &: \quad WTP_{(TEV(CF))} > WTP_{(TEV(Bag))} \\
H_6 &: \quad WTP_{(TEV(Bag))} > WTP_{(BV(Bag))} \\
H_7 &: \quad WTP_{(BV(CF))} > WTP_{(BV(Bag))}
\end{aligned}
$$

where H_3 assumes that WTP for the conservation of Campi Flegrei (CF) as a whole (total economic benefits (TEV)) is greater than WTP for preserving components of Campi Flegrei not yet available to the public (economic benefits associated with existence value (NAS)); H_4 states that WTP for the conservation of Campi Flegrei as a whole (total economic value) exceeds WTP for the conservation value of Campi Flegrei for future generations (bequest value (BV)); H_5 implies that WTP for the conservation of Campi Flegrei as a whole (total economic benefits) is greater than WTP for the conservation of only part of the site (Bagnoli (Bag)) (total economic benefit for conserving Bagnoli); similarly, H_6 assumes WTP for the conservation of archaeological remains at Bagnoli (total economic benefit) to be greater than WTP for the conservation of Bagnoli for future generations; and finally, H_7 considers WTP for the conservation value of Campi Flegrei for future generations (bequest value) to be larger than WTP for the conservation of the Bagnoli area of the site for future generations.

In terms of the nesting terminology used by Carson and Mitchell (1995), the conservation of Bagnoli expressed in WTP3 is a complement to the conservation of the wider Campi Flegrei area expressed by WTP1. Conservation for exclusive use of future generations in both Bagnoli and Campi Flegrei can also be seen as complements of their larger existing conservation plans. Finally, conservation of sites currently not available in the whole Campi Flegrei area, which is linked to the option value of gaining access to them at a later date, can be defined as a complement of the existing conservation plan.

RESULTS

The data analysis (1) identified and removed protest bids and outliers in both the 1995 and 1997 samples; (2) calculated welfare measures and confidence interval estimations for the pooled and adjusted 1995 and 1997 samples; (3) tested for embedding in both the pooled and the adjusted 1995 and 1997 samples; (4) used stepwise regression to estimate the best fit models for each of the WTP functions in the 1995, 1997 and pooled samples; (5) used dummy variables to check the consistency of estimates over time; and (6) undertook a comparative analysis of steps #3 and #5 and of the results.

Identification of Protests and Outliers

Although the questionnaire design aimed at helping the identification of protests through follow-up questions, the criteria used here to drop or retain an observation were linked with the offered bid, the stated WTP and the income recorded for each observation. The 1995 and 1997 samples were adjusted for *protests* which were identified as observations where the response to all five WTP questions was negative, given the lowest bid offer, and the level of income was above average. Similarly, those observations for which the response was positive for all WTP questions, when offered the highest bids, but for which the income of the respondent was very low were regarded as *outliers*. A total of 24 observations (protests and outliers), representing 5.3% of the whole, were dropped in the 1995 sample, whilst 17 observations, equal to 3.4% of the total number, were disregarded in the computation for the 1997 sample. The percentage in both samples is very small; varying the chosen criteria, e.g. increasing/decreasing the income level for inclusion, resulted in a negligible change in the number of observations. Most of the respondents defined as *outliers* had almost exhausted their yearly income with their offers, and it seemed sensible to exclude them from the analysis in order to obtain conservative results. On the other hand, those observations which were considered protests were checked against the follow-up question, and the cross check appeared satisfactory. In both samples the number of outliers and protests was approximately the same.

Welfare Measures and Within Subject Tests for Embedding

The WTP point estimates of each sample were computed using the Hanemann's approximation, while the 95% confidence intervals were obtained using the Delta method (Table 10.1). Table 10.2 shows a summary of the internal tests for both 1995 and 1997 samples, as well as the pooled one. The first three tests are all passed both at point estimates and at the 5% significance level, with the exception of the inequality WTP1 > WTP4, which appears inconsistent at the 5% level of significance when considering the 1995 sample. The remaining two inequalities do not hold, except when point estimates are considered in the 1995 sample.

Stepwise Regressions and Dummy Variable Approach

A logit regression for each WTPi was run on the adjusted 1997 (N=484) and the adjusted 1995 (N=424) sample. A backward stepwise regression based on the likelihood ratio test for deleting variables from the model was used for both samples (Tables 10.3 and 10.4). Table 10.5 gives the parameter estimates for the pooled sample obtained using the stepwise procedure. Both the variables BID and INCOME are consistently present in all models, whatever WTP is considered; they appear to be highly significant too (almost always at the 5% confidence level). Knowledge of the site appeared to be an important factor, as the variable KNOWL is significant at the 1% level in the 1997 sample for all WTPs except WTP2; while in the pooled sample it is not significant when considering WTP2 and WTP4, a result that is confirmed by the significance of the

Table 10.1   Mean WTPs for the adjusted samples

Sample	Features	WTP1	WTP2	WTP3	WTP4	WTP5
1997	No. of observations	480	476	475	476	476
	Hanemann's approximation	29.633	9.974	3.989	3.343	23.101
	95% CI	(27.066 to 32.200)	(1.428 to 18.519)	(−10.256 to 18.234)	(−8.234 to 14.920)	(1.119 to 45.083)
1995	No. of observations	422	420	424	424	424
	Hanemann's approximation	27.643	10.468	5.151	12.607	1.238
	95% CI	(19.850 to 35.436)	(3.110 to 18.001)	(−7.110 to 17.412)	(−9.060 to 34.274)	(−14.257 to 16.733)
1997 & 1995	No. of observations	902	896	899	900	900
	Hanemann's approximation	28.813	10.183	0.817	6.985	11.531
	95% CI	(23.248 to 34.378)	(4.487 to 15.879)	(0.628 to 1.006)	(−3.604 to 17.575)	(2.745 to 20.317)

Table 10.2   Summary of internal tests across samples

Implication	Type of benefit	Pooled sample		Sample 1995		Sample 1997	
		(1)	(2)	(1)	(2)	(1)	(2)
WTP1 > WTP2	Option value for not accessible	Yes	Yes	Yes	Yes	Yes	Yes
WTP1 > WTP3	Bequest value for park	Yes	Yes	Yes	Yes	Yes	Yes
WTP1 > WTP4	Magnitude conservation	Yes	Yes	Yes	No	Yes	Yes
WTP4 > WTP5	Bequest value for Bagnoli	No	–	Yes	No	No	–
WTP3 > WTP5	Magnitude of bequest value	No	–	Yes	No	No	–

Notes:
(1) Consistent at point estimates of WTPs.
(2) Consistent at 5% significance level.

two dummies KNNONE and KNSOME in the 1995 sample, for WTP2 and WTP4. The variable SEX is never significant when looking at the 1997 sample, but being a woman is highly significant in the 1995 sample for WTP3, WTP4 and WTP5, and in the pooled one for WTP2, WTP3 and WTP5. Being of young age also affects all WTPs for the 1995 sample, and WTP1 and WTP4 when analysing the 1997 sample. All the other variables appear to be significant for some of the WTPs, but without showing any specific pattern.

Table 10.3   Stepwise results for the adjusted 1997 sample (N=484)

Features	WTP1	WTP2	WTP3	WTP4	WTP5
No. of observations	415	412	412	412	411
−2 × Log–likelihood	439.277	439.261	451.815	414.920	430.421
% Correct predictions	74.46	74.76	73.79	74.51	73.24
Constant	−0.4523	−1.2260**	−2.953***	−0.9159**	−1.724***
Age	−0.1080**			−0.1304***	
Bid	−0.0324***	−0.0307***	−0.0202***	−0.0292***	−0.0194***
Educ	0.2733**				
Income	0.0105*	0.0160***	0.0495***	0.0168***	0.0150***
Incsq			−0.0003*		
Knowl	0.3227***		0.3276***	0.3177***	0.3019***
Member	0.5792**	0.6622**			
Car		0.9669**	0.8079*		
Sex					

Notes:
*** Significant at 1%.
** Significant at 5%.
* Significant at 10%.

In order to discuss the reliability of these results over time, we used the dummy variable approach, pooling the two samples and creating a variable, namely 1997, which assumed value 1 if the observation belongs to the 1997 sample, and 0 otherwise. Following Carson *et al.* (1997) we first considered the case of common slope. The new data set obtained by pooling the 1995 and 1997 adjusted samples consists of a total number of 902 observations, and Table 10.5 presents the parameter estimates obtained from the stepwise procedure. The variables BID and INCOME are always significant at the 1% level of confidence, whichever WTP one considers, and knowledge also appears to be highly significant for WTP1, WTP3 and WTP5. In this case, the dummy 1997 appears to be significant only when WTP4 is the dependent variable. When all variables, including non-statistically significant ones, are included in the model, 1997 was only significant for the WTP4 and WTP5 models.

Table 10.4   Stepwise results for the adjusted 1995 sample (N=424)

Features	WTP1	WTP2	WTP3	WTP4	WTP5
No. of observations	413	411	415	415	415
$-2 \times$ Log–likelihood	470.673	442.292	472.331	481.295	470.041
% Correct predictions	71.67	70.07	71.81	69.88	70.36
Constant	0.3456*	–0.5467**	–0.6217***	–0.8647***	–0.8050***
Bid	–0.0291***	–0.0332***	–0.0210***	–0.0153***	–0.0191***
College					
Income	0.0273***	0.0505***	0.0258***	0.0156**	0.0303***
Knnone		0.372**		0.4633***	
Knsome		0.4070**		0.2949**	
Mage					
Member	–0.2717**				
Napol					
Sex			0.3722***	0.3100**	0.3564***
Yage	–0.3165***	0.2540**	–0.4214***	–0.2411**	–0.3437***
Incsq		–0.0004**			

Notes:
*** Significant at 1%.
** Significant at 5%.
* Significant at 10%.

Table 10.5   Stepwise results for the pooled 1995 & 1997 sample (N=902)

Features	WTP1	WTP2	WTP3	WTP4	WTP5
No. of observations	800	796	800	800	799
$-2 \times$ Log–likelihood	898.490	870.303	919.032	903.016	896.345
% Correct predictions	72.63	72.74	68.75	70.38	71.21
Constant	–0.4273	–0.0507	–1.1461***	0.5062	–1.5369***
Age				–0.0329**	
Bid	–0.0301***	–0.0308***	–0.0202***	–0.0218***	–0.0191***
1997				1.0530**	
Educ	0.03319***				
Income	0.0156***	0.0172***	0.0233***	0.0167***	0.0197***
Incsq					
Knowl	0.1225**		0.1730***		0.2125***
Member	–0.2465**	–0.2157**			
Napol			0.1906**		
Sex		0.1790**	0.1725**		0.2064**

Notes:
*** Significant at 1%.
** Significant at 5%.
* Significant at 10%.

Therefore, we can conclude that when implying a common slope assumption, *there is* a shift in the choice model for WTP4 and WTP5, which is the WTP for the conservation of a part of the Campi Flegrei, namely Bagnoli, but none for the rest of Campi Flegrei. It is interesting to note that the political scenario in terms of the conservation of Bagnoli has partially changed in the last two years, as a step towards the requalification of the area has been taken on board by the local government. This results in the non-transferability over time of parameter estimates for WTP4 and WTP5. This is not a contradiction *a priori*, if we regard the CV method as a technique capable of measuring true preferences. Moreover, the results also seem to be confirmed by the rejection of the null hypothesis for the within subject tests regarding Bagnoli, WTP4 > WTP5 and WTP3 > WTP5, as shown in Table 10.2, which highlights the fact that the welfare measures are neither comparable nor transferable.

Table 10.6 presents the parameter estimates obtained when relaxing the common slope assumption. In this case the dummy 1997 is never significant, but the interaction slope effect determined by knowledge is consistently and highly significant for all WTPs. This result is interesting with respect to both what has been argued above, and the results described by Carson *et al.* (1997) in their analysis on temporal reliability: the concern about too little a change seems to be overcome, and the knowledge of the site appears to have a significant impact on WTPs. People who stated during the interview that they had a good knowledge of the site were also likely to have heard about the latest requalification programmes for Bagnoli, and this could have influenced their willingness to pay, making the results incomparable even over a short time period.

Discussion

The study presented in this chapter aims at verifying component reliability of CV estimates for complex historic goods over time. The recent literature debate has shed some light on the problems which may be encountered when applying the CV method to estimate WTP for complex goods; that is, when the object of valuation can be broken down into individual components or subsets which function as complements to each other. In such cases the relative orders of magnitude of the estimates may not be consistent with theoretical expectations. Since the work by Kahneman and Knetsch (1992), this has generally been referred to as the "embedding" effect, because the value of separate smaller components of a larger good are "embedded" into the latter. Disentangling these values in hypothetical markets constitutes a challenge, and has spurred much controversy (see e.g., Diamond *et al.*, 1992; Loomis *et al.*, 1993). However, Randall and Hoehn (1996) find that embedding is not peculiar to CV hypothetical framing, but is also observed in actual markets for private goods. They show that "embedding effects are standard economic phenomena induced

Table 10.6   Parameter estimates for the pooled 1995 & 1997 sample (N=902)

Features	WTP1	WTP2	WTP3	WTP4	WTP5
No. of observations	800	796	800	800	799
$-2 \times$ Log–likelihood	883.003	851.767	904.638	871.506	878.389
% Correct predictions	72.00	74.25	70.88	72.38	71.71
Constant	0.0838	0.5914	−1.6944	0.0738	−0.1530
Age	0.0072	0.0006	0.0275	−0.0164	−0.0209
Bid	−0.0277***	−0.0323***	−0.0203***	−0.0150***	−0.0193***
1997	0.5545	1.0432	0.3274	1.1618	1.2204
Educ	0.4631*	0.1618	0.2136	0.0228	0.0894
Income	0.0328**	0.0384**	0.0106	0.0166	0.0145
Incsq	−0.0002	−0.0003*	8.70E–05	−4.8E–05	0.0001
Knowl	−0.2202	−0.3573**	−0.0600	−0.2608*	−0.0863
Member	−0.1865	−0.0503	0.0046	0.0349	−0.0841
Napol	0.1356	0.0320	0.2091	−0.1598	0.0843
Sex	0.0263	0.1836	0.3477***	0.2682**	0.3251***
D_Age	−0.1042**	−0.0833	−0.0675	−0.1091**	−0.0503
D_Bid	−0.0041	0.0018	0.0005	−0.0152***	−7.3E–05
D_Educ	−0.1381	0.0012	−0.1334	0.0277	−0.1670
D_Income	−0.0155	−0.0122	0.0405*	0.0229	0.0197
D_Incsq	0.0001	0.0002	−0.0004	−0.0002	−0.0003
D_Knowl	0.4830***	0.3398**	0.3562**	0.5522***	0.3895**
D_Member	−0.0020	−0.1884	−0.0886	−0.0371**	0.0547
D_Napol	−0.2608	−0.2937	−0.0677	0.4630*	0.2205
D_Sex	−0.0158	0.0097	−0.3131*	−0.2426	−0.2598

Notes:
*** Significant at 1%.
** Significant at 5%.
* Significant at 10%.

by substitution relationships and constrained endowments" and, therefore, cannot be considered as a CV artifact (Randall and Hoehn, 1996). Nevertheless, CV practitioners still need to tackle this issue in designing effective survey instruments.

Hanemann (1994) distinguishes three different specifications of the embedding phenomenon: sequencing effects, sub-additivity effects, and scope effects. Empirical results seem to show that when eliciting the WTP for a set of goods, there is evidence of a bias associated with the position of the question in the overall sequence (see "sequence bias" in Cummings *et al.*, 1986, p. 33 or "question ordering bias" in Mitchell and Carson, 1989, p. 237). When considering improvements from baseline scenarios an item tends to receive a higher valuation when its elicitation question is located towards the first positions of the sequence.

Sub-additivity effects have been postulated as a result of some studies where the WTP for the whole set of goods was found to be much less than the sum of the WTPs elicited for its constituents (Desvousges *et al.*, 1993). Finally, a scope effect is present when the mean WTP does not conform to the declining marginal utility hypothesis.

POLICY IMPLICATIONS

The above discussion has focused on some issues that often raise concerns with policy makers about the acceptability of results based on hypothetical market experiments. Valuing cultural heritage should not represent a purely academic economic activity, but *must be* linked with *urban planning decisions*, in an *ex-ante* framework. In fact, the characteristics of *cultural goods* themselves, the values that people attach to *man-made capital*, open up a new perspective on the debate about sustainable cities. Attaching a value to cultural heritage is linked to the concept of intentional reconstruction of *cultural urban landscape*, of an assessment of urban planning alternatives, inside the framework of a more general planning policy. In this perspective, the costs of implementing studies such as CVs would be compensated by the social benefits gained, in terms of knowledge of the priorities that the relevant population may express for the development or management of an important cultural area. This ensures participative grounds upon which to base policy and management decisions.

The study presented here was not commissioned by the local authority (which in Italy is the *Sovrintendenza per i Beni Archeologici*) to provide an answer to a specific management issue, but was designed purely for methodological purposes. Nevertheless, the WTPs estimates obtained for different parts of the site at Campi Flegrei have shown a good degree of reliability, despite the limitations of the study, and represent a useful piece of information to feed local policy decision making. In fact, it would be possible to estimate the social surplus generated by different policy strategies, with their associated costs to the population. For example, one could estimate the effects of new management strategies, such as introducing an entrance fee for *restricted access* sites. Furthermore, one could analyse the income elasticity of demand for archaeological sites, congestion disutilities at sites, and the carrying capacity of sites according to some sustainability criterion. This could allow forecasts of primary and secondary benefits of alternative policies, both in terms of positive and negative externalities. In other words, it could be possible to define *management models* for this peculiar *non-renewable resource*.

CONCLUSION

This study reveals that people have different values for different elements of cultural goods. It also shows the possibility of minimizing the bias of CV estimates of welfare measures, using appropriate questionnaire design. In fact, as Randall and Hoehn (1996) have stressed, embedding effects appear not to be a CV artifact, but a phenomenon predicted by economic theory and reliable measurements should exhibit this effect.

We have performed within subject tests for embedding and regard this as a *necessary condition* for rejecting the null hypothesis of component insensitivity. The dichotomous choice format applied in the CV studies reported here seems capable of limiting the bias due to sequencing effects, despite the small sample size. The stability over time of the first three tests for embedding shown in Table 10.2, which are passed both at point estimates and at the 5% level of significance, confirm that appropriate design can substantially reduce these effects, although other formats, such as contingent ranking and stated preference approaches,[8] may be more adequate.

The results discussed above also stress the need, for methodological purposes, of more CV applications in the cultural heritage sector and further research in this direction. In fact, cultural heritage goods, such as the one presented here, can easily be desegregated into their component elements. The study also confirms what is highlighted by Carson and Mitchell (1995), namely the importance of presenting respondents with a scenario description where the difference among components of goods is meaningful, and the use of a survey which promotes respondents' participation during the interview process.

The other interesting result is the role played by the knowledge that the respondents have of the commodity (in this case an archaeological site) presented in the scenario. When dealing with passive use values, such as existence and intrinsic values, knowledge of the characteristic of the commodity being valued becomes crucial.

A major problem with many CV responses and CV estimates of maximum WTP is that they are often subject to large variances. A consequence of large variance is that the null hypothesis of no difference between WTPs for various elements of cultural goods sometimes cannot be rejected. However, careful survey design in this study meant that this was not a problem, except for valuing sub-areas of the conservation site and for estimating bequest value. This means that for Campi Flegrei there is reasonable certainty over the total value of this specific cultural good, but DC CV is less helpful in indicating with any degree of certainty which management options to pursue in determining the extent to which different elements of the archaeological site should be further developed archaeologically (and which parts should just be preserved or abandoned). This uncertainty about whether it is worth preserving parts of archaeological sites increases as we move further away from use value alone, i.e. as the preservation decision becomes increasingly dependent upon non-use (e.g. bequest) value elements. Tackling this problem requires surveys with large sample sizes.

ENDNOTES

1. For example, archaeological remains associated with Hadrian's Roman Wall in Northumberland and Cumbria in England (a World Heritage Site), comprise the wall itself, milecastles, major Roman forts at periodic intervals along the wall, other settlements connected to this Roman presence at some distance from the wall, roads and other remains such as temples, as well as contemporary museums displaying Roman artifacts, etc.
2. The etymology of the name means *Burning Fields*. The Romans defined the whole region as such due to the intense volcanic activity.
3. For environmental pollution damages the NOAA report recognizes that passive use value will vary over time as natural resource recovery and restoration takes place. But this is a separate issue.
4. Over the long term values for natural resource goods may not remain constant, depending on elasticity of income for different goods, changes in preferences, availability of substitutes, etc.
5. Among others, Carson and Mitchell (1995) have outlined a test for nested goods; a study by Downing and Ozuna (1996), followed by a similar one by Carson *et al.* (1997) focused on temporal reliability of welfare measures.
6. The differences in the two versions of the questionnaire were deliberately introduced in order to test for other aspects of reliability over time and consistency of estimates which are beyond this study.
7. This will be the subject of further analysis and discussion in a forthcoming paper.
8. The study of Campi Flegrei implemented in 1997 contemplated also the use of a contingent ranking approach in order to compare the effect on component sensitivity of different CV formats.

REFERENCES

Carson, R.T. and Mitchell, R.C. (1995), Sequencing and nesting in contingent valuation surveys, *Journal of Environmental Economics and Management* **28**: 155–73.

Carson, R.T., Hanemann, W.M., Kopp, R.J., Krosnick, J.A., Mitchell, R.C., Presser, S., Ruud, P.A., Smith, V.K., Conaway, M. and Martin, K. (1997) Temporal reliability of estimates from contingent valuation, *Land Economics* **73** (2): 151–63.

Cummings, R.G., Brookshire, D.S. and W.D. Schultze (1986), *Valuing environmental goods: a state of the art assessment of contingent valuation*, Rowland and Allanheld Publishers, Totawa, N.J., USA.

Desvousges, W.H., Johnson, F.R. Dunford, R.W., Muudson, S.P., Wilson, K.N. and K. Boyle (1993), Measuring natural resource damages with contingent valuation: Test of validity and reliability, pp. 91–164 in Hausman, J.A. (ed.) 1993: *Contingent valuation. A Critical Assessment*, Elsevier Science Publishers (North Holland), Amsterdam.

Diamond, P.A., Hausman, J.A., Leonard, G.K. and M.A. Denning (1993), 'Does Contingent Valuation Measure Preferences? Experimental Evidence', pp. 41–89 in Hausman, J.A. (ed.) 1993: *Contingent Valuation. A Critical Assessment*, Elsevier Science Publishers (North Holland), Amsterdam.

Downing, M. and Ozuna, T. (1996) Testing the reliability of the benefit function transfer approach, *Journal of Environmental Economics and Management* **30**: 316–22.

Fusco Girard, L., Riganti, P. and Cerreta, M. (1998) Towards a post-economic culture: conservation and evaluation of cultural man-made capital, *paper presented at the* 10th International Conference on Cultural Economics, Barcelona, 16–19 June 1998.

Hanemann, M. (1994) Valuing the environment through contingent valuation, *Journal of Economic Perspectives* **8**(4): 19–43.

Kahneman, D. and Knetsch, J.L. (1992) Valuing public goods: the purchase of moral satisfaction, *Journal of Environmental Economics and Management* **22**: 57–70.

Loomis, J., Lockwood, M. and DeLacy, T. (1993), Some empirical evidence on embedding effects in contingent valuation of forest protection, *Journal of Environmental Economics and Management* **24**: 45–55.

Mitchell, R. and Carson, R., (1989), *Using Surveys to Value Public Goods: the Contingent Valuation Method*, Resources for the Future, Washington.

Randall, A. and Hoehn, J.P. (1996), Embedding in demand systems, *Journal of Environmental Economics and Management* **30**: 369–80.

11. Valuing reduced acid deposition injuries to cultural resources: marble monuments in Washington, DC

Edward R. Morey, Kathleen Greer Rossmann, Lauraine G. Chestnut and Shannon Ragland

INTRODUCTION

Numerous elicitation methods have been employed to gather stated preference data for use in estimating the value of environmental goods. The most commonly used methods have been various forms of the contingent valuation method (CVM), for example payment cards, open-ended willingness-to-pay (WTP) questions, and referenda. More recently, choice experiments (CEs) have been used to gather valuation data for environmental goods for which the value of the good is primarily direct use. This study uses pairwise choice experiments to estimate the total value (direct and passive use) of an environmental good. The CEs were contained in a survey administered in person in a group setting. This approach exploits many of the benefits of individual in person interviews, while maintaining a more consistent presentation of the information across respondents and lower implementation costs.

This study estimates the benefits of reducing acid deposition injuries to an important set of cultural resources: the 100 outdoor marble monuments in Washington, DC. The reductions in injuries are presented as hypothetical preservation programs that mimic the likely range of injury reductions resulting from the reductions in sulfur dioxide (SO_2) emissions required by Title IV of the 1990 US Clean Air Act Amendments.

Group interviews were conducted in the Philadelphia and Boston metropolitan areas. The results indicate that, on average, households in these areas are willing to make a one-time payment of $33 to $69, depending on the level of preservation, to slow down the rate of deterioration of the 100 outdoor marble monuments in Washington, DC. The remainder of this chapter is organized as follows. The next section introduces the elicitation method and the theoretical model. The following two sections discuss the collection of the CE data and present the empirical results. Finally, the last section provides concluding remarks and suggestions for further research.

CHOICE EXPERIMENTS AND MODELING WTP

Valuing Environmental Goods with Choice Experiments

Choice experiments evolved from conjoint analysis, a method used extensively in marketing and transportation research (Louviere, 1988; Green and Srinavasen, 1990; Batsell and Louviere, 1991; Louviere, 1992). Conjoint analysis requires respondents to rank or rate multiple alternatives where each alternative is characterized by multiple attributes (e.g. Johnson *et al.*, 1995; Roe *et al.*, 1996). Typically, CEs require respondents to choose the most preferred alternative (a partial ranking) from multiple alternative goods—i.e. a choice set—where the alternatives within a choice set are differentiated by their attributes. When using CEs to value environmental goods a price, often a tax or a measure of travel costs, is included as one of the attributes of each alternative, so that preferences towards the other attributes can be measured in terms of dollars, i.e. WTP or willingness to accept (WTA).

Choice experiments have been used to estimate the value of public goods. For example, Magat *et al.* (1988) and Viscusi *et al.* (1991) estimated the value of reducing health risks; Adamowicz *et al.* (1994), Buchanan *et al.* (1998), and Adamowicz *et al.* (1997) estimated recreational site choice models for fishing, mountain biking, and moose hunting, respectively; Adamowicz *et al.* (1996) estimated the value of enhancing the population of a threatened species; and Layton and Brown (1998) estimated the value of mitigating forest loss resulting from global climate change.[1] Except for Adamowicz *et al.* (1996) and Layton and Brown (1998), each of these studies measured only direct-use values. In each of the studies, respondents were presented with multiple choice sets from which they chose their most preferred alternatives.

There are many desirable aspects of CEs, not least of which is the nature of the choice being made.[2] To choose the most preferred alternative from some set of alternatives is a very common decision experience, especially when one of the attributes of the alternatives is a price. One need only walk the isles of a grocery store to experience this type of decision environment. In a hypothetical market, multiple sets of alternative goods can be constructed with varying attribute levels for each alternative. The task of the respondent is to choose the most preferred alternative from each of these choice sets. In this respect, this type of CE is markedly different from the CVM. Rather than being presented with one hypothetical state of the world and either voting for or against, or stating or choosing one's WTP for it, the CE requires respondents to choose the good that is most preferred from multiple choice sets. One can argue that such a decision task encourages respondents to concentrate on the trade-offs between attributes rather than to take a position for or against an initiative or policy. This type of repeated decision process may also diffuse the strong emotions often associated with environmental goods, thereby reducing the likelihood of "yea-saying". [3]

Like conjoint analysis, CEs allow for the construction of goods characterized by attribute levels that (currently) do not exist. This feature is particularly useful in marketing studies when the purpose is to estimate preferences for new products. Similarly, researchers estimating the value of environmental goods are often valuing a good or condition that does not currently exist. In this study, we estimate the value of changes in the future condition of a good—up to 300 years from now—which cannot be observed in goods currently available.

Choice Model

The CE framework is consistent with the discrete choice random utility model, the same theoretical framework often used with CVM and travel cost data (McFadden, 1974; Ben-Akiva and Lerman, 1985; Mitchell and Carson, 1989). Within this framework, we assume that individuals have preferences over any pair of goods, for example, preservation alternatives. Individual i chooses the preservation alternative j that provides the greatest utility, U_{ij}, where alternative j is a member of the choice set of C possible alternatives. The probability that individual i will choose preservation alternative j over k is:[4]

$$\text{Pr}_i\{j \text{ over } k\} = \text{Pr}_i\{U_{ij} \geq U_{ik}; j \neq k\} \ i = 1,2,...,I \text{ and } j,k = 1,2,...,23. \quad (11.1)$$

The utility individual i receives from choosing preservation alternative j is:

$$U_{ij} = V_{ij} + \varepsilon_{ij} \quad (11.2)$$

where V_{ij} is assumed deterministic from both the researcher's and the individual's perspective, and ε_{ij} is random from the researcher's perspective, but known by the individual. Equation (11.2) is the conditional indirect utility function and identifies maximum utility conditional on the choice of preservation alternative j. By substituting equation (11.2) into equation (11.1) and rearranging, the probability of choosing alternative j over alternative k becomes:

$$\text{Pr}_i\{j \text{ over } k\} = \text{Pr}_i\{V_{ij} - V_{ik} \geq \varepsilon_{ik} - \varepsilon_{ij}; j \neq k\} \quad (11.3)$$

It is assumed that each ε_{ij} is independently drawn from a univariate Type I Extreme Value Distribution (McFadden, 1974) with the cumulative distribution function:

$$F(\varepsilon_i) = \exp[-e^{-r_i(\varepsilon_i - \alpha)}] \tag{11.4}$$

where α is a location parameter set equal to zero and r_i is a positive scale parameter. This distribution has a mode of α, mean of $\alpha + \gamma/r_i$, where γ is Euler's constant (~ 0.57721), and variance $\sigma_\varepsilon^2 = \pi^2/6r_i^2$. We assume that the random components of the conditional indirect utility function, ε_{ij}, are independent and identically distributed across individuals and choice occasions; that is, $r_i = r \; \forall i$. Without loss of generality, r is set equal to 1. The probability that individual i will choose preservation alternative j over k becomes:

$$\Pr_i\{j \text{ over } k\} = \frac{e^{V_{ij}}}{e^{V_{ij}} + e^{V_{ik}}} \quad \text{and} \quad \frac{\Pr_i\{j \text{ over } k\}}{\Pr_i\{k \text{ over } j\}} = \frac{e^{V_{ij}}}{e^{V_{ik}}}. \tag{11.5}$$

CHOICE EXPERIMENT DATA COLLECTION

Application

Society values cultural resources such as monuments, building facades, and outdoor sculpture for a variety of aesthetic, cultural, and historical reasons. Value may be derived from direct use (e.g. visiting monuments), indirect use (e.g. viewing pictures of monuments), and passive use (e.g. knowing that monuments will teach current and future generations about historical events). Given the vast distribution of cultural resources, it is likely that their value to society is significant. Nevertheless, relatively little is known about how the public values these resources. Aside from what can be inferred from visitation data or maintenance and renovation expenditures, there are few quantitative estimates of the overall value of these resources. Even less is known about how the value of cultural resources may be affected by changes in the condition of these resources.

Some cultural resources that are made of carbonate stone, e.g. marble or limestone, or bronze are injured by exposure to air pollutants such as SO_2, which in the US is being reduced by Title IV of the 1990 Clean Air Act Amendments. These injuries, which include surface erosion and soiling, alter the appearance of the resource to an extent that might diminish value. For example, a bronze statue that has lost its original patina may no longer be aesthetically pleasing, or a marble monument that has lost its inscription may have less historical value. Society may derive benefits by avoiding such injuries, or by slowing the rate at which they occur, which is one of the potential benefits of Title IV.

Survey Instrument Development

The survey instrument was developed after a scoping effort, which included a literature review, consultation with an expert review panel, and scoping interviews regarding preferences and attitudes toward monuments and their condition. Nine focus groups were then conducted to further develop and refine the presentation materials and the survey instrument.[5]

The goal of the study was to develop estimates of the value of expected reductions in injury to cultural resources as a result of the Title IV required reductions in SO_2 emissions. Because there are many types of materials and many different kinds of cultural resources that might benefit from reductions in SO_2 emissions, the first step in the study was to select a category of cultural resources on which to focus. We chose the set of outdoor marble monuments and historic buildings in the Washington, DC area because these have national significance. For many types of building materials, the value of the damage caused by air pollution is adequately measured by the costs of replacement or repair, but this is likely not true for monuments and buildings with historic significance. We limited the material to marble to keep the description of the effects of air pollution manageable (it varies for different materials) and because marble is quite vulnerable to the effects of SO_2 and was a commonly used material for monuments and building facades between 1850 and 1940 in Washington, DC.

Although the Title IV requirements will result in substantial emission reductions throughout the eastern half of the United States (reducing SO_2 emissions by about 40% from 1980 levels), we limited this study to the potential effects on marble monuments and the marble facades of select historic buildings in the Washington, DC area. Covering a larger area would be difficult because of the wide variation in the numbers and types of monuments in different locations. Limiting the study to a single monument would make the description of the monument easier, but would not reflect the regional nature of the impact of changes in air quality on the resource. Because Washington, DC is the nation's capital and contains a large collection of nationally known monuments, we expect that the value of reducing the injury to these monuments will exceed the value of reducing the injury to monuments in other eastern US cities, at least for non-residents.

The approximately 100 outdoor marble monuments in Washington, DC were listed for survey respondents along with a map showing their locations. A few photographs of selected monuments were also shown, including a few of the best known and a few of the less well known monuments. About 75% of the respondents said they had visited outdoor monuments in Washington, DC. Although people often commented on moving personal experiences when visiting certain monuments, the primary reason they offered for being willing to pay to preserve these monuments was so that the monuments would be available for other people to visit, both now and in the future.[6] Respondents stressed the importance of conveying the historical and inspirational messages of monuments to future generations; indeed, more than 70% of the respondents said that it mattered to them that these monuments still existed 100 years or more from now, which is long after their own expected lifetimes. Thus, passive-use values appeared to be a more important component of WTP than direct-use values.

There were two key challenges to the development of the valuation scenario for this survey. The first was how to describe the change in the rate of injury to the monuments that would be achieved, and the second was finding a plausible hypothetical mechanism for achieving these changes with plausible alternative costs to individual households.

To develop the descriptions of the effects of SO_2-related pollutants on outdoor monuments, we reviewed summaries of the scientific literature and consulted with researchers on this topic. SO_2-related pollutants have been linked to erosion and chemical alteration of marble. These processes lead to loss of surface detail and discoloration. Some erosion occurs with exposure to rain alone, but SO_2-related air pollutants accelerate this process and are responsible for certain types of discoloration. However, most of the quantitative analysis has focused on the chemistry and not on the impact of these processes on the overall appearance of the monument. We concluded that, although the effects of SO_2-related air pollutants on marble monuments can be described, a specific quantitative estimate of the reduction in the rate of deterioration in the appearance of marble monuments as a result of Title IV emission reductions is not feasible at this time. However, a plausible range for these effects was defined based on consultation with experts in this area. We presented this to survey respondents as changes in the amount of time it would take before certain changes in appearance would occur, which were illustrated with computer-generated photographs.

The second challenge was to develop a plausible hypothetical mechanism by which these changes in the rate of injury could be achieved. One option was to pose a change in air pollution emissions, but this caused several difficulties because there are so many joint benefits of reducing air pollution, including improvements in health and visibility. To focus the valuation questions on these 100 marble monuments, we posed three alternative treatment processes that would reduce the susceptibility of the marble to air pollution and weathering and slow the rate of deterioration in the appearance of the monuments. There are no such treatment processes available, but subjects in the focus groups seemed to readily accept the plausibility of such treatments existing. Using this hypothetical mechanism mimicked the expected effects on the monuments of reducing air pollution and allowed the valuation exercise to focus on just these 100 monuments.

Preceding the description of the preservation programs, the nature of the effects of pollution on marble was described with verbal descriptions and photographic illustrations. Of the roughly 100 outdoor marble monuments and historic buildings in Washington, DC, almost all were erected between 1850 and 1940. These monuments and historic buildings were listed by name and their locations were shown on a map of the area. A few illustrative photographs of some well known and not so well known monuments were also shown.

Given the varying shapes of the monuments, the different types and quality of marble, the different weathering conditions, and the different ages of the monuments, the condition of the monuments is quite varied today. Two monuments were chosen to represent the average condition of the monuments today and the average expected future condition (Photograph 11.1). The first is a statue of Benjamin Franklin in Washington, DC. The second is a capital, or top, of a column, similar to those on the US Capitol, the Supreme Court, and the Lincoln and Jefferson Memorials.

A photograph of each of these monuments was digitally altered to represent the average current condition of the group of monuments and the estimated average condition in 75 and 150 years from now if no preservation program is undertaken (that is, without the Title IV pollution reductions). These six images were displayed on a timeline to illustrate how air pollution and weathering injuries are expected to affect the monuments' appearance over time. The baseline timeline spans 300 years, from 1850, the beginning of the monument installation period, to 2150, with the three pairs of pictures spaced along the timeline at 1996 (today), 2075 (about 75 years from now), and 2150 (about 150 years from now).[7]

The three preservation programs were described in terms of the extent to which they would proportionately alter the injury timeline. For Option A, which extends by 25% the amount of time it will take for the injuries in the picture series to occur, the second pair of pictures is shown at 94 years from now and the third pair at 188 years from now. Option B extends the amount of time by 50% to 113 years and 225 years, respectively; Option C extends the amount of time by 100%, doubling the years to 150 and 300 from now, respectively.

Four large posters displayed the various timelines, the first poster showed the baseline timeline without any preservation program; the next three illustrated each preservation option in comparison to the baseline. Images of the latter three posters are shown in photograph 11.1. In addition, each respondent had a large copy of the six-picture series to examine independently and at close range.

Photograph 11.1   Digitally altered photographs used in the survey

For our study, each set of choices consisted of two alternatives. Respondents were instructed to select the more preferred alternative from each pair. An alternative is a combination of one of the preservation options (Option A, Option B, Option C, or status quo) and a dollar value that the household would pay as a one-time payment for that option.[8] The dollar values were selected from the following: $0 (for status quo only), $0.25, $1, $3, $7, $10, $15, $25, and $50.[9]

To help respondents understand the choice task, the pairwise choice section began with two example pairs. The example pairs were:

Example 1:   No Preservation for $0   or   Preservation Option
                                                   C for $25

and

Example 2:   Preservation Option B for $10   or   Preservation Option
                                                   C for $15

For each pair, the survey administrator provided reasons why people might select either option. These reasons were included to let participants know that there are good reasons for selecting either alternative in a pair.

The choice task for each respondent then consisted of 10 pairwise choices. Twenty versions of the choice sets were used. The task of designing the choice sets was relatively straightforward, because the alternatives are described in terms of only two attributes.[10] Preservation level takes one of four values and price takes one of nine values. All dominant pairs—pairs with more effective options for an equal or lower dollar amount (e.g. Option B at $3 and Option A at $7)—were excluded, leaving 108 pairs. Each of the 108 pairs appeared on at least one version. In addition, each survey had five pairs containing the status quo (No Preservation at $0) as an alternative.[11]

Survey Administration

The survey data were collected during a series of group sessions. These sessions lasted an average of 1.5 hours and were attended by 7 to 31 respondents. The sessions were divided into two parts. During the first part, which lasted about 50 minutes, respondents alternated between listening to the administrator present information, reviewing the information in their response booklets, and providing written answers to survey questions. During the second part, respondents worked at their own pace, reading survey questions and providing written answers. Information was provided verbally by the survey administrator, reinforced with written summaries in the response booklets, and visually on large posters at the front of the room and in illustration booklets.[12]

This group survey approach exploits many of the advantages of in-person interviews: extensive use of visual aids; greater comprehension of complex hypothetical scenarios; and greater opportunity to motivate respondents to answer difficult questions.[13] Furthermore, the group sessions allow for greater consistency in presentation across individuals and more privacy for the respondent than individual surveying.[14] While the presentation of the information used in the group survey sessions was developed and tested in focus groups, the survey sessions were not conducted as focus groups. There were no discussions among participants and it was explained at the outset that survey responses would not be revealed during the session.

This survey required that an extensive amount of verbal and visual information be presented to respondents about the good, the injuries, and the hypothetical scenario. The amount of information in the survey and the need for extensive visual materials precluded the use of a telephone-only survey (without accompanying materials). Since we were able to refine the presentation of the information during the focus groups, producing the materials and administering the group surveys was less costly than adapting the presentation to a combination mail–telephone survey. It may be feasible to adapt the materials for presentation in a mail survey, but this would require extensive testing to ensure its effectiveness in communicating the necessary information.

In each city we selected two survey areas to represent the city. In Boston, the areas were Dedham and Woburn; in Philadelphia, the areas were downtown and Ft. Washington. The sample was recruited from a list of randomly selected households who resided in these areas. Individuals at 908 households completed a telephone screening survey (several demographic questions) and were offered $50 to participate in a group survey on a national policy issue.[15] Of these, 409 (45%) agreed to attend; 272 (67%) actually attended a session and completed a survey. Because we did not specify the subject of the survey, contacts were not able to self-select based on their preferences for monument preservation. Four survey groups were conducted at each survey center in each area for a total of 8 groups per city and 16 overall. The size of the group ranged from 7 to 31, averaging 17 people per session.

That participants were required to attend a session and were compensated for doing so may compromise the degree to which our sample represents the population of Boston and Philadelphia.[16] Our sample somewhat underrepresents younger (under 35 years) and older (over 64 years) individuals, and over-represents Caucasian and non-low-income individuals. Table 11.1 shows the demographic characteristics of our sample and the study population, metropolitan Philadelphia and Boston. Given the demographic differences of the sample and population, the sample mean WTP does not represent the population WTP unless it is weighted for these differences.

Table 11.1   Demographic characteristics for study sample and population

Demographic characteristic		Sample		Population
Age (18 and older)	18 to 24	23	9%	16%
	25 to 34	37	14%	24%
	35 to 44	67	26%	18%
	45 to 64	106	41%	24%
	65+	26	10%	18%
Ethnicity	Caucasian	197	76%	70%
	Non-Caucasian	62	24%	30%
Income[17]	Less than $12,000	21	8%	20%
	More than $12,000	238	92%	80%

EMPIRICAL RESULTS

Estimation of Conditional Indirect Utility Function

We have data for $I=259$ individuals, and choices of preservation alternatives for up to 10 pairs of alternatives per individual, yielding a total of 2,568 choices.[18] For each pair, p, an individual chooses alternative A or B. Given the binary logit model of pairwise choices, the parameters in the conditional indirect utility function have been estimated by maximizing the following likelihood function using the Gauss programming language:[19]

$$L = \sum_{i=1}^{I} \sum_{p=1}^{P_i} \left\{ y_{ip} \ln\left(\frac{e^{V_{iAp}}}{e^{V_{iAp}} + e^{V_{iBp}}} \right) + \left(1 - y_{ip}\right) \ln\left(\frac{e^{V_{iBp}}}{e^{V_{iAp}} + e^{V_{iBp}}} \right) \right\} \quad (11.6)$$

where y_{ip} equals one if individual i chooses alternative A from pair p and zero if alternative B is chosen.

The deterministic part of conditional indirect utility from equation (11.2), V_{ij}, is a function of the two attributes characterizing alternative j: the level of preservation alternative j (Level$_j$) and the amount of money the individual has left to spend on all other goods after choosing preservation alternative j (Income$_i$–Price$_j$), and other characteristics of individual i (S_i) such that:

$$V_{ij} = V(\text{Level}_j, (\text{Income}_i\text{--Price}_j), S_i \quad i = 1,2,...,I \text{ and } j = 1,2 \quad (11.7)$$

Level$_j$ can take on one of four values: 0 for the status quo, 0.25 for Option A, 0.50 for Option B, and 1.00 for Option C. Price$_j$, the dollar amount associated with preservation alternative j, can take on one of nine values: $p = \{0, 0.25, 1.00, 3, 7, 10, 15, 25, 50\}$. Income$_i$ is the midpoint of the household income range specified by the respondent.[20]

Numerous non-linear relationships were tested for both (Income$_i$--Price$_j$) and Level$_j$. The specification of conditional indirect utility that best explains the choices made is:

$$V_{ij} = (b_1 + b_2\text{Gender}_i + b_3\text{Low-income}_i)\,(\text{Income}_i\text{--Price}_j)$$
$$+(b_4 + b_5\text{Age}_i + b_6\text{Ethnicity}_i)\,\text{Level}_j$$
$$+(b_7 + b_8\text{Age}_i + b_9\,\text{Ethnicity}_i)\,(\text{Level}_j)^{0.5} \quad (11.8)$$

Age$_i$ is the respondent's age in years, and Gender$_i$, Low-income$_i$, and Ethnicity$_i$ are dummy variables with the following assignments:

Gender$_i$: 0—Male, 1—Female
Ethnicity$_i$: 0—Caucasian, 1—Non-Caucasian
Low-income$_i$: 0—Household annual income $\geq$ \$12,000; 1—Household annual income $<$ \$12,000

The parameter estimates are reported in Table 11.2. Likelihood ratio tests indicate each variable adds significantly to the model's explanatory power.

Table 11.2 Maximum likelihood parameter estimates for conditional indirect utility function

Parameters	Estimates	t-Statistics
b_1	0.0521	12.056
b_2	−0.0241	−5.515
b_3	0.0346	3.311
b_4	−1.1652	−1.431
b_5	0.0387	2.234
b_6	−0.7507	−1.390
b_7	3.2849	3.792
b_8	−0.0122	−0.661
b_9	−0.9611	−1.730

Log of the likelihood function = −1,356.75

The estimated model correctly predicted 75% of the choices. The model is better able to predict the choices of some respondents than others: the model predicts all the choices of 55 respondents (21%) and at least 70% of the choices of 192 respondents (74%). The model incorrectly predicts all choices for 3 respondents (1%). Another measure of goodness-of-fit is the ρ^2 index described by Ben-Akiva and Lerman (1985). For our model, the index $\rho^2 = 1 - L(\hat{\beta})/L(0)$ equals 0.24.

The parameter $\beta_1 \equiv (b_1 + b_2\text{Gender}_i + b_3\text{Low-income}_i)$ is the marginal utility of money. Given the estimates of these parameters, the marginal utility of money is positive and constant for each respondent, though it varies across respondents. The marginal utility of money is a step function of income; people with annual household income less than $12,000 have a greater marginal utility of money than those with higher incomes. The marginal utility of money also varies by gender: women have a lower marginal utility of money than men.

The marginal utility of the level of preservation $(\beta_2 + 0.5\beta_3(\text{Level}_j)^{-0.5})$, where $\beta_2 \equiv (b_4 + b_5\text{Age}_i + b_6\text{Ethnicity}_i)$ and $\beta_3 \equiv (b_7 + b_8\text{Age}_i + b_9\text{Ethnicity}_i)$, is positive and declining for all respondents over the range of preservation levels considered (0 to 1), except for young, non-Caucasian respondents.[21] Marginal utility from preservation increases with age and is lower for non-Caucasians.

These differences among individuals are consistent with answers to the attitudinal survey questions. Repeatedly, female and Caucasian respondents expressed attitudes consistent with experiencing greater utility from monument preservation than their counterparts. Also, some non-Caucasian respondents, especially African-Americans, expressed some negative attitudes toward these monuments which they felt did not reflect their own history and culture.

Welfare Estimates

To estimate the welfare changes, or WTP, associated with changes in the rate of deterioration of the marble monuments in Washington, DC, we estimate each individual's willingness to pay, WTP_i, for changes in the level of preservation.[22] Given that the marginal utility of money is a step function of income, there is no choice of alternatives once the state is specified, and the policies considered have small welfare effects, the WTP for a change from state 0 (the status quo) to Option j is:

$$\text{WTP}\{0j\} = \frac{1}{\beta_1}\left[U_{ij} - U_{i0}\right] \qquad (11.9)$$

where $U_{ij} = V_{ij} + \varepsilon_{ij}$. Substituting the estimated conditional indirect utility function and simplifying:[23]

$$\mathrm{WTP}\{0j\} = \frac{1}{\beta_1}\left[\beta_2\left(\mathrm{Level}_j\right) + \beta_3\left(\mathrm{Level}_j\right)\right]^{0.5}. \qquad (11.10)$$

We are interested in the WTP for changes from the status quo, the level of preservation in the absence of the Title IV reductions in SO_2, to states of the world with one of the preservation options. The estimated WTP for Options A, B, and C for every individual in the sample is significantly different from zero. Table 11.3 reports the minimum, maximum, median, and mean estimated WTP as a one-time payment and the confidence interval of the mean for the 259 respondents.

Table 11.3.   Estimated sample household WTP: one-time payment

	Min	Max	Median	Mean	95% Confidence interval of mean[24]
WTP for Option A	$8.91	$60.62	$30.86	$38.16	$31.67–$48.37
WTP for Option B	$10.77	$95.63	$46.98	$55.68	$47.34–$69.27
WTP for Option C	$11.59	$155.04	$73.31	$82.24	$71.33–$100.15

As suggested by the parameter estimates for the conditional indirect utility function, females, Caucasians, non-low-income people, and older people are willing to pay more than their counterparts. In general terms, the estimated WTP of non-low-income males is 53% that of non-low-income females, and the estimated WTP of low-income males is 72% that of low-income females. The estimated WTP of low-income males is 60% that of other males, and the estimated WTP of low-income females is 44% that of other females.[25] Depending on the age of the individual, a representative non-Caucasian's estimated WTP ranges from 34% to 60% that of a Caucasian. For any 10-year increase in age, the estimated WTP for a Caucasian increases from 2% to 10%.

These mean WTP estimates can be adjusted to represent the urban populations of Boston and Philadelphia by weighting the WTP of sample respondents to correct for the fact that their demographic characteristics are, on average, somewhat different from those of the study population. Our sample under-represents those under 35 years and those over 65 years, non-Caucasians, and those having low income (see Table 11.1). Table 11.4 reports weighted estimates for the study population.[26]

For some policy analysis applications, such as comparing the benefits to annualized costs of air pollution control, it is useful to have estimates of annual WTP. The one-time household payment can be converted to equivalent perpetual annual payments by assuming some discount rate. Table 11.5 provides these calculations assuming a 7% real discount rate. It is uncertain what the correct discount rate is for this purpose, but 7% is used here to illustrate the calculation. A higher discount rate would give a higher annualized value, and a lower discount rate would give a lower annualized value.

Table 11.4   Weighted estimated household WTP: one-time payment

	Min	Max	Median	Mean	95% Confidence interval of mean
WTP for Option A	$10.85	$100.31	$25.18	$32.69	$27.27–$41.32
WTP for Option B	$15.45	$156.65	$37.38	$47.14	$40.51–$58.50
WTP for Option C	$20.52	$251.13	$56.63	$68.49	$60.28–$83.27

Table 11.5   Annual weighted estimated household WTP: perpetual annual payment given a 7% discount rate

	Median perpetual annual payment	Mean perpetual annual payment
WTP for Option A	$1.76	$2.29
WTP for Option B	$2.62	$3.30
WTP for Option C	$3.96	$4.79

Comparison of Welfare Estimates

This section compares the WTP estimates derived here with WTP estimates generated from other studies which value reductions in pollution more generally. We also compare our CEWTP estimates with the results of a payment-card question included in our survey.

Comparison of estimates: estimates of benefits associated with reducing pollution

There have been a few studies that have estimated WTP for other types of benefits associated with reducing pollution. For example, McClelland *et al.* (1991) conducted a CVM study in Atlanta and Chicago to estimate the WTP of local residents for a reduction in air pollution comparable in magnitude to that expected in eastern cities under Title IV. Respondents were asked their maximum annual household WTP for this reduction and then asked to allocate that amount among the various effects of air pollution that would be realized.

They estimated a mean annual WTP of $121 (1996 dollars). The average split among the various pollution effects was: $26 for reduced soiling, materials, and vegetation effects, $23 for visual air quality improvements, $59 for reduced human health effects, and $13 for other reduced effects. This study did not ask for WTP for air quality improvements in locations other than the city where the respondents lived. WTP for reducing air pollution injury to marble monuments in Washington, DC would therefore be in addition to WTP for local air quality improvements for most residents of the United States. Compared to a mean annual WTP for reducing local soiling, materials, and vegetation injury of $26 per household, a mean annual WTP of $2.29–$4.79 for reducing injury to marble monuments in Washington, DC is plausible.

Comparison of estimates: payment-card data

Within our survey, valuation data were also gathered using a payment-card question for the most effective preservation program, Option C. Respondents were asked to indicate their maximum WTP for Option C by circling one of 22 values ranging from $0 to $200, "More than $200" or "Don't know".

The data were analyzed using an interval model assuming that the random component is distributed normally (Payment Card Model 1) and assuming that the random component is distributed log-normally (Payment Card Model 2). The models maximize the likelihood that each individual's $E[WTP]$ lies between the amount circled on the payment card and the next highest amount. For Payment Card Model 1, the estimated $E[WTP]$ function that best fits the data specifies $E[WTP]$ as a function of ethnicity and a two-step income variable. For Payment Card Model 2, $E[WTP]$ is a function of a stepped-age variable, gender, a stepped-income variable, and ethnicity. The results of both payment card models and the CE model are shown in Table 11.6.

Table 11.6   Comparison of estimated sample household WTP for option C: one-time payment

	Median	Mean	95% Confidence interval of mean
Payment Card Model 1 (normal)	$68.06	$57.29	$49.26–$64.93
CE model	$73.31	$82.24	$71.33–$100.15
Payment Card Model 2 (log-normal)	$107.89	$96.95	$71.78–$134.48

The CE mean and median WTP estimates lie between the two payment-card $E[WTP]$ estimates; the CE mean estimated WTP is significantly greater than the Payment Card Model 1 estimate, but is not significantly different from the

Payment Card Model 2 estimate. Since the payment-card question followed the pairwise choices for all respondents, we are not able to test the extent to which this ordering affected the payment-card responses. In addition, there may be systematic differences in how people answer CE questions versus payment-card questions. Therefore, at best this comparison provides only a rough benchmark.

DISCUSSION AND CONCLUSION

This chapter estimates the value of reducing the effects of air pollution on a set of important cultural resources. The valuation scenario used and the use of choice experiments allowed us to isolate an environmental change in a way that encouraged survey respondents to focus on one of the effects of air pollution while diffusing the strong emotions often associated with pollution reduction. We feel that the use of choice experiments is uniquely suited for such an analysis; it requires survey respondents to focus their attention on the various changes in attributes of an environmental good rather than requiring them to indicate the extent of their support for an environmental policy.

The welfare estimates presented are for the total value associated with slowing the rate of deterioration of (or reducing the effects of pollution on) the outdoor marble monuments in Washington, DC. We find that households in metropolitan Boston and Philadelphia are, on average, willing to pay a one-time payment of $33 to $68 to slow the rate of injury to these monuments, depending on the level of preservation (pollution reduction). This study finds that WTP is a function of gender, income group, age, and ethnicity: female, non-low-income, older, and Caucasian individuals are willing to pay more than their counterparts. Without further study, though, the extent to which these results can be generalized to a larger population is unknown. In particular, WTP may be a function of other demographic characteristics for which variation within our sample was limited. For example, WTP may depend upon region of residence or whether one lives in a rural or urban environment.

One of the motivations for this study is the requirement by the US Congress that the costs and benefits of the Title IV program of the 1990 Clean Air Act Amendments be assessed as the program is implemented. Estimates of the expected benefits to human health (Ostro *et al.*, 1999) and visibility aesthetics (Chestnut and Dennis, 1997) have been completed and will be updated as the actual emissions reductions are achieved. This study provides a step toward quantitative estimates of the expected benefits from slowed rates of injury to a set of nationally important monuments and historic buildings, although more information is needed before aggregate national estimates of the Title IV-related benefits regarding this set of national monuments can be developed. More information in two areas is needed. First, the physical science needs to be better able to quantify the change in the rate of visible injury associated with the change in SO_2 emissions. Second, more must be learned about how values vary across the country for this set of monuments. Because of their national significance, we presume that their condition would have value to residents throughout the country, but this study only sampled urban and suburban residents in two eastern US cities (both within a day's drive of Washington, DC.).

The valuation methodology and findings presented in this chapter are of interest for several reasons. This is one of only a few studies where choice experiments have been used to estimate passive-use values and one of few studies to estimate the value of slowing the rate of deterioration of cultural resources. The welfare estimates we derive are significant and reasonable; they fall within the range of amounts estimated in studies of similar environmental goods and are supported by the follow-up payment-card question within this study. These results add to the support for use of choice experiments in valuing environmental goods in general, and show the strengths of using this valuation technique for estimating passive-use values.

This study collected survey data in a group setting. This approach provides a low-cost method of implementing in-person surveys requiring extensive and detailed information describing a hypothetical good and a valuation scenario. Finally, the marginal utility of money is modeled as a step function of income, an approach supported by the data and one which simplifies the derivation of welfare estimates. Each of these innovations contributes to the development of a methodology that can reliably estimate the value of non-market goods and, in particular, goods for which values are derived from passive use.

Collecting multiple observations, in this case multiple choices, from each individual allows for the examination of differences across individuals. One possible extension of this study is to examine the extent of heterogeneity of preferences toward cultural resources. This can be done by relaxing our assumption that the scale parameter, r_i, is equal across all individuals and instead allow it to vary either by individual or type of individual. Relaxing this constraint would allow the parameter estimates to vary proportionally across individuals. Another approach is to employ a random parameters model, whereby one or more of the taste parameters is randomly drawn from a known distribution yet the parameters for any specific individual are unknown. Given that 10 choices are observed for each individual, it may also be possible to allow complete heterogeneity of preferences by estimating a separate model for each respondent.

ACKNOWLEDGEMENTS

This research was supported by the National Acid Precipitation Assessment Program. Support for and development of the initial idea for the study were greatly assisted by Susan Sherwood, Dennis Leaf, Robert Rowe, and J. Mac Callaway. Technical guidance and review were provided throughout the study by Robert Rowe, William Schulze, A. Myrick Freeman III, Victor Mossotti, Rodney Weiher, Elaine McGee, Michael Uhart, Robert Baumgartner, and Pam Rathbun. Concepts3 developed the digitally-enhanced photograph series. Photographs were provided by Nick Wyman, Sarah Richardson, Mark Tribble, Barry Hinkle, and Elaine McGee. Additional assistance was provided by Peggy Searcy, Tamara Anderson, Janice Pagel, Sally Keefe, Murray Whitehead, Chad Bierman, and Greg Pitts.

ENDNOTES

1. In contrast, several environmental valuation studies have used a rating technique, one in which survey respondents choose from among multiple choice sets by rating the degree to which they prefer one alternative over another. For example, Opaluch *et al.* (1993) and Kline and Wichelns (1996) use choice experiments to develop a utility index for the attributes associated with potential noxious facility sites and farm land preservation, respectively. Johnson and Desvousges (1997) estimate WTP for various electricity generation scenarios using a rating scale in which respondents indicate their strength of preference for one of two alternatives within each choice set.
2. The authors of the choice experiment studies mentioned above make note of these and other advantages of using choice experiments to gather stated preference data.
3. Adamowicz *et al.* (1996) discuss this possible effect and also suggest that respondents are less able to behave strategically when responding to choice experiments.
4. Morey (1999) provides a thorough description and derivation of the multinomial logit model.
5. A more complete description of the survey development process and a copy of the survey are available at http://spot.colorado.edu/~morey/monument/index.html.
6. Although focus group participants and, later, survey respondents expressed strong feelings about the importance of these monuments, they rated the importance of the condition of the monuments significantly lower than other issues such as crime, public education, and health care.
7. The original condition of the monuments is not portrayed in the timeline.
8. More complex alternatives are common, e.g. the goods in Adamowicz *et al.* (1996) have seven attributes. However, the simplicity of our bundles avoids a potential criticism of more complex alternatives. This criticism suggests that respondents might make their choices based on simplifying decision rules that ignore some attributes (Tversky *et al.*, 1989).
9. These amounts were chosen based on information about WTP provided by focus group respondents.
10. When each alternative is characterized by more than two attributes, the efficient selection of choice sets is more complex. See Adamowicz *et al.* (1997).
11. Across the 272 surveys, the correlation coefficient for the change in price and the change in level of preservation is 0.2590.
12. A copy of the survey is available at http://spot.colorado.edu/~morey/monument/index.html.
13. The advantages of in-person interviews for stated preference surveys have been described by many, including Mitchell and Carson (1989), Arrow *et al.* (1993), and Mitchell and Carson (1995).
14. This benefit, discussed by Weinberg (1983), suggests that respondents will be more comfortable not revealing their answers about personal issues (e.g. drug use) to an interviewer. It

may also be that respondents answer more truthfully in response to questions about environmental or other social issues when they are not required to reveal their answer to an interviewer.

15. Given the political climate at the time (August, 1996), it was necessary to say that the subject of the survey was not related to any election issues or candidates, nor health care.

16. Most of the research on monetary incentives has focused on the degree to which such incentives—usually small payments of $5 or less—increase response rates for mail surveys (e.g. Mizes *et al.*, 1984; Hopkins and Gullickson, 1992; Robertson and Bellenger, 1978; Church, 1993) and in-person interviews (Willmack *et al.*, 1995; Goyder, 1994). Some studies have also tested for significant differences in the demographic characteristics and responses of those paid an incentive and a control group (e.g. Robertson and Bellenger, 1978; Willmack *et al.*, 1995; Jobber *et al.*, 1988; Finlay and Thistlethwaite, 1992; Lorenzi *et al.*, 1988; James and Bolstein, 1992; Trice, 1984). In most of these studies, no response bias or demographic differences were found. Trice (1984) and James and Bolstein (1992) find some evidence of response effects due to incentive payments, though no response bias *per se*.

17. This is for annual household income of less than $12,500 for the study population.

18. Thirteen of the 272 respondents did not provide all of the demographic data used in the model. Of the remaining 259 respondents, some did not make a choice for each of the 10 pairs.

19. Since $r_i = 1 \ \forall_i$ it is omitted here.

20. The dollar amount of $120,000 was assigned to the variable $Income_i$ for respondents who indicated that their household income is greater than $100,000. The results of the model are not sensitive to this choice.

21. Non-Caucasian respondents under age 24 have an estimated negative marginal utility of preservation for levels greater than 0.8.

22. Typically, one is constrained to estimate the expected value of the individual's WTP, $E[WTP]$, rather than the WTP_i. This is because the individual's WTP is a function of his or her epsilon draw. However, this is not the case when the policy is a change in states and there is no choice in either state—our case. The epsilon is the same on both sides of the equality that defines WTP, so WTP is not a function of the epsilon, and one estimates it rather than its expectation. See Morey and Rossmann (2000).

23. Note that equations (11.9) and (11.10) contain additional terms if paying the WTP associated with a policy is of sufficient magnitude to cause an individual to change income categories (e.g. become poor). See Morey and Rossmann (2000) for details. Given the magnitude of the WTP estimates in this application, it is unlikely that any individuals are so effected.

24. This confidence interval is calculated using an order statistic on 2,000 Monte Carlo simulations of the mean WTP for the sample. This Monte Carlo sampling experiment uses a random number generator to draw independent observations of the estimated parameters from a normal distribution with a mean equal to the parameter estimates and variance equal to the estimated parameter covariance matrix. This is repeated 20,000 times for each of the 259 respondents.

25. The differences by gender complicate the interpretation of these estimates as household WTP estimates. For households in which there is a man and a woman, the household WTP is likely to depend on the roles of the man and woman in the household expenditure decision-making process. A conservative approach would be to use the estimate of the decision maker with the lower WTP, in this case males.

26. We have data on the distribution of the population by age, income, and ethnicity categories but do not know the extent to which age, income, and ethnicity are correlated. Therefore we must weight WTP as though these characteristics are not correlated. As a result, our weighted estimates are likely to be conservative estimates for the population, since income and ethnicity are likely to be positively correlated; the assumption that they are not will overweight the WTP of non-Caucasians and low-income households.

REFERENCES

Adamowicz, W., J. Louviere and M. Williams (1994), Combining Revealed and Stated Preference Methods for Valuing Environmental Amenities, *Journal of Environmental Economics and Management*, 26, 271–92.

Adamowicz, W., P. Boxall, M. Williams and J. Louviere (1996), Stated Preference Approaches for Measuring Passive Use Values: Choice Experiments versus Contingent Valuation, Working Paper.

Adamowicz, W., S. Swait, P. Boxall, J. Louviere and M. Williams (1997), Perceptions versus Objective Measures of Environmental Quality in Combined Revealed and Stated Preference Models of Environmental Valuation, *Journal of Environmental Economics and Management*, 32, 65–84.

Arrow, K., R. Solow, R.R. Portney, E.E. Leamer, R. Radner and H. Schuman (1993), Report of the NOAA Panel on Contingent Valuation, *Federal Register*, 4601–14.

Batsell, R.R. and J.J. Louviere (1991), Experimental Analysis of Choice, *Marketing Letters*, 2, 199–214.

Ben-Akiva, M. and S. Lerman (1985), *Discrete Choice Analysis: Theory and Application to Travel Demand*. Cambridge, MA: The MIT Press.

Buchanan, T., E.R. Morey and D.M. Waldman (1998), Happy Trails to You: The Impact of Trail Characteristics and Access Fees on a Mountain Biker's Trail Selection and Consumer's Surplus, Discussion Paper, Department of Economics, University of Colorado at Boulder.

Chestnut, L.G. and R.L. Dennis (1997), Economic Benefits of Improvements in Visibility: Acid Rain Provisions of the 1990 Clean Air Act Amendments, *Journal of Air and Waste Management Association*, 47, 395–402.

Church, A.H. (1993), Estimating the Effect of Incentives on Mail Survey Response Rates: A Meta-Analysis, *Public Opinion Quarterly*, 57 (1), 62–80.

Finlay, J. and P.C. Thistlethwaite (1992), Applying Mail Response Enhancement Techniques to Health Care Surveys: A Cost–Benefit Approach, *Health Marketing Quarterly*, 10 (1), 91–102.

Goyder, J. (1994), An Experiment with Cash Incentives on a Personal Interview Survey, *Journal of Market Research Society*, 36 (4), 360–6.

Green, P.E. and V. Srinavasen (1990), Conjoint Analysis in Marketing: New Developments with Implications for Research and Practice, *Journal of Marketing*, 54 (4), 3–19.

Hopkins, K.D. and A.R. Gullickson (1992), Response Rates in Survey Research: A Meta-analysis of the Effects of Monetary Gratuities, *Journal of Experimental Education*, 61 (1), 52–62.

James, J.M. and R. Bolstein (1992), Large Monetary Incentives and their Effect on Mail Survey Response Rates, *Public Opinion Quarterly*, 56, 442–53.

Jobber, D. K. Birro and S.M. Sanderson (1988), A Factorial Investigation of Methods of Stimulating Response to a Mail Survey, *European Journal of Operational Research*, 37 (2), 158–64.

Johnson, F.R. and W.D. Desvousges (1997), Estimating Stated Preferences with Rated-pair Data: Environmental, Health, and Employment Effects of Energy Programs, *Journal of Environmental Economics and Management*, 34, 79–99.

Johnson, F.R., W.H. Desvousges, E. Fries, and L.L. Wood (1995), Conjoint Analysis of Individual and Aggregate Environmental Preferences, Triangle Economic Research Technical Working Paper No. T-9502.

Kline, J. and D. Wichelns (1996), Measuring Public Preferences for the Environmental Amenities Provided by Farmland, *European Review of Agricultural Economics*, 23, 421–36.

Layton, D. and G. Brown (1998), Heterogeneous Preferences Regarding Global Climate Change, Working Paper.

Lorenzi, P., R. Friedmann and J. Paolillo (1988), Consumer Mail Survey Responses: More (Unbiases) Bang for the Buck, *Journal of Consumer Marketing*, 5 (4), 31–40.

Louviere, J.J. (1988), Conjoint Analysis Modeling of Stated Preferences: A Review of Theory, Methods, Recent Developments and External Validity, *Journal of Transport, Economics and Policy*, 10, 93–119.

Louviere, J.J. (1992), Experimental Choice Analysis: Introduction and Overview, *Journal of Business Research*, 24, 89–95.

Magat, W.A., W.K. Viscusi and J. Huber (1988), Paired Comparison and Contingent Valuation Approaches to Morbidity Risk Valuation, *Journal of Environmental Economics and Management*, 15, 395–411.

McClelland, G., W. Schulze, D. Waldman, J. Irwin and D. Schenk (1991), Valuing Eastern Visibility: A Field Test of the Contingent Valuation Method, Cooperative Agreement #CR-815183–0103. Report prepared for the US Environmental Protection Agency, Washington, DC.

McFadden, D. (1974), Conditional Logit Analysis of Qualitative Choice Behavior, In *Frontiers in Econometrics*, ed. P. Zerembka. New York: Academic Press.

Mitchell, R.C. and R.T. Carson (1989), *Using Surveys to Value Public Goods: The Contingent Valuation Method*. Washington, DC: Resources for the Future.

Mitchell, R.C. and R.T. Carson (1995), Current Issues in the Design, Administration, and Analysis of Contingent Valuation Surveys, In *Current Issues in Environmental Economics*, eds. P. Johansson, B. Kristroem and K. Maeler. New York: Manchester University Press.

Mizes, J.S., E.L. Fleece and C. Roos (1984), Incentives for Increasing Return Rates: Magnitude Levels, Response Bias, and Format, *Public Opinion Quarterly*, 48 (4), 794–800.

Morey, E.R. (1999), Two RUMs Uncloaked: Nested-Logit Models of Site-Choice and Nested-Logit Models of Participation and Site Choice, In *Valuing the Environment Using Recreation Demand Models*, eds. C.L. Kling and H. Herriges. Cheltenham: Edward Elgar.

Morey, E.R. and K.G. Rossmann (2000), The Compensating Variation for a Change in States When There is Only One Alternative in Each State and Where Utility is Assumed a Linear Spline Function of Income, Working Paper.

Opaluch, J., S. Swallow, T. Weaver, C. Wessels and D. Wichelns (1993), Evaluating Impacts from Noxious Facilities: Including Public Preferences in Current Siting Mechanisms, *Journal of Environmental Economics and Management*, 24, 41–59.

Ostro, B.D., L.G. Chestnut, D.M. Mills and A.M. Watkins (1999), Estimating the Effects of Air Pollutants on the Population: Human Health Benefits of Sulfate Aerosol Reductions under Title IV of the 1990 Clean Air Act Amendments, In *Air Pollutant and Effects on Health*, eds. S.T. Holgate *et al.* London: Academic Press, pp. 899–915.

Robertson, D.H. and D.N. Bellenger (1978), A New Method of Increasing Mail Survey Responses: Contributions to Charity, *Journal of Marketing Research*, 15 (4), 632–3.

Roe, B., K.J. Boyle and M.F. Teisl (1996), Using Conjoint Analysis to Derive Estimates of Compensating Variation, *Journal of Environmental Economics and Management*, 31, 145–59.

Trice, A.D. (1984), Hotel Ratings: Recruitment and Incentives, *Psychological Reports*, 55, 58.

Tversky, A., S. Sattath and P. Slovic (1989), Contingent Weighting, Judgement and Choice, *Psychology Review*, 95, 352–71.

Viscusi, W.K., W.A. Magat and J. Huber (1991), Pricing Environmental Health Risks: Survey Assessments of Risk–Risk and Risk–Dollar Trade-offs for Chronic Bronchitis, *Journal of Environmental Economics and Management*, 21, 32–51.

Weinberg, E. (1983), Data Collection: Planning and Management, In *Handbook of Survey Research*, ed. P.H. Rossi. New York: Academic Press.

Willmack, D.K., H. Schuman and B. Pennell (1995), Effects of a Prepaid Nonmonetary Incentive on Response Rates and Response Quality in a Face-to-Face Survey, *Public Opinion Quarterly*, 59, 78–92.

12. Valuing cultural services in Italian museums: a contingent valuation study

Marina Bravi, Riccardo Scarpa and Gemma Sirchia

INTRODUCTION

Italian museums are experiencing a transformation in terms of both institutional arrangement and public management. In this transformation, two different management systems find themselves face to face. On the one hand, the public museum system, which is strongly linked to and controlled by central government through the Ministry of Culture. On the other hand, the mixed private–public museum system, characterized by a faster decision making, but suffering sharp management constraints due to chronic tight budgets.

Positive experiences from other western countries (UK, USA, etc.) offer food for thought about both the limits and the potential gains achievable via institutional change in the provision of cultural goods in the Italian museum system. The distinctive characteristic of these countries, *vis-à-vis* Italy, is that less public money is poured into the management of museums. Both in the UK and USA cuts have been made possible by the implementation of corporate tax-relief provisions. These allow museums to rely more on private funding and corporate donations, while private contributors promote their image and influence as art patrons.

In a world of increasingly scarce public resources for cultural activities, one may argue that the main policy goal is to strike the right balance between reliance on public funding and broader opening to market forces. In this context, pricing and product/service differentiation strategies become crucial for the implementation of any marketing action.

However, only some marketing techniques from the private sector can be transferred to this non-profit sector. This chapter seeks to answer the following question: can the use of contingent valuation (CV) be effectively employed in the context of defining access charges for enjoying cultural goods provided by a local museum system? More specifically, our study concentrates on benefit valuation and its related charge policies in relation to two modern art galleries in Turin: the *Galleria Civica* and *Rivoli Castle*. These have marked differences in management systems and sources of revenue, but both offer comparable cultural services and goods to a prevalently local public. In this specific context, we examine how willingness to pay (WTP) distributions for the same hypothetical change in provision differ between the two museums.

The remainder of the chapter is divided into five sections. In the second section, we present the argument in support of the use of CV as a method for estimating WTP to avoid the loss of existing levels of provisions of cultural services by museums. The third section describes the CV surveys conducted to derive WTP estimates for two modern art galleries. The fourth deals with some of the econometric issues associated with the use of discrete-choice elicitation. In the fifth section we present parametric and non-parametric estimates of WTP distributions and discuss our findings. The sixth concludes.

CV AND THE MARKETING OF PUBLIC CULTURAL SERVICES

Effective marketing of any good and service requires some knowledge of value. Ever since one can remember, Italian museums and art exhibitions have managed public access on the basis of administrative and populistic charges. In other words, charges were designed to supplement running costs only marginally, as the public sector was expected to bear most of the burden of running museums. In recent years, however, the rising levels of education have brought about an increased cultural awareness and appreciation for cultural heritage. This in turn has increased demand in terms of both quality (increased expectations on standards of access and conservation) and quantity (number of visitors per year). Meeting these changes in demand meant an increase in management costs.

In Italy, the adoption of marketing strategies to investigate the value that the public at large places on different forms of cultural services was much delayed with respect to that for other private goods and services. The delay was due to: (a) the existence of monopsonistic forces in the supply of public services; (b) a strongly rooted reluctance to consider marketing policies applicable to social institutions and non-profit organizations; and (c) the prevalence of intangible contents in the production/consumption activity of this sector.

The history of the Italian Public Administration is marked by an essentially bureaucratic approach. Decision makers have traditionally been more interested in designing protocols of tasks and functions than in achieving management objectives. The museum sector is a typical example of this phenomenon. Here, in fact, the function of protecting the public cultural heritage has clearly prevailed over that of promoting and improving public access to the available assets. Nevertheless, Italy has not been immune from the crisis of the welfare state that has taken place throughout the western world. Scarcity of public money is forcing museum managers to find alternative ways of covering their costs. However, conventional demand analysis is not adequate to investigate the structure of reservation prices for changes in provision levels of public cultural goods. Hence, non-market valuation methods are of immediate interest to applied economists involved in advising museum management.

Recent and current government policies have shown a tendency to pull out of public funding of cultural goods and services. In this climate, a very realistic prospect for the consumers enjoying these benefits is that of a reduction or qualitative worsening of the provision, unless increased access charges are enforced. Individual WTPs to prevent losses in public access to cultural goods are therefore an indicator of paramount importance for museum managers. The two studies reported in this chapter were both centred around this hypothetical scenario. However, they concerned two museums with very different forms of management, as well as distinctive features in their supply of cultural goods.

The measurement of WTP becomes an important indicator if one wishes to establish a relationship between input costs (the resources used to produce the service) and the benefits enjoyed by the community. WTP estimation is vital to identify: (a) the cost component that can be paid by the user; (b) the extent to which different segments of demand have to contribute to cover costs; and (c) how many and what resources, relating to the non-covered of charges share of costs, will be used.

CV is a direct non-market method often employed to estimate WTP distributions for changes in public good provisions. The CV technique consists of interviewing a random sample of the target population. During this interview, respondents are presented with a detailed description of a baseline scenario and of another alternative one. Then a monetary valuation of the change between the described scenarios is elicited using one of a variety of elicitation techniques. This allows the analyst to identify the hypothetical WTP or willingness to accept (WTA), depending on whether the change presented in the scenario represents a welfare gain or loss for the respondent.

Because it is based on interviews and hypothetical scenarios, the technique is highly flexible, but tight protocols have been developed for its credible implementation. It is particularly suitable for addressing aspects of demand for cultural goods and services which are characterized by intangibility, heterogeneity and inseparability. The CV survey is also a means of obtaining information about the demographic, social, professional and cultural characteristics of the consumer with reference to actual or potential users (with subsequent inferences for a population of cases).

Through the formulation of the question eliciting WTP/WTA, it is possible to hypothesize the supply of additional services against a price increase, or else to predict a scenario in which, for example due to a cut in financial resources, some aspects of supply decrease.

The reliability performance of CV results was tested for almost 30 years in an attempt to check their theoretical and methodological consistency and plausibility. The hypothetical character of the evaluation has led to critical considerations (Diamond and Hausman, 1994) which have highlighted the bias effects—strategic behaviour, complacency, identification of price vectors, scenario mis-specification, etc.—to which the elicitation question is potentially subject. Nonetheless, if used as part of a cultural service marketing strategy, this technique may reveal its utility to resolve what have been identified as causes of its intrinsic weakness in this context.

Summing up, CV may be used flexibly as a market simulation technique, like all the other tools long established in marketing studies, such as, for example, conjoint analysis (see Louviere, 1992).

BACKGROUND AND CV SURVEY

We present two experimental applications of the CV method to derive WTP distributions from populations of visitors to two museums. These are very similar in terms of functions and target public but, at the same time, are institutionally counterpoised. The *Galleria Civica d'Arte Moderna e Contemporanea* (henceforth *Civica*) in Turin is a gallery of nineteenth and twentieth century Italian painting and sculpture publicly managed by the City Council, while the *Museo d'Arte Contemporanea* at *Rivoli Castle* (henceforth *Rivoli*) specializes in the visual arts of the last 40 years and is at least partially privately managed.

Civica was founded in 1863 in Turin as a *Museo Civico*, and was the first institution in Italy set up to collect contemporary works. Since 1950 the collection has been hosted in a new building, which had to be completely restructured in the 1980s due to bad degradation. The remodelling of the building was completed in 1992. Then the exhibition was re-opened to the public, under a new set of regulations, and featured, among other things, a variety of connected activities, such as its book and photographic collections, conference room, temporary exhibitions and periodical educational projects for Turin schools.

Rivoli Castle, instead, was originally built as a Savoy royal residence. It was transformed in the course of the seventeenth century according to the designs of famous architects, such as Castellamonte, Garove and Bertola and, after 1715, Filippo Juvarra. The idea of restructuring the *Castle* and converting it into a museum of contemporary arts dates from 1978, but the new structure only opened in 1984, with the exhibition *Overture*, dedicated to the main trends in European and American contemporary art.

The *Galleria Civica* is the property of the City of Turin, which pays the staff and keeps a centralized management. The coordination of Turin museum activities is disciplined by the *Regolamento dei Musei Civici e delle Mostre* (Civic Museum and Exhibition Regulations), approved in 1994. A director is appointed for the administrative sector, but there is no professional manager for external services (cafeteria, bookshop, etc.) or promotion and marketing activities.

The *Rivoli Castle* museum, on the other hand, is structured autonomously, along the lines of a private company. The management body includes not only the Piedmont Regional Authority but also banks and private companies (FIAT, GFT, CRT, etc.), which represent the local economy. The museum has its own autonomous budget and is free to programme its activities and make decisions on initiatives, new accessioning, staff management and the like.

A comparison of the balance sheets of the two museums between 1993 and 1996 (Mattone, 1998) can be conducted by examining some *ratios*. These are indicators of financial and operating efficiency which, *inter alia*, reflect their differing cost structures. The average costs incurred per service production in proportion to numbers of visitors (Table 12.1) represent the first important evidence to reflect upon. The figures reveal somewhat marked differences between the two museums. Although, in 1994, *Rivoli Castle* attracted almost twice as many visitors as the *Galleria Civica*, the latter shows a cost-to-visitor ratio considerably higher than that of *Rivoli Castle* (almost three times higher in 1994). This is largely due to excessive spending for caretakers (50% of outlay against 20%) and extraordinary expenses (Table 12.2), which are not offset by an increase in the flow of visitors. In proportion to staff numbers, attendance figures show that the two museums have different degrees of managerial and personnel efficiency. During the two-year period 1994–95, there was an average of 25,000 visitors per employee at *Rivoli*, while *Civica* had 300 visitors per employee.

For the CV survey, 1,500 interviews were attempted in a random sample of direct users of *Rivoli Castle* in 1996 and about 1,000 for direct users of the *Galleria Civica* in 1997; 1,323 and 854 interviews, respectively were completed to be used in this study. The elicitation question was formulated by opting for a dichotomous-choice response to reduce the effects of strategic behaviour of respondents to a minimum. The proposed change of scenario was dictated by the museum's management, and after many different formulations it was decided to ask the following question:

> *The museum you are visiting is financed by ... and its direct revenue (admission, bookshop, merchandising) corresponds to about 5% of its budget. Hypothesizing a*

Table 12.1 *Financial and management efficiency indicators—Rivoli and Civica, 1993–94–95–96*

	Museo d'arte contemporanea Castello di Rivoli				Galleria Civica d'arte moderna di Torino		
	1993	1994	1995	1996	1994	1995	1996
Average cost per visitor	99	49	59	86	167	117	
Average cost per opening hour	1,306	1,694	2,021	2,095	2,342	2,841	
Average cost per square metre of exhibition space	536	696	830	860	1084	1315	
Annual visitors per employee	1,158	2,569	2,718	1,935	234	429	347
Square metres per employee	214	182	194	194	36	38	38
Annual visitors per opening hour	13.2	34.4	34.2	24	14	24.2	20
Annual visitors	32,413	84,763	84,267	59,995	34,651	59,660	48,170
Annual opening days	308	308	308	308	308	308	308
Total employees	28	33	31	31	148	139	139
Hours of daily opening	8	8	8	8	10	10	10
Sqare metres of exhibition space	6,000	6,000	6,000	6,000	5,324	5,324	5,324
Annual temporary exhibitions	4	4	5	5	3	4	

Table 12.2 Balance sheet structure—Rivoli and Civica, 1993–94–95–96

	Rivoli Castle				Civica Gallery	
	1993	1994	1995	1996	1994	1995
INCOME STRUCTURE						
Total public funding/Total	93.9	35.7	52.6	47.1	100	100
Total private funding/Total		37	31.6	43.3	0.32	0.26
Total indirect funding/Total	5.7	26.5	14.5	9.3	3.08	3.92
Miscellaneous income/Total	0.4	0.7	0.07	0.3	0.93	0.52
	100	100	100	100	100	100
SPENDING STRUCTURE						
Total personnel expenses/Total	23.2	17.6	19.6	19.2	53	46.6
Total spending on cultural activities/Total	30.7	36.7	30.9	36	3.96	20.5
Total ordinary expenditure/Total	29.9	36.5	41.4	36.8	33	25.1
Total extraordinary expenditure/Total	5.2	5.3	5.6	4.6	9.26	7.78
Miscellaneous expenditure/Total	10.7	3.8	2.5	3.5	0	0
	100	100	100	100	100	100

cut in public funding such as to significantly decrease the cultural services offered by the museum, would you be prepared to spend an annual sum of L. ... (to be devolved to the body responsible for the service) to be able to continue to use the museum at present conditions, bearing in mind the present admission fee? Yes .... No ....

The questionnaire thus emphasizes the problem of the meagre and dwindling availability of public funds. It then appeals to the individual visitor's sense of responsibility to involve him in financial support of a local public good. The price vector was chosen on the basis of previous pilot studies, and ranges from 5 to 100 thousand Lit. (Lit. 5–100k). The proposed scenario leaves much to the respondent's interpretation of "significant decrease", but other attempts to specify scenario changes in a more detailed fashion produced quite cumbersome elicitation questions. The final wording is considered acceptable given the experimental nature of these two first studies and considering that the main objective is to elicit a general WTP distribution to prevent service deterioration so as to design a pricing policy in case of budget shortages. The scenario refers to a change in the level of utility identified by economic theory as an equivalent variation.

The payment vehicle is chosen to be a yearly contribution to the institution managing the museum. This is an analogue form of payment to cultural club memberships and is considered quite believable in the context of provision of a cultural service with predominantly local customers.

ECONOMETRIC ISSUES

When the analyst needs to derive estimates of welfare measures from discrete-choice CV responses, a number of assumptions are in order. As usual, the estimation will be most robust to potential model mis-specifications when the assumptions are least restrictive. Models of structural behaviour normally require the specification of a formal model of choice. Each of the alternatives faced by the respondent can be associated with different utility levels. Random utility models (RUMs) have been successfully proposed (Hanemann, 1984) and widely employed. The parametric estimation of these models is based on quite restrictive assumptions. First, one needs to assume a specific form of the deterministic component of utility, v. The attributes of the alternative, as well as the respondents' characteristics, are often included amongst the vector of variables x which determines the value of this component, up to a vector of estimable parameters β. Second, one also needs to assume a given distribution of the unobservable component u of the RUM model. Eventually, a specification linking the probability of a positive response to the WTP question,

Pr(Yes|x;β), is defined. Then, sample likelihood maximization algorithms are employed to find the values of β that maximize the sample likelihood over the parameter space. The estimated parameter vector β_{ML} is then employed to compute the various welfare measures, based on the untruncated or truncated expectations or on the distribution percentiles of the estimated density Pr(Yes|x_i;β_{ML}).

To validate the estimated parameter vector, we can also employ distribution-free methods (semi-parametric or semi-non-parametric) in order to derive more robust estimates of the β vector and then compare them with the parametric ones in order to detect the sensitivity of the β_{ML} to the given distributional specification employed (Li, 1996). If distribution-free methods produce β estimates close to β_{ML}, we can feel more comfortable about employing the latter to determine the density extrapolation needed to compute the welfare measures or other simulations.

However, one may be uniquely interested in the estimation of welfare measures, and not in that of structural parameters of choice. In this case, the estimation of Pr(Yes|x) is sufficient and total non-parametric estimation is viable by means of density estimators (survival curve estimators). One such estimator, that has received some degree of attention and application in DC-CVM data, is the Turnbull–Kaplan–Meier (TKM) estimator (Haab and McConnell, 1996). However, this estimator represents only a lower bound on conditional density estimation, and hence its derived welfare measures are also a lower bound on real ones. The TKM estimator imposes weak monotonicity on the probability estimates, reflecting the theoretical implication and intuitive concept that, as the bid amount decreases, the expected probability of a "yes" response cannot decrease. Other non-parametric density estimators, without systematic biases, have also been employed (Scarpa *et al.*, 1998), but these do not impose weak monotonicity.

Structural estimation of choice models is clearly required when it is necessary to extrapolate off the support of the observed covariate. For example, when the welfare measure of choice is a truncated expectation beyond the investigated bid range (see Hanemann, 1984, 1989; Duffield and Patterson, 1991), it may happen that the frequency of positive response at the maximum bid amount employed is still quite high. This may be due to the poor performance of the pre-survey pilot study, or to a bid design that happens not to investigate the upper range of the population bid amounts well. In these cases, an unbiased estimate of the welfare measure requires a correct assumption on the behaviour of the Pr(Yes|x) of the support of x. In this context, the choice of distributional assumption becomes a driving force behind the estimation of the welfare measure.

ESTIMATION OF WTP DISTRIBUTIONS

In this study the estimation was designed to assess and compare the WTP distributions from the population of visitors of the two museums. Despite the differences in cost structure and managerial objectives, the cultural services offered by the two museums and the customer profiles are very similar, so not much difference was expected *a priori* in the main distributional features. The main objective of the econometric analysis is the derivation of unconditional WTP distributions, via estimation of Pr(Yes|bid). As pointed out by McFadden (1994), unconditional distributions are sufficient to derive welfare estimates. Probability estimates of distributions conditional on socio-economic covariates could be useful in a context in which discriminatory access charges could realistically be implemented. However, discriminatory pricing is not a policy option that museum managers were ready to entertain in Turin.

The observed empirical distribution of discrete responses across bid amounts from the two random samples is reported in Table 12.3. A cursory glance at this data already shows that the two empirical distributions present different traits, especially with respect to the frequencies of "yes" responses at high bid amounts. At the maximum bid amount of Lit. 100k, the empirical frequency is 10% higher in *Rivoli* than in *Civica*. Further, the behaviour around the range Lit. 20–40k shows a sharp 30% decline in *Civica*, but only 16% in *Rivoli*. In general, *Rivoli*'s empirical distribution declines more gently, while *Civica*'s shows a sharp decline around the median and towards the tails.

Table 12.3   Observed CV Responses

	Civica *N*=854			Rivoli *N*=1,323		
Bid	"Yes"	Responses	Rel. Freq.	"Yes"	Responses	Rel. Freq.
5	54	69	0.783	93	113	0.823
10	53	69	0.768	66	93	0.710
15	51	74	0.689	74	118	0.627
20	54	80	0.675	64	111	0.577
30	52	71	0.732	62	114	0.544
40	26	70	0.371	45	108	0.417
50	26	76	0.342	58	125	0.464
60	31	69	0.449	40	115	0.348
70	20	71	0.282	45	115	0.391
80	18	66	0.273	21	97	0.217
90	19	73	0.260	25	102	0.245
100	9	66	0.136	27	112	0.241

The TKM non-parametric probability and lower bound welfare estimates, which are maximum likelihood estimates under weak monotonicity, are reported in Table 12.4 and charted in Figure 12.1. The pool-adjacent-violator algorithm is responsible for the pooling of probability estimates at bid amounts 10, 15, 40 and 50 in *Civica*, as well as bid amounts 40, 60, 80 and 90 in *Rivoli*. The median WTP, M(WTP), estimates under linear interpolation over the relevant percentiles are very close for both museums (about Lit. 31–34k, currently equivalent to 15–17 euro), as are the lower bounds on expected WTP, E(WTP) (about Lit. 30k, 15 euro). Examining the TKM probability graphs in Figure 12.1 confirms the existence of a difference in the shape of the two unconditional distributions.

Conventional linear logit random utility consistent parameter estimates are reported in the first two columns of Table 12.5, along with welfare estimates

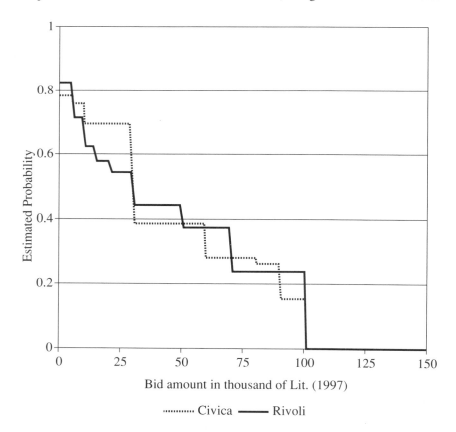

Figure 12.1   Estimated probablility densities of positive response from Turnbull–Kaplan–Meier non-parametric estimator

derived using the formula in Hanemann (1989; see also Hanemann and Kanninen, 1999). Confidence intervals were derived using the Krinsky and Robb (1986) parametric bootstrap procedure. The estimated medians, truncated mean (at the maximum bid amount of Lit. 100k) and mean over the non-negative orthant are all very similar, with widely overlapping confidence intervals. However, as is apparent from the individual contributions to the sample likelihood of each sample observation, the *Rivoli* sample fits this parametric specification worse than the *Civica* one. Further, parameter estimates obtained by pooling the samples and using constant (α_c) and slope-specific (β_c) dummies for *Civica* museum (third column in Table 12.5) show that both dummies have significant *t*-values. This indicates what is also borne out by likelihood ratio tests for model specification (not presented here), which is that the two distributions are significantly different. The negative sign of β_c indicates that *Civica*'s visitors have a higher marginal utility of money than those for *Rivoli*.

Table 12.4   Nonparametric analysis based on Turnbull–Kaplan–Meier probability estimates

	Civica				Rivoli		
Bid	Pr(Yes)	N	Yes	Bid	Pr(Yes)	N	Yes
5	0.783	69	54	5	0.823	113	93
10	0.768	69	53	10	0.710	93	66
30	0.698	225	157	15	0.627	118	74
60	0.386	215	83	20	0.577	111	64
70	0.282	71	20	30	0.544	114	62
80	0.273	66	18	50	0.442	233	103
90	0.260	73	19	70	0.370	230	85
100	0.136	66	9	100	0.235	311	73

Lower bound on E(WTP)=36 (±2.04) Lower bound on E(WTP)=35.6 (±1.07)
Lower bound on M(WTP)=30.9[*]   Lower bound on M(WTP)=34.3

Note: Estimates of M(WTP) marked with an asterisk were obtained by linear interpolation over the relevant interval.

To investigate further this difference in a parametric context, a more flexible specification is adopted, still maintaining the logit distributional assumption. Box–Cox transformed bids (λ(bid)=(bid$^\lambda$ – 1)/λ) are used in a grid search over the λ parameter, with approximations to the third decimal digit. As is well known, as λ tends to zero the distribution gradually acquires the characteristics of a natural log transform (log-logistic model), and as it tends to one those of the linear-logistic model. The resulting maximum likelihood estimates and

Table 12.5 *Parametric analysis based on logit models*

	Civica	Rivoli	Joint	Civica Box-Cox	Rivoli Box-Cox
N	854	1323	2177	854	1323
Mean log-likelihood	-0.6004	-0.6284	-0.6174	-0.5994	-0.6243
α	1.3291*	1.0091	1.0078	1.6768	2.2351
	(0.1402)	(0.1072)	(0.1126)	(0.1671)	(0.2000)
β	-0.0304	-0.0245	-0.0245	-0.1004	-0.4382
	(0.0026)	(0.0020)	(0.0021)	(0.0086)	(0.0353)
α_c	–	–	0.3199	–	–
			(0.1997)		
β_c	–	–	-0.0058	–	–
			(0.0037)		
λ		–	–	0.679	0.207
Median	43.8**	41.1	–	–	–
	(39.0–48.3)	(36.3–45.5)			
Mean (truncated at bid max)	46.0	45.2	–	45.8	44.9
	(43.0–48.9)	(42.6–47.6)		(42.7–48.8)	(42.4–47.8)
Mean (on R+)	51.5	53.8	–	–	–
	(47.1–56.6)	(49.6–59.2)			
Mean (truncated at Lit. 200k)	–	–	–	53.7	61.9
				(48.9–59.8)	(57.0–67.8)
Mean (truncated at Lit. 300k)	–	–	–	55.0	71.3
				(50.0–61.4)	(63.3–80.1)

Notes:
* Asymptotic standard errors in parentheses.
** In thousand Lit. with Krinsky and Robb's 95% confidence interval in parentheses.

welfare measures are reported in the last two columns of Table 12.5. The estimated densities are plotted in Figure 12.2. The values of mean log-likelihood indicate that this flexible functional form significantly improves the likelihood of both samples (this is also borne out by formal likelihood tests not presented here). As is clear from the estimates for the λ parameter (λ=0.207), *Rivoli* museum faces a WTP distribution with quite a fat tail, while *Civica* (λ=0.679) suffers much less from this problem. This is reflected in the sensitivity of welfare estimates based on extrapolations of the estimated parametric distribution beyond the maximum bid amount of Lit. 100k. In fact, when the integral for the expected WTP is truncated at this amount, the estimates are very similar across all models, while moving the truncation point beyond this to Lit. 200k and Lit. 300k affects *Rivoli*'s estimates much more than *Civica*'s.

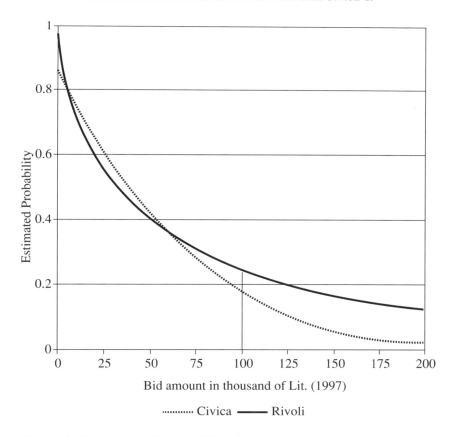

Figure 12.2   Estimated probability densities of positive response from Box–Cox logit model

The overall conclusion that can be drawn from the econometric analysis is that the location parameters of the distribution of WTP are very close in the two samples. However, the behaviour of the WTP distribution in the upper percentiles seems to differ strongly between the two samples. This suggests that *Rivoli* museum has a comparatively larger up-market segment of visitors, who are willing to pay high amounts in a larger proportion than those visiting *Civica*. In terms of management implications, this may be interpreted as providing the possibility to secure a given level of revenue by asking higher access charges and relying on a smaller level of visitation.

CONCLUSIONS

Italian policies regulating provision of cultural services are generally oriented towards a scant diversification of the product, targeted at a generalized and non-segmented audience of consumers. This is why charges have traditionally been positioned at medium–low levels. Increase in demand and a shortage in public funds pose new challenges to museum managers. These require some knowledge of WTP for access to cultural services and products and contingent valuation is one of the non-market methods that can provide this information.

This study has presented the results of two CV surveys designed to estimate WTPs to avoid service deterioration in two modern art exhibitions: the *Galleria Civica* and *Rivoli Castle*. Although these are under substantially different forms of management, they provide similar services to similar consumer targets. Estimates of location parameters for WTPs obtained with single-bounded discrete-choice CV are very similar across parametric and non-parametric estimation methods. The behaviour of parametric estimates of WTP distributions, however, differs markedly at higher percentiles. *Rivoli*'s visitors seem to have a higher probability of being willing to pay a given bid amount than *Civica*'s visitors. This despite the fact that cost-efficiency ratios revealed that *Rivoli* is managed more cost-effectively than *Civica*.

Overall, WTP estimation for the two museums has highlighted the existence of a sizeable consumer surplus, which could be exploited by adequate access pricing. More specifically, the comparison of the two case studies highlights that, in the face of a different cost and management structure and a different number of visitors, the populations of visitors in the two museums express similar mean WTP amounts coming from different distributions. The greatest volume of annual benefit is produced by the exhibition hosted in *Rivoli Castle*, which attracts a high number of users. We speculate that this is at least in part due to a more efficient management and a more qualified supply.

Services and charges diversification, accompanied by greater internal efficiency, would appear to be the alternative to total deregulation and privatization, apparently unfeasible in Italy, especially in a sector responsible for the task of protecting and promoting the appreciation of culture. CV may represent a useful non-market tool to investigate visitors' preferences in this context, where reliance on competitive market behaviour to derive estimates of reservation price schedules would clearly be misplaced.

ACKNOWLEDGEMENTS

The CV study was designed and conducted by M. Bravi and G. Sirchia, while the econometric analysis was conducted by R. Scarpa, the writing of the chapter, however, was a joint effort. The authors wish to acknowledge useful comments from the editors of this book and the participants of the Xth International Conference on Cultural Economics held in Barcelona, Spain, 14–17 June 1998, where this material was first presented. The usual disclaimer applies.

REFERENCES

Diamond, P.A. and J.A. Hausman. 1994. Contingent Valuation: Is Some Number Better Than No Number?, *Journal of Economic Perspectives*, 8, 45–64.

Duffield, J.W. and D.A. Patterson. 1991. Inference and Optimal Design for a Welfare Measure in Dichotomous Choice Contingent Valuation, *Land Economics*, 67, 225–39.

Haab, T.C. and K.E. McConnell. 1996. Referendum Models and Negative WTP: Alternative Solutions, *Journal of Environmental Economics and Management*, 32, 251–70.

Hanemann, W.M. 1984. Welfare Evaluations in Contingent Valuation Experiments with Discrete Response Data, *American Journal of Agricultural Economics*, 66, 332–41.

Hanemann, W.M. 1989. Welfare Evaluations in Contingent Valuation Experiments with Discrete Response Data: a Reply, *American Journal of Agricultural Economics*, 71, 1057–61.

Hanemann, W.M. and B. Kanninen. 1999. The Statistical Analysis of Discrete-Response CV Data, in *Valuing Environmental Preferences*, I. Bateman and G.K. Willis (eds.), Oxford University Press, Oxford, pp. 302–441.

Krinsky, I. and A. Robb. 1986. Approximating the Statistical Properties of Elasticities, *Review of Economics and Statistics*, 68, 715–19.

Li, C.-Z. 1996. Semiparametric Estimation of the Binary Choice Model for Contingent Valuation, *Land Economics*, 72, 462–73.

Louviere, J.J. (1992), Experimental Choice Analysis: Introduction and Overview, *Journal of Business Research*, 24, 89–95.

Mattone, F. 1998. Il museo-Impresa: strategie di marketing e valorizzazione, *Unpublished Bachelor Thesis*, 1997–98, Facoltà di Architettura, Politecnico di Torino.

McFadden, D. 1994. Contingent Valuation and Social Choice, *American Journal of Agricultural Economics*, 76, 689–708.

Scarpa, R., M. Bravi and G. Sirchia. 1998. Kernel vs. Logit Modeling of Single Bounded CV Responses: Valuing Access to Architectural and Visual Arts Heritage in Italy, in *Environmental Resource Valuation: Application of the Contingent Valuation Method in Italy*, R. Bishop and D. Romano (eds.), Kluwer Academic Publishers, Norwell, pp. 232–44.

13. A contingent valuation study of the Royal Theatre in Copenhagen

Trine Bille

Reprinted from Hume Papers on Public Policy, Volume 6, No. 3, 1998; Heritage, the Environment and the Arts: Pricing the priceless, pp. 38–66, with permission from Edinburgh University Press

BACKGROUND AND PURPOSE

In this chapter some of the results of a study, with the purpose of valuing a quasi-private cultural good, namely the Royal Theatre in Copenhagen, Denmark, using the contingent valuation method (CVM), are presented.[1] The intention is to investigate if CVM can be used in order to estimate the total value of the Royal Theatre to the Danish population and to study whether the value of the Royal Theatre's non-market benefits can justify the public grants given to the theatre. A CV study of the Royal Theatre is therefore of direct political interest, as it can reveal whether the Royal Theatre "is worth the money" from the taxpayers' point of view.

This application of CVM is quite new. For the most part CVM has been used on environmental goods.[2] In the literature there are only a few examples of utilization of CVM for cultural goods (e.g. Martin, 1994; Throsby and Withers, 1983; Morrison and West, 1986), and most of these studies have used CVM on very broadly defined goods, i.e. public support for the arts in general.

This limited use of CVM in the literature of cultural economics is quite surprising, as much of this literature deals with legitimizing public subsidies to the arts, which clearly appears from the following quotation of Professor David Throsby in the Journal of Economic Literature (1994): "*Finding a rational and guiding principles for government support of the arts was one of the major areas of concern of the earliest postwar writings in cultural economics, and these issues have continued to recur in the literature ever since*". Throsby and Withers (1979) and Frey and Pommerehne (1989) among others have discussed theoretical arguments for public support to cultural activities. There is wide agreement that the main arguments are to be found in positive consumer externalities of different kinds, and CVM is more or less the only benefit measurement approach which can be used to quantify the level of consumer externalities generated.

In the second section of this chapter a short description of the Royal Theatre's activities is given and different kinds of benefits connected to the Royal Theatre are mentioned. In the third section the CV study is designed. The main results are presented in the fourth section, where the individual willingness to pay (WTP) is aggregated to the total WTP for the Royal Theatre for the whole of the Danish population. In the fifth section the WTP is divided into use, non-use and option values using a reductionistic method. In the sixth section determinants of WTP are analysed, estimating a Poisson model and a self-selection model. The last section concludes the chapter.

THE ROYAL THEATRE

The theatre was founded in 1748 and is the Danish national theatre.[3] It has three stages in Copenhagen, an old stage from 1874, a newer stage and a small stage for experimental plays. It also carries out tours in the rest of Denmark. It is one of the few theatres in the world offering both opera, ballet and drama performances. Around 400,000 tickets are sold every year, but more than two-thirds of the Danish population has never visited the theatre. It receives about DKKm 266 (about £25 million) in support from the state every year, which is more than 80% of its total budget and about 35% of the total public support for theatres in Denmark, which is given to about 75 different theatres.

There are several reasons why the Royal Theatre is chosen as a case. *Firstly*, it is a very well defined cultural good. All Danes are familiar with it and know they are already paying for it through taxes. Besides, everybody seems to have an opinion of it. In other words: there is a very high degree of familiarity with the good, which means it is a good which the respondents are expected to have relatively well defined preferences for. *Secondly*, the Royal Theatre is one of Denmark's most elitist cultural institutions and only a very small percentage of the population actually goes to the theatre (7% has been there within the last year). *Thirdly*, as the Royal Theatre is mainly financed by public subsidies it means that the non-users are financing the main part of the theatre's budget through taxes.

Besides, it is shown in Bille Hansen (1996) that consumer surplus for visits at the Royal Theatre only makes up a small part of the public grants given to the theatre. In Bille Hansen (1991) a demand model for subscription sales is estimated on the basis of data for the number of subscriptions sold, average ticket prices, consumer incomes, the number of productions offered, etc. in the period 1971/72 to 1988/89. From this model a price elasticity of –0.33 is calculated.[4] Assuming a price elasticity of –0.33 is applicable to the total number of tickets sold at the Royal Theatre,[5] a total consumer surplus for visits at the theatre of about DKKm 42 can be estimated, although with a large uncertainty in the estimate. This corresponds to a little more than the theatre's total box office receipts, which in 1991/92 amounted to about DKKm 36. This consumer surplus estimate only covers about 15% of the public grants the theatre receives. Thus, if the subsidy shall be justified, it has to be on account of the non-market benefits of the Royal Theatre.

Benefits Connected to the Royal Theatre

In a deterministic world without uncertainty one usually distinguishes between use values and non-use values. In most of the CV-literature there is consensus about the fact that *the total value* of a good in a deterministic world can be estimated using the following definition:

$$TV \equiv UV + NUV \qquad (13.1)$$

where TV = total value, UV = use value and NUV = non-use value

Use Value

The use value is the value which is connected to direct consumption of the private part of the good. Using the Royal Theatre as an example the direct use value would of course be the experience of a theatrical performance. This value can either be recreational, lead to bigger personal insight and perspective for the individual or be commercial in the sense that it inspires the individual theatre-goer who might use the inspiration in his/her professional career and development. These motives for the demand will, however, not be discussed further.[6] The experience of a performance in the Royal Theatre is a private good understood in such a way that exclusion is possible via the sale of tickets and the consumption is rival because there is a limited number of seats for each performance. By charging a ticket price, part of the use value can be expressed through the box-office takings. By using the usual assumption of a decreasing demand curve the whole use value will, however, not be caught in the box-office takings because the audience will also have a consumer surplus in connection with their visit to the theatre.[7]

Non-Use Values

Different forms or motives of non-use values in relation to the Royal Theatre can be defined.

- *Vicarious consumption*: e.g. the pleasure derived from reading critical reviews of the Royal Theatre's performances, even though one has no wish to see them. The entertainment derived from reading about the repeated scandals at the theatre. A sacked director of the opera, strike among stage technicians and the actors' private lives are "hot material". Another and more important form of vicarious consumption is *television transmissions* of the Royal Theatre's performances.
- *Educational benefit*: the Royal Theatre forms part of the general education and contributes towards developing abilities and qualifications like, for example, the provision of public creative ideas and aesthetic standards, of social comment and criticism, etc. Besides, the film industry and the media utilize the acting skills and talents which are developed at the Royal Theatre, so that the viewers of a television drama, for example, have an indirect utility of the Royal Theatre.
- *Bequest benefit*: the Royal Theatre comprises an important part of the national cultural heritage and identity, and the continued existence of the Royal Theatre is a significant factor in ensuring that important elements of the Danish cultural heritage, including the Holberg and the Bournonville tradition, are preserved and made accessible to future generations.
- *Prestige benefit*: e.g. an international recognition of the Royal Ballet can contribute towards national pride and identity, spread Denmark's name abroad, attract tourists, etc.

Even though it is analytically possible to differentiate various motives which explain why the existence of the Royal Theatre is incorporated in the consumers' utility function, it is difficult to isolate and measure each element separately. Therefore, breaking down the non-use value into sub-components will not be done.

Option Value

In a world with uncertainty the utility will become the ex ante expected value. In accordance with Cicchetti and Freeman (1971) the option value (OV) can be defined as the difference between the option price (OP) and the expected consumer surplus ($E(\text{CS})$):

$$\text{OV} = \text{OP} - E(\text{CS}). \tag{13.2}$$

It is hereby presumed that the option value should not be seen as a separate benefit category, but as a correction factor to the total value in a deterministic world (Mitchell and Carson, 1989; Randall, 1991). The option value can be positive, negative or zero, and several contributions in the literature have dealt with the conditions under which one can predict the size and sign of the option value (for example Smith, 1984; Freeman, 1984; Plummer and Hartman, 1986). There is agreement about the fact that for practical empirical purposes, option price is the correct benefit measurement (see for example Bohm, 1975; Graham, 1981; Bishop, 1982; Freeman, 1993). In relation to CVM it is thus the option price which must be revealed, in other words, the maximum amount the consumer is willing to pay under conditions of uncertainty about future preferences, personal income, prices and supply.

DESIGN OF THE CV STUDY

CVM is a survey-based methodology where a sample of a population is asked about their maximum WTP for (a specified change in) a (public) good. Values for the good are then inferred from these respondents' decisions.[8] CVM has created a vehement debate among economists because traditionally economists have a strong bias in favour of estimates that are inferred from observed behaviour as opposed to stated preferences such as those revealed in CV studies. On the other hand, CVM is more or less the only method capable of estimating the total value (use, non-use and option value) of a good.[9]

The Sample

The study encompasses a random sample of the Danish population more than 16 years old. In all 1,843 people have been interviewed by telephone, with a follow-up visit for those who did not have a telephone or could not be reached by telephone. The interviews took place in the autumn of 1993 in connection with an extensive study of the population's cultural and leisure-time habits (Fridberg, 1994).[10]

The data set is good in the sense that the whole population was asked—not just those who go to the Royal Theatre. In this respect, this CV study differs from other studies (e.g. Dubgaard, 1996), where it is exclusively the direct users who have been asked. It could be claimed that the sample has its limitations because it is only Danes who have been interviewed (see criticisms by Frey, 1997). The foreign WTP has been assumed to be zero, and thus the tourists' WTP is supposed not to exceed the ticket price. This could be seen as a shortcoming because part of the Royal Theatre's audience are tourists,[11] who probably also have a consumer surplus for their visits to the theatre. On the other hand, the tourists do not pay Danish taxes and for this reason it seems reasonable only to estimate the Danes' WTP.

Welfare Concept

It is the maximum WTP for the Royal Theatre continuing its activity at the present level which is to be estimated—or expressed in a different way: the isolated welfare loss as a result of closing down the Royal Theatre. The correct welfare measure in connection with valuation of the Royal Theatre is therefore WTA—in other words the smallest amount respondents are willing to accept in compensation for doing without the good. Using Mitchell and Carson's (1989, p. 41) new interpretation of property rights,[12] it is, however, clear that the question of the citizens' WTP can be put in two ways (which is also in accordance with Gordon and Knetsch, 1979):

1. What is the maximum amount the citizens are willing to pay (WTP) for the Royal Theatre to continue its activities at the present level?
2. What is the minimum level of compensation the citizens are willing to accept (WTA) if the Royal Theatre is closed down?

On account of the many disappointing results with the WTA measure,[13] the WTP measure is used in this study. The NOAA panel (Arrow *et al.*, 1993) likewise recommend a conservative design in CV studies, which among other things is achieved by using WTP instead of WTA measures.[14] For theoretical discussions and explanations of the disparity between WTP and WTA, see e.g. Hanemann (1991), Knetsch and Sinden (1984, 1987), Kahneman and Tversky (1979).

It should be noted that it has been implicitly presumed that the Royal Theatre is an *indivisible good*. Either we have the Royal Theatre—or we do not. Alternatively, a question could have been asked concerning the WTP for *marginal changes in the level of activity*, as the number of performances can of course be varied. But here the purpose of the analysis should be considered. First and foremost it is the intention to investigate if CVM can be used in order to estimate the total value of the Royal Theatre to the Danish population and to study whether the value of the Royal Theatre's non-market benefits can justify the public grants given to the theatre. The citizenry's WTP for marginal changes in the supply is therefore of limited interest.[15]

Besides, another problem should be noted, namely that CVM does not include an optimizing algorithm, i.e. the good is presented to the respondents as it is. It is assumed the supply is already technically efficient in the sense that the activities are so perfectly run that no improvement is possible without having to give up some other goal (x-efficiency). This assumption is rarely met, and in Bille Hansen (1991) it is shown that large opportunities actually exist for improvements in technical efficiency at the Royal Theatre.

Elicitation Methods

There are a large number of different question formats each with their own strengths and weaknesses.[16] In this study *direct, open-ended questions* have been chosen.[17] This choice is based on the following considerations. *Firstly*, the WTP questions had to be fitted into a larger study of the cultural habits of the Danes (Fridberg, 1994). This meant a number of limitations in the study design, as it was given beforehand that the study was to be carried out as telephone interviews. Dichotomous choice seems to be the method which is most in favour at the moment (cf. Arrow *et al.*, 1993). The problem is that it is expensive to use, and on account of economic limitations it was, therefore, not possible to use this format. *Secondly*, a number of positive reasons can be given for choosing open-ended questions. Open-ended questions will always be preferred in an ideal world as they provide most information. The reason for dichotomous choice being recommended is that it facilitates the respondents' choices, which makes sense if the valuation of a good is such an unusual task for the respondent that s/he finds it difficult to offer a satisfactory answer. It can thus be difficult on the spur of the moment to say how much one is willing to pay to rescue the "black-spotted toad" if one has never seen it and never given a thought to its worth, or perhaps been totally unaware that it even existed. The Royal Theatre is, however, known to everybody, and having to pay for the Royal Theatre through taxes is familiar. Perhaps they do not know how much they pay,[18] but they know that they pay something. In a situation like this where the good is familiar, and not least where the fact that the respondent has to pay for the good is a commonplace one, experience shows that open-ended questions function in a satisfactory manner (Mitchell and Carson, 1989).

The influence of how much information should be given to the respondents before the interview has been tested in a small experiment using a split sample. The sample was divided randomly into two equally large groups. One half received the information that all Danes above the age of 18 pay on average about DKK 60 (about £5.5) a year to the Royal Theatre through taxes. The other half did not get this information.[19]

The NOAA panel (Arrow *et al.*, 1993) places decisive emphasis on the fact that the respondents are explicitly made aware of their budget restriction as well as possible substitutes for the good to be valued. The respondents were made aware of their budget restriction by being asked if they *"would still pay more if it was necessary to raise taxes"*.[20]

In addition, the respondents were asked a question with the purpose of revealing whether they consider the Royal Theatre to have non-use value or not. They were asked whether they go to the Royal Theatre, and if this is the case, how often. They were also asked a lot of questions about their other cultural activities, and likewise asked a number of questions concerning their socioeconomic status, including gender, age, level of schooling, occupational training, marital status, number of dependent children, income, etc. The questions are presented in the Appendix to this chapter.

WILLINGNESS TO PAY FOR THE ROYAL THEATRE: RESULTS

Stated Individual WTP

The individual WTP for the Royal Theatre varies from DKK 0 to DKK 8,000, and the same variation is found in the amount the respondents believe they pay towards the theatre. The median is DKK 60—equal to the actual average amount paid to the theatre a year by each taxpayer—and this is regardless of whether the respondent has received this information or not. On the other hand, a clear tendency can be seen for the respondents who have received information to have a lower WTP compared with those who have not received information. This is clear in both the 95% and 75% fractiles (Table 13.1).

Table 13.1   Fractiles for the individual WTP per year for the Royal Theatre

Fractiles (%)	All	With information (DKK)	Without information (DKK)	Believed payment (DKK)
0	0	0	0	0
5	0	0	0	0
25	8	50	0	50
50	60	60	60	100
75	100	90	200	400
95	600	200	1,000	1,250
100	8,000	5,000	8,000	8,000

The distribution of the WTP responses for the whole sample is also presented in Figure 13.1, where the amounts any of the respondents are willing to pay are plotted on the X axis, while the number of respondents who have stated this amount is plotted on the Y axis.

Figure 13.1 illustrates an interesting picture. Firstly, there is a relatively large proportion of zero bids, although this is hardly surprising. Indeed, one might in fact have expected it to be larger since only approximately 7% of the Danish population has been to the Royal Theatre within the last year. 340 people, the equivalent of 18% of the respondents, have stated a WTP for the Royal Theatre of DKK 0. Secondly, the WTP clusters around a few round figures, namely DKK 50–60, DKK 100, DKK 200, DKK 500, DKK 1,000, and DKK 2,000.

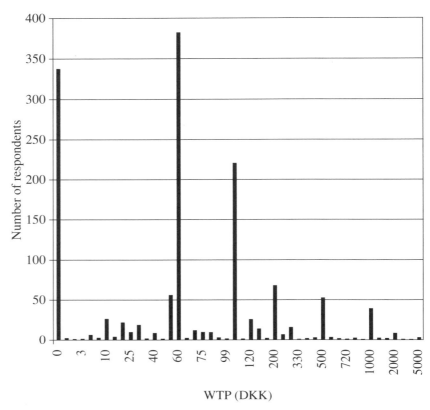

Figure 13.1   Distribution of WTP bids

Thirdly, the growth in the bids given can, approximately, be described using a logarithmic distribution (exclusive of the zero bids). The higher the amount given, the greater the distance to the next bid on the scale.

The WTP behaviour which the figure reflects is not particularly surprising. The respondents do not know their preferences well enough to be able to state whether they are willing to pay DKK 89.50 or DKK 107.75 towards the Royal Theatre. On the other hand, they are quite clear about whether the theatre is worth DKK 100, DKK 200 or DKK 500 to them. In addition to this, the increasing distance between the amounts reflects a falling marginal utility per DKK. If a respondent is willing to pay approx. DKK 50, then it is important whether the price is DKK 50 or DKK 100. If, on the other hand, the respondent is willing to pay approx. DKK 3,000, it does not matter whether the price is DKK 3,000 or DKK 3,050.

Non-Response

It is usual to receive a high non-response rate to open-ended valuation questions. It can cause problems for the representativeness of the study if a large number of respondents have not responded to single questions (item non-response). The response rate is shown in Table 13.2.

Table 13.2   Response rate for the open-ended valuation questions

	Sample group	Don't know	Responses	Response rate
With information	903	74	829	92
Without information	925	342	583	63
Believed payment	926	552	374	40
In all	1,843*	431*	1,412	77

Note   * Of these, 15 not available.

It can be seen from Table 13.2 that only 8% have responded "don't know" to the question about their WTP for the Royal Theatre, when they received information about the amount taxpayers contribute on average towards the theatre. On the other hand, 37% found it impossible to form an opinion about the valuation question without having any information about the actual expenses. All in all, this adds up to a response rate of 77 to the open-ended valuation question, which must be said to be satisfactory.

The question is, however, whether the average WTP for the 1,412 people who have responded to the question can be presumed to be representative for the whole sample of 1,843 people. If different groups of the population have different WTP and these groups in addition have a different tendency to respond to the valuation question, this will give rise to a *sample non-response bias*. When the "don't know" respondents' characteristics are compared with the whole sample, the "don't know" respondents do not stand out to any significant degree. Sample non-response bias does not, therefore, seem to be a serious problem.[21]

Aggregated WTP for the Royal Theatre

The individual WTP bids can be aggregated to the total WTP in the Danish population for the Royal Theatre using Kaldor–Hicks' compensation criterion. The aggregated, unadjusted WTP for the Royal Theatre is illustrated in Table 13.3.

Table 13.3 Aggregated (unadjusted) WTP for the Royal Theatre

	Average (DKK)	Median (DKK)	Dispersion	Taxpayer (1,000) 1992	Aggregated average (DKKm)	Aggregated median (DKKm)	Public subsidy to Royal Theatre (DKKm) 1994
With information	79	60	205		350	270	
Without information	259	60	627		1,165	270	
Believed payment	399	100	891		1,795	450	
In all	154	60	442	4,498	690	270	266

It can be seen that an annual subsidy of DKKm 266 is paid to the Royal Theatre. Therefore, one can *conclude that the citizenry's WTP is of a magnitude which at least measures up to the public subsidy which is given to the theatre.*[22]

There is, however, no unequivocal measure of the aggregated WTP, as it depends upon assumptions made with regard to which estimate best reflects the citizenry's "true" preferences.

The aggregated WTP for the Royal Theatre can be found by either using the median or the average, and subsequently multiplying this figure by the number of taxpayers. If the *median* is used it can be seen that the aggregated WTP adds up to DKKm 270 in all, which is about the same as the subsidy which is actually given to the theatre. It can also be seen that the median has the convenient property of being stable regardless of whether the respondents have received information about the average expenses or not. This indicates that *the political process actually functions well and the result is in accordance with the preferences of the median voter.*

On the other hand, it is the average WTP which is in harmony with the potential Pareto criterion and economic efficiency. *The average* is bigger than the median, because the distribution is clearly skewed to the right. If the average is used for aggregating WTP, a far higher value is obtained, namely DKKm 690. Besides, there is a big difference between the samples who received or did not receive information respectively. If the average for respondents *receiving information* is used, an aggregate WTP of DKKm 350 is obtained, while the average for the sample *not receiving information* gives an aggregated WTP of more than DKKb 1, which is four times as much as the subsidy which is in fact given to the Royal Theatre.

A serious problem is thus the significant difference in the average for respondents with and without information about actual expenditure on the Royal Theatre. The question is, which situation best elicits the respondents' "true" preferences. Arguments both for and against information can be put forward.[23]

Against information is the fact that respondents who are unsure will often tend to make a valuation on the basis of an initial value (Mitchell and Carson, 1989, p. 240). The final evaluation will therefore be biased towards the initial value with an associated anchoring bias. Information about the actual average amount paid to the Royal Theatre can be interpreted as "the correct value", which clearly in this study has led to anchoring bias and thereby prevented the respondents' "true" WTP from being expressed.

On the other hand, *in favour of information* is the fact that it can be of assistance to the respondent in the valuation process. In the same way that the consumer is confronted with the price of a good in trade on the private market, after which s/he can decide whether the good is worth the money, the information about an average "price" for the Royal Theatre can help the respondent in his/her deliberations about whether the theatre is worth DKK 60 in relation to his/her income and the price for other goods, or whether it is worth more or less than DKK 60 and if so by how much. This is first and foremost confirmed by the smaller proportion of "don't know" answers and zero bids for the group with information.

More generally, it is a question as to whether we look at the "technical" problem of anchoring bias as more serious than the danger that respondents give more or less random answers because they are uncertain about the hypothetical valuation situation.[24] Arrow *et al.* (1993) argue in favour of the fact that one should always choose the conservative estimate, and that a conservative estimate can be encouraged by giving the respondents information about the money which is currently being spent on the good. But in this study we are not especially interested in a conservative estimate, but in a »true« estimate. It is, however, difficult to know which one of the two averages best reflects the respondents' "true" preferences, and the truth possibly has to be found somewhere in the middle. Inspired by Bohm's (1979) interval method regarding strategic bias, there is reason to believe that the "true" WTP is somewhere in the middle of the averages for the groups with and respectively without information. The average of DKK 154 for the whole sample is possibly not far from the truth. The question about information is treated in more depth elsewhere (Bille Hansen, 1996, 1997).

Other aspects influencing which estimate to choose and which corrections to make in order to reflect the aggregated WTP for the Royal Theatre in the best possible way can be discussed. Problems concerning protest bids and truncation, strategic behaviour and overstatement of WTP are—among other things— treated in depth elsewhere (Bille Hansen, 1996, 1997) and shall just be mentioned here.

Protest bids do not seem to be a serious problem, but a small number of the zero bids in the sample without information are possibly protest bids. Besides, it seems reasonable to remove the highest bid of DKK 8,000,[25] which reduces the average to DKK 146.

No effort was made to try to measure the extension of strategic behaviour, e.g. by means of Bohm's interval method, where half the sample is given incentives to overstate their true WTP while the other half is given incentives to understate it. Therefore, no definitive evidence can be given, but the results show no strong indications of *strategic answers*,[26] even though about 8% of the respondents may answer strategically (see Table 13.5).

CVM reveals responses to *hypothetical questions* and therefore it has been claimed that CVM often leads to an overstatement of WTP (e.g. Bohm, 1994). One very common way of dealing with this problem is to make the respondents explicitly aware of their budget restrictions, for instance by asking if they still want to pay their stated amount if it becomes necessary to raise taxes. In this study we tried setting the WTP at DKK 60 for all respondents who have answered "no" to higher taxes and who have a WTP exceeding DKK 60. By doing this, the aggregated WTP is reduced by about 27%, but one does not reach a correct estimate of the aggregate WTP, since there may be respondents who want to pay their stated WTP even though they do not want taxes to rise. However, the correction is a way to ensure that the benefit estimate reached is a conservative estimate. It can therefore be viewed as a response to the general problem that CVM reveals responses to hypothetical questions and, especially when CV-studies relate to a single issue, they can lead to an overstatement of WTP or lack of consistency with other expenditures in the respondents' overall budget.

Having made these corrections an average WTP of DKK 104 appears, and thus an aggregated WTP of DKKm 467.

THE WTP DIVIDED INTO USE, NON-USE AND OPTION VALUES

The way in which WTP can be disaggregated into different benefit categories has previously only been discussed sporadically in the literature. Two methods predominate: (a) the direct method and (b) the reductionistic method.

In *the direct method* the respondents are asked either to state a WTP for the individual benefit categories (for example Greenley *et al.*, 1981), or to first state a total WTP and subsequently divide this into different benefit categories.[27] It is characteristic of these studies that the estimates for non-use categories are considerably larger than the estimates for use values. Smith and Desvousges (1986) have also asked the respondents about both E(CS) and OP, so that it is possible to calculate an estimate for OV. The results showed, among other things, that OV accounted for a considerable portion of OP for the users, and that this value generally exceeded the use value. This method must be said to place a relatively large requirement on the respondents, on the one hand with regard to their comprehension of the theory, including not least the difference between OV, OP and E(CS), and on the other hand with regard to the extent to which they have well-defined preferences, and thus the extent to which they are able to supply meaningful responses to these very detailed valuation questions. Mitchell and Carson (1989) call this "*the fallacy of motivational precision*", and they are very sceptical towards the direct method. They believe that the respondents' WTP is based on a holistic consideration, and that the respondents are unable to give meaningful responses regarding separate categories.

In *the reductionistic method* the problem with "the fallacy of motivational precision" is avoided.[28] Individuals are classified either as users or non-users, and it is presumed that only users have use value. Besides, it is assumed that the non-users' WTP is the equivalent of non-use value for the users. The problem with the method is that the users could have another attitude to the non-use component than the non-users. Neither is a distinction made between option and non-use values, even though the non-users' WTP must be presumed to contain both components.

In this study the reductionistic method is used, and in addition an attempt is made to separate option value from non-use value, as the respondents cannot only be classified as a user/non-user, but can also be divided according to whether they believe that the Royal Theatre has non-use value or not.

A Reductionistic Division into Benefit Categories

A positive WTP for non-users can be explained by the fact that the Royal Theatre has non-use value and that they want to pay an option price.

The sample group can be divided into eight groups according to three criteria.

1. User/non-user: a user has visited the Royal Theatre within the last year.
2. Considers the Royal Theatre to have non-use value/not to have this: if an affirmative response is given to the question "Do you consider the Royal Theatre to have a *value for people other than those who go there,* because it has an importance for the country's cultural level, attracts tourists or for any other reason?", it is presumed that the respondent considers the Royal Theatre to have non-use value.
3. Have a positive/zero WTP: everybody who has a WTP above DKK 0 has a positive WTP.

This division has been made in Table 13.4, and the following hypotheses can be made.

Hypotheses

The respondents in *group 4*—who are non-users and do not feel that the Royal Theatre has non-use values, but have a positive WTP—can be interpreted as being willing to pay an option price. In other words, they would like to pay for the possibility of being able to go to the Royal Theatre some day in the future. It is reasonable to assume that this option price contains an expected CS and an option value.

The respondents in *group 3* are non-users, too, but they think that the Royal Theatre has non-use values. Therefore, the assumption is that they will pay both an option price and for the theatre's non-use values.

The respondents in *group 2* are assumed to be willing to pay an option price and a CS for a private consumption ex post. They have no non-use values.

Table 13.4 Model for a reductionistic division into benefit categories

	User		Non-user	
	Non-use values	No non-use values	Non-use values	No non-use values
Positive WTP	*Group 1*	*Group 2*	*Group 3*	*Group 4*
	Option price Non-use values CS for private consumption	Option price CS for private consumption	Option price Non-use values	Option price
No WTP	*Group 5*	*Group 6*	*Group 7*	*Group 8*
	Irrational answers	No CS	Answers strategically, egoistically	No value

Likewise, it must be assumed that the respondents in *group 1* will pay an option price, for the theatre's non-use values and a CS for their private consumption ex post.

Therefore, it must be assumed—ceteris paribus—that there is a growing WTP from group 4 to group 3 and further on to group 1:

$$\text{WTP}(group \ 1) > \text{WTP}(group \ 3) > \text{WTP}(group \ 4).$$

Furthermore, it is assumed that:

$$\text{WTP}(group \ 1) > \text{WTP}(group \ 2) > \text{WTP}(group \ 4).$$

However, it is uncertain whether:

$$\text{WTP}(group \ 2) >/< \text{WTP}(group \ 3)$$

because it depends on whether the average WTP for non-use values is bigger or smaller than the average WTP for private consumption ex post.

The respondents in *group 8* do not attach any value to the Royal Theatre. The respondents in *group 7* are non-users and attach non-use values to the Royal Theatre, but they have no WTP. They are assumed to give strategic or egoistic answers. The respondents in *group 6* are users who do not attach non-use values to the Royal Theatre and do not have any WTP. Thus, the respondents in this group have no CS, either ex post or ex ante. The respondents in *group 5* are users who attach non-use values to the Royal Theatre, but have no WTP. Whether there are any respondents in this group at all, they have answered irrationally, and it is expected that there will be no respondents in this group.

Results

Of the, in all, 1,843 people interviewed, there are 1,286—the equivalent of 70%—who have responded to all the above-mentioned questions and have not responded "don't know" to any of them. In Table 13.5 the respondents are divided according to the three criteria.

When the respondents are divided into the eight groups (Table 13.5) *the main impression is that the respondents' answers make sense altogether*. This is elaborated in the following.

It can be seen from the table that 22.5% have no WTP for the Royal Theatre.

Of the four groups *without WTP*, it is in particular *group 7* which is interesting. They are non-users, consider the Royal Theatre to have non-use values,

Table 13.5 The respondents divided into users, non-users, respondents with non-use values, no non-use values, positive WTP and no WTP

		User		Non-user		Total
		Non-use values	No non-use values	Non-use values	No non-use values	
Positive WTP	No. of respondents	*Group 1*	*Group 2*	*Group 3*	*Group 4*	
		87 (6.8%)	8 (0.6%)	784 (60.9%)	118 (9.1%)	997 (77.5%)
	Average WTP	DKK 331	DKK 938	DKK 201	DKK 116	DKK 208
No WTP	No. of respondents	*Group 5*	*Group 6*	*Group 7*	*Group 8*	
		0 (0%)	2 (0.2%)	102 (7.9%)	185 (14.4%)	289 (22.5%)
	Average WTP	DKK 0	DKK 0	DKK 0	DKK 0	DKK 0
Total	No. of respondents	87 (6.8%)	10 (0.8%)	886 (68.8%)	303 (23.8%)	1,286 (100%)
	Average WTP	DKK 331	DKK 150	DKK 178	DKK 45	DKK 160

but have no WTP. 7.9% of the responses lie in this group, about whom it must be presumed that they respond strategically or egoistically.

The respondents in *group 8*—14.4% of the respondents—do not attach any value to the Royal Theatre.

By and large there are no users who do not want to pay. There are only two respondents in *group 6* who do not have any CS, either ex post or ex ante, and as expected there are no respondents in *group 5*.

If we look at the group *with positive WTP*, which comprises 77.5% in all, groups 1, 3 and 4 seem to be directly comparable as expected. There is a rising average WTP from group 4 to 3 to 1.

Group 4, who are not users themselves and who do not consider that the Royal Theatre has a value for others than those who go there themselves, but who have a positive WTP, must be interpreted as wanting to pay an option price. This option price has an average size of DKK 116. There are 118 people in this group, of whom 21% have visited the Royal Theatre more than one year ago. In other words they are sporadic users. These sporadic users have an average WTP of DKK 167, while those who have never been to the Royal Theatre have an average WTP of DKK 102.

Group 3, who are not users themselves either, but who consider that the Royal Theatre has a value to people other than those who go there themselves, and who have a positive WTP, must be interpreted as attaching a non-use value to the Royal Theatre and as wanting to pay an option price. The average WTP for these respondents is DKK 201, and if it is presumed that the average option price is the same as for the respondents in group 4, the average non-use value can be calculated as DKK 85. The largest number of answers (60.9%) lies in this group, and the statistical uncertainty in the answers is thus relatively small in this group compared with the other groups.

Group 1, who comprise 6.8% and who have an average WTP of DKK 331, have both a CS in connection with a private consumption, attach non-use value to the Royal Theatre and want to pay an option price.[29] If a reductionistic method is also used here, the average CS for private consumption can be calculated as DKK 130.

The responses in *group 2* seem unrealistically high. If one is to follow a logical course, the average WTP ought to be less than in group 1, as this group does not attach any non-use value to the Royal Theatre. It should, however, be noted that group 2 only contains 8 responses, and the statistical uncertainty of the responses is therefore large.[30]

Division into Benefit Categories

On the basis of this reductionistic analysis it is possible to give an estimate of the size of various benefit categories (Table 13.6).

The calculation includes *all respondents*, which means that the zero bids (i.e. groups 5, 6, 7 and 8) are included, too. In this case the average option price is calculated to be DKK 45, the average WTP for non-use values is calculated to be DKK 133, and the average CS for private consumption ex post is calculated to be DKK 148.[31]

Table 13.6   The different benefit categories' share of the total WTP for the Royal Theatre

	Exclusive of zero bid	Inclusive of zero bid		
	Average WTP (DKK)	Average WTP (DKK)	No. of respondents	Share of total WTP
Option price	116	45	1,286	29%
Non-use values (X_{nu})	85	133	973	64%
CS for private consumption ex post (X_u)	130	148	97	7%

Of the aggregated WTP for the Royal Theatre the option price thus amounts to about 29%, the non-use values amount to about 64% and CS for private consumption ex post amounts to about 7%.

This calculation requires that the average option price in the other groups is the same as in group 4 plus 8, and that the average non-use value in the other groups is the same as in group 3 plus 7. This is of course a relatively restrictive assumption, as it is, for example, not inconceivable that users have another attitude to the non-use component in their WTP than non-users. Besides, when the users have a higher WTP it might not only be on account of a CS for their private consumption ex post, but also because they e.g. have a higher income which determines a higher WTP. It is possible to take this into account in a model-based division into benefit categories, in which different socioeconomic explanatory factors which also have an influence on the WTP are taken into account. This will be done in the following section.

DETERMINANTS OF WTP

The following simple model is constructed to explain WTP:

$$WTP_i = f(I_i, X_{ui}, X_{nui}, K_i, Z_{1i}, ..., Z_{ni}) \tag{13.3}$$

$i = 1,...,N$, where N is the number of individuals and:

WTP_i = willingness to pay for the Royal Theatre

I_i = a dummy variable which indicates whether the respondent has received information about the actual average subsidy per taxpayer or not

X_{ui} = a user of the Royal Theatre[32]

X_{nui} = a dummy variable, which indicates whether the respondent considers the Royal Theatre to have non-use value or not

K_i = a subjective indicator of cultural interest (or a substitution effect)

Z_{1i}, ... ,Z_{ni} = objective socioeconomic criteria: (1) income, (2) geographical distance to the Royal Theatre, (3) gender, (4) age, (5) level of schooling, (6) occupational training, (7) employment, (8) marital status, (9) number of dependent children.

(3) to (9) are considered to be preference-shaping factors.

The variables used in the model are defined in Table 13.7.

Table 13.7   Variables

Variable	Definition of variable	Expected sign*
WTP	WTP in DKK	
I	Dummy variable 0 = has not received information 1 = has received information	–
X_u	Dummy variable 0 = non-user (has not been to the Royal Theatre within the last year) 1 = user (has been to the Royal Theatre within the last year)	+
X_{nu}	Dummy variable 0 = does not consider the Royal Theatre to have non-use value 1 = considers the Royal Theatre to have non-use value	+
K	Cultural indicator An attempt has been made to capture the respondents general level of activity in the cultural area using an indicator, which increases from 0 to 5, depending on how many of the following activities one has taken part in, during the past year: been to the cinema, been to a classical concert, been to an art exhibition, been to another kind of museum, seen a play. The sign for this variable can be both positive and negative, depending on whether a large consumption of other cultural activities is a substitute for a visit to the Royal Theatre or whether a large general interest in the arts increases the number of visits to the Royal Theatre (cultural capital).	+/–

Table 13.7   continued

Variable	Definition of variable	Expected sign*
Income	The respondents' net income Interval midpoints are used in 14 income groups	+
Gender	Dummy variable 0 = man 1 = woman	+
Age	Continuous variable	+/−
Schooling	Dummy variable 0 = does not hold upper secondary certificate or equivalent 1 = holds upper secondary certificate or equivalent	+
Training/education	Occupational training 0 = no occupational training 1 = specific occupational training 2 = higher education	+
Employment	Two dummy variables 1 = self-employed, 0 = white-collar/civil servant 1 = unemployed, 0 = white-collar/civil servant	− −
Marital status	Dummy variable 1 = spouse/partner 0 = single	+/−
Children	Number of dependent children Continuous variable	−
Geography	Geographic distance to the Royal Theatre, where 1 = capital 2 = West Zealand, Storstrøm, Funen 3 = Jutland and Bornholm	−

Note: * See e.g. Schulze and Ursprung (1996) and Frey and Pommerehne (1989) for testable hypotheses about determinants of preferences.

It is, however, not completely without complications to estimate this model. As the dependent variable is censored (limited) at zero, OLS cannot be used. The Tobit model is suitable for this situation, but because the error term is presumed to follow a normal distribution the model will generate negative predicted values,[33] which means that the parameter estimates cannot be used as a starting point for a division into benefit categories. One solution could be to use a distribution which cannot take on negative values, for example a Poisson distribution.

The problem with the *negative predicted values* has not really been discussed in the CV literature, supposedly for two reasons. *Firstly*, by and large CVM has not been used to value a specific cultural good previously, but has primarily been used for the valuation of environmental goods, where to a great extent it is reasonable to imagine negative external effects and thus a negative WTP. *Secondly*, it is not a big problem when the valuation function is used solely to validate CVM. For this purpose the precise size of the parameter estimates is of less importance. The crucial thing is first and foremost the signs of the parameter estimates.

Another problem is that the two variables of interest if the model is going to be used as a starting point for a division into benefit categories, namely X_u and X_{nu}, are really *endogenous variables* which could possibly be explained by more or less the same background variables as the WTP. In principle we thus have three equations:

$$\text{WTP}_i = f(I_i, X_{ui}, X_{nui}, K_i, Z_{1i}, ..., Z_{ni}) \tag{13.4a}$$
$$X_{ui} = h(K_i, Z_{1i}, ..., Z_{ni}) \tag{13.4b}$$
$$X_{nui} = g(X_{ui}, K_i, Z_{1i}, ..., Z_{ni}) \tag{13.4c}$$

One solution to this is self-selection or dummy endogenous models, which are discussed and estimated later in this chapter.

The *endogenetic problem* has never been thoroughly discussed in the CV literature. Sliberman *et al.* (1992) discuss the problem, but "solves" it by estimating an independent valuation function for users and non-users. Self-selection models and dummy endogenous models are hardly discussed in the CV literature.[34]

It is, however, very difficult to estimate a model which at the same time considers these problems, i.e. first and foremost the endogenetic problem and the problem with negative WTP estimates. A model which simultaneously takes into account these special conditions in the data cannot be estimated with any standard econometric/statistical programme package. Besides, no CVM articles have previously discussed exactly these statistical problems coherently. Most CV studies use the Tobit model or logistic regressions in order to appraise the theoretical validity of the method. It appears that no one has tried to use the valuation function as a starting point for a division of the total WTP into benefit categories before.

A Model-Based Division into Benefit Categories (the Poisson Model)

The Poisson model has exactly the advantage that the dependent variable cannot assume negative values.[35] Besides, the dependent variable can only assume discrete values which are in agreement with the picture in Figure 13.1, but the disadvantage is that information is thrown away by using a discrete distribution.[36]

Let us assume that the dependent variables WTP_1, WTP_2, ..., WTP_n follow independent Poisson distributions with the respective parameters λ_1, λ_2, ..., λ_n. This leads to:

$$\text{Prob}(WTP_i = r) = \exp(-\lambda_i)\frac{(\lambda_i)^r}{\lambda!}. \tag{13.5}$$

If we assume that λ_i is log-linearly dependent on the explanatory variables, this leads to:

$$\ln \lambda_i = \beta_0 + \sum_{j=1}^{p} \beta_i X_{ij}. \tag{13.6}$$

In this model it is assumed that the WTP falls into six intervals:

$$WTP_0, \text{ if } WTP_i^* = 0,$$
$$WTP_1, \text{ if } 0 < WTP_i^* \leq 75,$$
$$WTP_2, \text{ if } 75 < WTP_i^* \leq 150,$$
$$WTP_3, \text{ if } 150 < WTP_i^* \leq 250,$$
$$WTP_4, \text{ if } 250 < WTP_i^* \leq 750,$$
$$WTP_5, \text{ if } WTP_i^* > 750.$$

Hereby the distribution in Figure 13.2 appears.

A Poisson regression gives the results in Table 13.8.[37]

The result of the Poisson regression shows that information, on self-employed or unemployed and the respondent's age has a significantly negative effect on the WTP, whereas to attach importance to the Royal Theatre's non-use value, a high cultural indicator, a high income and living in the metropolitan region has a positive, significant effect on the WTP. On the other hand, schooling, gender, marital status and number of children living at home do not seem to be of any importance for the WTP. To be a user of the Royal Theatre does not seem to be of any importance either. *By and large, the results are in accordance with expectations concerning the determinants of WTP (see Table 13.7).*

The size and parameter estimates for X_u and X_{nu} can be calculated as:

$$\lambda_i = \exp(\beta X) \tag{13.7}$$

Table 13.8   Regression results

	Poisson regression	Probit user/ non-user	Heckman selection model
Intercept	−0.1942 (0.0896)	−3.8891 (0.0000)	162.9 (0.0008)
I	−0.5304 (0.0000)		−195.6 (0.0000)
X_u	0.1349 (0.1140)		427.6 (0.0005)
X_{nu}	0.8084 (0.0000)		87.7 (0.0015)
K	0.0976 (0.0000)	0.5019 (0.0000)	1.2149 (0.9107)
Income	0.10×10^{-5} (0.0036)	0.21×10^{-5} (0.0152)	0.64×10^{-3} (0.0007)
Gender	0.0776 (0.1546)	0.2041 (0.1968)	36.1 (0.1508)
Age	−0.0040 (0.0263)		−1.5 (0.0410)
Schooling Upper secondary certificate or equivalent	0.0386 (0.5203)	0.3541 (0.0190)	5.2 (0.8649)
Education*			
Employment Self-employed	−0.3941 (0.0033)		−121.7 (0.0150)
Unemployed	−0.3096 (0.0053)		−86.7 (0.0464)
White-collar/civil servant			
Marital status	0.0041 (0.9465)		−5.5 (0.8420)
Children	−0.0393 (0.1794)	−0.1819 (0.0440)	−10.6 (0.4244)

Table 13.8   continued

	Poisson regression	Probit user/ non-user	Heckman selection model
Geographical distance			
1	0.1725	1.2430	9.82
	(0.0032)	(0.0000)	(0.7564)
2	0.0691	0.6645	15.0
	(0.3475)	(0.0085)	(0.6493)
3			
Heckman's λ			−162.4
			(0.0215)
σ			327.07
			(0.0000)
Rho			−0.43
Log-likelihood	−1,490.3	−184.9	
N	1,057	1,057	1,057

Notes:
The figures in brackets are significance levels for the parameter estimates.
* Education is not included in the regressions because schooling and education are highly correlated.

which for X_u gives:

$$\lambda_i = 1.01 \qquad\qquad (13.8)$$

and for X_{nu} leads to:

$$\lambda_i = 1.85 \qquad\qquad (13.9)$$

If converted into DKK taking the six intervals as the point of departure this leads to:

$$X_u = \text{DKK } 76 \text{ and } X_{nu} = \text{DKK } 139. \qquad (13.10)$$

If we compare these estimates with the estimates arrived at using the reductionistic method (see Table 13.6), namely:

$$X_u = \text{DKK } 148 \text{ and } X_{nu} = \text{DKK } 133 \qquad (13.11)$$

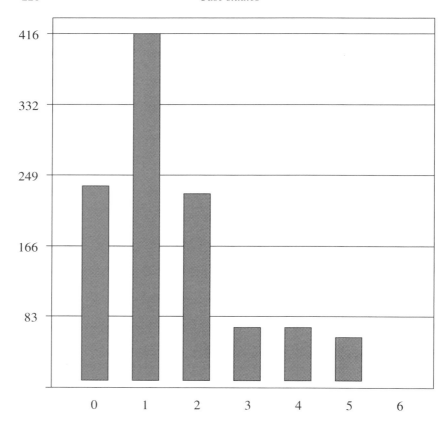

Figure 13.2   WTP distribution on intervals

we find that the estimates for X_{nu} are almost identical, whereas the estimates for X_u are somewhat smaller in the Poisson model. Firstly, this could be due to the fact that the model has been estimated on a scale where the WTP assumes values from 0 to 5, whereby the influence of very high values of the WTP is eliminated. Secondly, the parameter estimate for X_u is insignificant, which is probably due to problems with the self-selection in the model.

All in all, *a model-based division into benefit categories does not seem to produce results significantly different from the reductionistic method.*

Self-Selection Models

In the Poisson model being a user of the Royal Theatre has been considered an exogenous variable on equal terms with other personal characteristics. However, this could be characterized as an unsatisfactory way to analyse the problem because being a user of the Royal Theatre is not an exogenous, but an endogenous variable. The same problem applies to the variable indicating whether the respondent thinks the Royal Theatre has non-use values or not.[38] In other words, the correct model is a *self-selection model* where the individuals themselves choose if they are users of the Royal Theatre and whether they think that the theatre has non-use values. If the model is not specified in this way, it can lead to mis-specification problems.

If being a user or a non-user of the Royal Theatre and the size of the WTP in addition are dependent on the same *unobserved* explanatory variables, the variable X_u will be correlated with the residual in the equation for WTP. In this case sample selection bias arises and the estimated parameters will be biased. The same would apply for X_{nu}.[39]

A simple way to solve the problem with self-selection for X_u is via a model where being a user/non-user as well as the size of the WTP is estimated in two equations:[40]

$$\text{WTP}_i = X_i \beta^1 + X_{ui} \beta^2 + u_i \qquad (13.12)$$

$$X_{ui}^* = Z_i Y + \varepsilon_i, \qquad X_{ui} = 1 \text{ if } X_{ui}^* > 0$$
$$X_{ui} = 0 \text{ if } X_{ui}^* = 0. \qquad (13.13)$$

The equation system can be estimated simultaneously with Heckman's two-stage method or the maximum likelihood method (in this study Heckman's method is used). The user decision function can be estimated by a probit function and the equation for the WTP can be estimated by OLS or Tobit where a dummy variable for being users is included.

Table 13.8 shows the results of the estimation of this self-selection model. Contrary to the Poisson model, this model is estimated on continuous data.

The probit estimation for being a user or not[41] shows what could be expected, i.e. the cultural indicator, upper secondary certificate or equivalent, income, geographical distance to the Royal Theatre and number of children living at home are of significant importance for being a user of the Royal Theatre or not. The probability of being a user is higher the higher the cultural indicator, if the respondent holds an upper secondary certificate or equivalent, has a high income and/or a dwelling in the metropolitan region, while on the other hand a greater number of children living at home reduces the probability.

Compared with the Poisson model, where to be a user of the Royal Theatre does not have any significant importance for the size of the WTP, this variable is of significant importance in Heckman's model. On the other hand, the cultural indicator and the geographical distance from the Royal Theatre lose their importance in Heckman's model, which is probably due to the fact that they are of significant importance for being a user and of less importance for the size of the WTP.

If the residual in the equation for the size of the WTP is correlated with the residual in the user decision function because one or more *unobserved* personal characteristics have been left out in both equations, sample selection bias arises, as previously mentioned. As the parameter estimate for lambda is significant, the estimation result indicates that this is the case. In other words, there seems to be *unobserved heterogeneity* between the two groups. This can be due to the WTP being dependent on one or more extra explanatory variables, not included in the estimation.[42]

In Heckman's model the parameter estimate for X_u becomes DKK 427 and that for X_{nu} DKK 87, but because there is an unobserved heterogeneity in the model the parameter estimates are possibly biased. Besides, the model—as well as the Tobit model—predicts a negative WTP for some respondents, which influences the average and therefore also the size of the parameter estimates. The parameters estimated cannot therefore be used for a division of the total WTP into benefit categories.

The ideal thing to do would probably be to estimate a Poisson model with self-selection, but this is not a trivial task.

Theoretical Validity

Even though the parameter estimates in Heckman's model cannot be assumed to have the correct size because of the above-mentioned problems, they are suitable for a valuation of the theoretical validity of the CVM analysis. The estimated results indicate that different socioeconomic factors are able to explain the WTP in a way predicted by theory, as both the significance of the parameter estimates and the signs are equivalent to expectations. However, this check of the theoretical validity of the CV study does of course say nothing about whether the *size* of the WTP is correct, since it is only a check on the variation.

CONCLUSION

CVM has not previously been used for this type of cultural good, and the results provide reason for a certain optimism.

Firstly, CVM seems to be well suited in order to estimate the total value of the Royal Theatre to the Danish population. The main impression is that the respondents' answers make sense altogether. The determinants of WTP are in accordance with expectations, in both the Poisson and the self-selection model, and the theoretical validity of the study can thereby be confirmed. However, a serious problem in the study is the significant difference in the average WTP for respondents respectively with and without information about actual, average tax payments per taxpayer to the Royal Theatre. Further research is needed regarding this question.

Secondly, the results show that the Danish population is in fact willing to pay at least the amount the theatre costs in state subsidies. Even though a large proportion of the Danish population never visit the theatre, they are willing to pay an option price for the possibility of being able to go there and for the non-use value of the theatre, i.e. educational value, bequest value, prestige value and vicarious consumption. In this way the public subsidy to the Royal Theatre can be legitimized on the basis of the preferences of the population. Besides, the results show that of the aggregated WTP for the Royal Theatre, the option price amounts to about 29%, the non-use values amount to about 64% and CS for private consumption ex post amounts to only about 7%, if the reductionistic method is used.

It is another matter whether CVM can be used to cope with day-to-day political decisions. The answer is no. For this purpose the method is too expensive, requires too much work and the uncertainty of the estimates is too large. CVM can only be used regarding big policy questions—e.g. state grants for the Royal Theatre. In these cases CVM is, however, well suited to get an estimate of the total value of a cultural good which has public good characteristics.

APPENDIX

The Questionnaire

One half of the sample received information about actual average tax payments to the Royal Theatre and were asked the open-ended valuation question:

All Danes over the age of 18 pay on average about DKK 60 (about £5.5) a year to the Royal Theatre through taxes. How much are you willing to pay at the most to the Royal Theatre through taxes?
Response categories: amount in DKK..., don't know.

The other half was not given information about the average tax payments to the Royal Theatre and was asked the following two questions:

All Danes pay to the Royal Theatre through taxes. How much are you willing to pay at the most to the Royal Theatre through taxes?
Response categories: amount in DKK..., don't know.

How much do you think Danes over the age of 18 pay on average to the Royal Theatre each year through taxes?
Response categories: amount in DKK..., don't know.

Besides, the respondents were asked if they think the state uses "*too much, the right amount, or too little money*" for a number of cultural purposes, including the Royal Theatre. These questions have been included in order to compare the responses to the open-ended questions with the preferences revealed in public opinion surveys. In this chapter, however, only the results of the direct, open-ended questions are presented and discussed.

In addition, the respondents were asked a question with the purpose of revealing whether they consider the Royal Theatre to have a non-use value:

Do you think that the Royal Theatre has value for people other than those who go there, because it has a significance for the country's cultural level, attracts tourists or for other reasons?
Response categories: yes, no, don't know.

Finally, the respondents were asked whether they go to the Royal Theatre, and if this is the case, how often. They were also asked about their other cultural activities, and likewise asked a number of questions concerning their socioeconomic status, including gender, age, level of schooling, occupational training, marital status, number of dependent children, income, etc.

ENDNOTES

1. This study constitutes a main part of my Ph.D. thesis in economics: "Studies in cultural economics", University of Copenhagen, Institute of Economics, 1996.
2. A recent bibliography (Carson *et al.*, 1995) lists 2,000 studies and papers from more than 40 countries on many topics, mainly environment, but also transportation, sanitation, health, the arts and education.
3. In Bille Hansen (1991), the activities of the Royal Theatre are described in more detail.
4. The estimate is around the same size as estimates found in other studies, e.g. O'Hagan (1994) found a price elasticity of –0.41 for visits to "the Abbey" theatre in Dublin, estimated on data for the period 1967–91. Gapinski (1984) found an own-price elasticity of –0.657 for the Royal Shakespeare Company, by estimating a demand function on data for the period 1965–80.
5. If we assume that selling by the piece is more inelastic than selling season tickets, because having a season ticket (eight performances) is connected with a far bigger total expense than buying a single ticket, this means that for the total ticket sale CS becomes bigger. On the other hand, the season-ticket holders are probably more experienced theatre-goers and more stable than the main part of the non-season-ticket holders, which indicates a more price-inelastic behaviour among the season-ticket holders, which means that CS for the total ticket sale becomes smaller than estimated with the same elasticity for the two different kinds of ticket sale.

6. Traditionally, economic theory does not deal with motives for a given demand because the individuals' preferences are assumed to be given exogenous. In this connection it is remarkable how big a part of the literature of non-use values deals with the motives for individuals having non-use values (see e.g. Madariaga and McConnell, 1987; Brookshire *et al.*, 1986).

7. Part of the visitors' consumer surplus can be included in the theatre's earnings by using price discrimination. Perfect price discrimination is, however, not possible.

8. For a general view of the theoretical and empirical issues involved see e.g. Mitchell and Carson (1989), Braden and Kolstad (1991) and Freeman (1993).

9. Much of the current debate in the United States about CVM is centred around the use of CVM involving litigation over natural resource damages, e.g. the State of Alaska used CVM to assess the natural resource damages from the Exxon Valdez oil spill (Carson *et al.*, 1992). In connection with the big catastrophe in March 1989, where the supertanker Exxon Valdez struck the rocks near Alaska and spilt 11 million gallons of crude oil in the ocean, the National Oceanic and Atmospheric Administration (NOAA) established an independent government panel chaired by the Nobel Prize winners Kenneth Arrow and Robert Solow. The panel were to advise NOAA on the following question: "Is the contingent valuation method capable of providing estimates of lost non-use or existence values that are reliable enough to be used in natural resource damage assessments?". The panel's conclusion was that "CV studies can produce estimates reliable enough to be a starting point for a judicial process of natural resource damages—including passive use values". The panel's guidelines and conclusions are to be found in Arrow *et al.* (1993). Hausman (1993) contains a set of papers highly critical of CV presented at a symposium sponsored by Exxon. A series of articles presenting a general view and different perspectives on CV have appeared in a 1994 issue of the Journal of Economic Perspectives (Diamond and Hausman, Hanemann, Portney).

10. The choice between whether the study should be carried out by way of postal, telephone or face-to-face interviews was thus given in advance. The general attitude in the literature seems to be that face-to-face interviews are preferred to telephone interviews, which are in turn preferred to postal interviews (for example, Arrow *et al.*, 1993; Mitchell and Carson, 1989). The reason given for this is that CV questions often involve complex scenarios, which require careful explanation and at times visual aids. This is, however, not the case in this study, because the Royal Theatre is a well-known good. Moreover, telephone interviews are less sensitive with regard to interviewer bias.

11. We do not know for certain how big a part of the Royal Theatre's audience are foreigners. From the Royal Theatre's analysis of the audience made in 1995 it is seen that tourists make up 4% of the tickets sold in August. This figure seems small compared with an earlier inquiry which showed that almost one-third of the visitors at the August performances were tourists. The two inquiries thus give quite different results. Besides, August is not a typical month, but a month when many tourists visit Denmark.

12. Mitchell and Carson (1989) have suggested a new interpretation of property rights in connection with public goods which require regular payment in order to maintain the present level of quality: "*Since the consumer is already paying for the good on a regular basis, the Hicksian compensating surplus for this case is the amount the consumer is willing to pay to forgo the reduction in the quality level of the good and still be as well off as before. This is measured in a CV study in the following way. The respondent would be informed that she is already making annual payments in some relevant form—higher prices and taxes, for example—to provide the current quality level of a good such as air visibility. She would then be asked to state the maximum payment that she is willing to make to preserve this quality level before she would prefer a quality reduction. To use a referendum analogy, the consumer is asked to set the highest amount she would be willing to pay annually in taxes for a given program which guarantees to maintain the present level of supply of a good for the next and succeeding fiscal years*".

13. A great number of empirical studies have shown that WTA is systematically larger than WTP for the same good, and the difference is far greater than can be explained by the income effect. The difference can in certain cases be of the magnitude 1:10. For an overview see Kahneman *et al.* (1990) and Cummings *et al.* (1986).

14. It should be noticed that the recommendations of the NOAA panel have not been immune to criticism, see e.g. Harrison (1993) and Mäler (1993).

15. I should also be noted that the response of those attending the Royal Theatre might be biased by the fact that it offers ballet, opera and drama productions and the "mix" might alter through time.

16. The different question formats are systematically compared in e.g. Sellar *et al.* (1985), Cummings *et al.* (1986) and Boyle and Bishop (1988).

17. Questions about whether the state shall spend "more/the same/less" money on different art forms including the Royal Theatre were also used for comparative reasons. However, only the results of the open-ended questions will be presented and discussed here.

18. In this study the respondents' information level has been tested as they were also asked how much *they believe they pay* on average through taxes to the Royal Theatre.

19. According to economic theory, supply and demand are separate notions which mean that the respondents' preferences and their WTP are independent of the production costs and the price of the good. It can therefore be claimed that it is irrelevant to give respondents information about the average price of the good in a CV study. This seems, however, not to be the case since the results show that this information has a significant effect on the respondents' valuation.

20. The more serious problem with "warm glow" (Diamond and Hausman, 1994), where respondents are willing to pay for "something beneficial for the arts", but do not mind what precisely they are paying for (the good has many close substitutes), does not seem to be a problem in this study, as the Royal Theatre is a very well-defined good which does not have any close substitutes.

21. *Sample selection bias* is more difficult to discover and correct as it is present if respondents who have not responded to the valuation question differ from the other respondents in their group (respondents with the same education, income, etc.) by being less interested in the good, and therefore also having a lower WTP. As no problems with sample non-response bias seem to occur in this study, no steps have been taken to make corrections for sample selection bias.

22. Luckily, in this survey the aggregated WTP is bigger than or equal to the public grant received by the theatre irrespective of which estimate is chosen. If this had not been the case, far bigger problems would have arisen concerning the conclusion of the study.

23. How much information respondents should be given in a CV interview is a question which is far from being settled in the literature, and surprisingly enough only very few studies have explicitly dealt with this important problem (see Hanley and Munro, 1992 for an overview of this literature). Almost all these studies have dealt with the influence of information about the good or information about substitutes or complementary goods—not information about the price of the good. Boyle (1989) is an exception.

24. The concept "hypothetical bias" is often mentioned in connection with CV studies. In this case where the good (the Royal Theatre) is well known to everybody and respondents know that they already pay something to the theatre through taxes, there is a high degree of familiarity, which, ceteris paribus, should minimize the "hypothetical bias".

25. It is a woman, 58 years old, who lives in Køge (a provincial town outside Copenhagen). She is unmarried, 9–10 years schooling and skilled labourer. She has a net income of about DKK 100,000 to DKK 119,000 per year and has never been to the Royal Theatre. She has not received information and she also believes that a Dane pays DKK 8,000 on average per year to the Royal Theatre through taxes.

26. Strategic behaviour might cause strategic bias in CV studies if the respondents believe that by giving misleading answers to the valuation questions they can influence the result to their own advantage. In the literature, experiments have been implemented to investigate empirically the extension of strategic behaviour (e.g. Bohm, 1972; Marwell and Armes, 1981; Schneider and Pommerehne, 1981). Most studies seem to conclude that strategic behaviour is not dominating (see Mitchell and Carson, 1989), but no clear evidence is established.

27. See for instance Walsh *et al.* (1984), Sutherland and Walsh (1985), Stevens *et al.* (1991) and Brookshire *et al.* (1983).

28. Carson and Mitchell (cited in Smith and Desvousges, 1986) and Sliberman *et al.* (1992) have used the reductionistic method.
29. This calculation of CS for private consumption is based on an ex post consideration; in other words, on previous behaviour. Included in the option price is, however, an ex ante expected CS—also for respondents who do not qualify as users.
30. For instance, there is an individual in this group who has a WTP of DKK 5,000. This observation alone alters the average from DKK 357 to DKK 938. The person in question is a man of age 38, who has received information about average expenditure on the Royal Theatre, has been to the Royal Theatre more than six times within the last year, and is generally very culturally active, has an upper secondary school certificate and has undergone higher education, lives in the capital, has one dependent child and a net income of more than DKK 450,000 p.a. Apart from this case there are two individuals in this group who have a WTP of DKK 1,000.
31. The 10 respondents in groups 2 and 6 are included in this calculation.
32. Here X_u and X_{nu} are regarded as exogenous variables included in the model on equal terms with the other exogenous variables. It is, however, more correct to look at X_u and X_{nu} as endogenous variables (see McConnell, 1990). The same also applies for K. This will be discussed further later in this chapter.
33. Alternatively, one can estimate a Tobit-like model where the dependent variable is non-negative (a survival model or a Tobit model where the residual follows a Weibull distribution). The problem in these models is, however, that the zero bids do not influence the parameter estimates.
34. Boeckstael *et al.* (1990) compare the Tobit, Heckman and Cragg models, estimating a demand model for fishing. However, CVM data are not used.
35. In the Poisson model the variance is equal to the average which limits the possible use of the model (Maddala, 1983, p. 51). In order to test the restriction about equal average and variance, a richer parameter model—namely a negative binominal regression model—is estimated, too. By doing this, a significantly better fit measured by a likelihood ratio test is not achieved, and the conditions of the Poisson model about equal average and variance can therefore be assumed.
36. It can be discussed whether it is more correct to look at the WTP as a *discrete or a continuous variable*. Actually, the WTP is a continuous variable. However, from Figure 13.1 it clearly appears that the WTP is concentrated on a few, round figures, i.e. 0, 50 (60), 100, 200, 500, 1,000 and 2,000. As previously mentioned, this is not very surprising. The question is whether the few respondents who state a WTP outside the above-mentioned amounts contribute with essential information, or whether they could be looked at as stochastic deviance from the round figures. About 237 respondents out of a total of 1,412 deviate in this way. In other words, 83% of the respondents have stated one of the round figures mentioned above. Arguments both for and against a discrete distribution can be put forward, but it is not surprising that the respondents do not know their preferences well enough to state if they want to pay DKK 89.50 or DKK 107.75 to the Royal Theatre. However, they do know if the theatre is worth DKK 100, DKK 200 or DKK 500 to them.
37. The models are estimated with the programme LIMDEP.
38. K is really endogenous, too, but as we are not interested in the precise size of the parameter estimate for K this is of lesser importance. K is included in order to get a better model by adjusting for sample selection bias.
39. In the literature there are many, similar cases where the data are partly generated by the individuals themselves choosing if they want to belong to one group or another (see Maddala, 1983). A classic example of the problem with self-selection is individuals choosing between two professions (hunters and fishermen) based on their productivity in these occupations. The observed distribution of income for hunters and fishermen is thus determined by these choices.
40. An extended self-selection model—where it is also taken into account that attaching non-use value to the Royal Theatre is an endogenous variable—can be as follows:

$$\text{WTP}_{1i} = X_i\,\beta_1 + u_{1i} \text{ (user with non-use values)}$$
$$\text{WTP}_{2i} = X_i\,\beta_2 + u_{2i} \text{ (non-user with non-use values)}$$
$$\text{WTP}_{3i} = X_i\,\beta_3 + u_{3i} \text{ (non-user without non-use values)}$$
$$X_{ui}^* = Z_i\,\lambda + \varepsilon_i$$
$$X_{nui}^* = Q_i\,\alpha + e_i$$
$$X_{ui} = 1, \text{ if } X_{ui}^* > 0$$
$$X_{ui} = 0, \text{ if } X_{ui}^* = 0$$
$$X_{ui} = 1 \text{ or } 0$$
$$\text{WTP}_i = \text{WTP}_{1i}, \text{ if } X_{ui} = 1 \text{ and } X_{nui} = 1$$
$$\text{WTP}_i = \text{WTP}_{2i}, \text{ if } X_{ui} = 0 \text{ and } X_{nui} = 1$$
$$\text{WTP}_i = \text{WTP}_{3i}, \text{ if } X_{ui} = 0 \text{ and } X_{nui} = 0$$

This model will, however, be very difficult to estimate with the present data set.

41. In the model the insignificant variables are sorted out.
42. The extra explanatory variable could for instance be "cultural ability and understanding". In the analysis there has already been an attempt to incorporate a measure for "cultural ability and understanding" by including the "cultural indicator" as an explanatory variable. Apparently, this does not, however, fully solve the problem with self-selection and there might be other reasons for the unobserved heterogeneity. If the model is estimated without the cultural indicator, the importance for sample selection bias of including this variable can be examined. If we try this the parameter estimate for X_u changes, increasing further to 716, and the parameter lambda decreases to −291 at the same time as the significance level for lambda is increased. This indicates that the cultural indicator actually adjusts for some of the sample selection bias which would otherwise be in the model.

REFERENCES

Arrow, K. R. Solow, E. Leamer, P. Portney, R. Radner and H. Schuman (1993): Report of the NOAA Panel on Contingent Valuation. *Federal Register*, **58** (10), 4601–14.

Bille Hansen, T. (1997): The Willingness-to-Pay for the Royal Theatre in Copenhagen as a Public Good. *Journal of Cultural Economics*, **21** (1), 1–28.

Bille Hansen, T. (1996): *Danskernes værdisætning af Det Kgl. Teater*. AKF Forlaget, Copenhagen.

Bille Hansen, T. (1991): *Det Kgl. Teater—et kulturøkonomisk studie*. AKF Forlaget, Copenhagen.

Bishop, R.C. (1982): Option Value: An Exposition and Extension. *Land Economics*, **58** (1), 1–15.

Boeckstael, N.E., I.E. Strand, K.E. McConnell and F. Arsanjani (1990): Sample Selection Bias in the Estimation of Recreation Demand Functions: An Application to Sport-fishing. *Land Economics*, **66** (1), 40–49.

Bohm, P. (1994): CVM Spells Responses to Hypothetical Questions. *Natural Resources Journal*, **34** (1), 37–50.

Bohm, P. (1979): Estimating Willingness to Pay: Why and How? *The Scandinavian Journal of Economics*, **81** (2), 142–53.

Bohm, P. (1975): Option Demand and Consumer Surplus: Comment. *American Economic Review*, **65**, 733–6.

Bohm, P. (1972): Estimating Demand for Public Goods: An Experiment. *European Economic Review*, **3** (2), 111–30.

Boyle, K.J. (1989): Commodity Specification and the Framing of Contingent Valuation Questions. *Land Economics*, **65** (1), 57–63.

Boyle, K.J. and R.C. Bishop (1988): Welfare Measurements Using Contingent Valuation: A Comparison of Techniques. *American Journal of Agricultural Economics*, **70** (1), 20–28.

Braden, J.B. and C.D. Kolstad (1991): *Measuring the Demand for Environmental Quality*. North-Holland Publishers, Amsterdam.

Brookshire, D.S., L.S. Eubanks and A. Randall (1983): Estimating Option Prices and Existence Values for Wildlife Resources. *Land Economics*, **59**, 1–15.

Brookshire, D.S., L.S. Eubanks and C.F. Sorg (1986): Existence Values and Normative Economics: Implementations for Valuing Water Resources. *Water Resources Research*, **22** (11), 1509–18.

Carson, R.T. *et al.* (1995): *A Bibliography of Contingent Valuation Studies and Papers*. Natural Resource Damage Assessment, Inc., La Jolla, California.

Carson, R.T. *et al.* (1992): *A Contingent Valuation Study of Lost Passive Use Values Resulting from the Exxon Valdez Oil Spill*. Report to the Attorney General and the State of Alaska. National Resource Damage Assessment, Inc., La Jolla, California.

Cicchetti, C.J. and A.M. Freeman (1971): Option Demand and Consumers Surplus: Further Comment. *Quarterly Journal of Economics*, **85**, 528–39.

Cummings, R.A. *et al.* (1986): *Valuing Environmental Goods: An Assessment of the Contingent Valuation Method*. Rowman & Allanheld Publishers, New Jersey.

Diamond, P.A. and J.A. Hausman (1994): Contingent Valuation: Is Some Number Better than No Number? *Journal of Economic Perspectives*, **8** (4), 45–69.

Dubgaard, A. (1996): *Economic Valuation of Recreation in Mols Bjerge*. SØMrapport, Copenhagen.

Freeman III, A.M. (1993): *The Measurement of Environmental and Resource Values. Theory and Methods*. Resources for the Future, Washington, DC.

Freeman III, A.M. (1984): The Size and Sign of Option Value. *Land Economics*, **60**, 1–13.

Frey, B.S. (1997): The Evaluation of Cultural Heritage. Some Critical Issues. In: Hutter, M. and I. Rizzo (eds), *Economic Perspectives on Cultural Heritage*. Macmillan Press, London, pp. 31–49.

Frey, B.S. and W.W. Pommerehne (1989): *Muses and Markets—Explorations in the Economics of Arts*. Basil Blackwell, Oxford.

Fridberg, T. (1994): *Kultur- og fritidsaktiviteter*, 1993. Socialforskningsinstituttet, Copenhagen.

Gapinski, J.H. (1984): The Economics of Performing Shakespeare. *American Economic Review*, **74** (3), 458–66.

Gordon, I.M. and J.L. Knetsch (1979): Consumer's Surplus Measures and the Evaluation of Resources. *Land Economics*, **55** (1), 1–10.

Graham, D.A. (1981): Cost–Benefit Analysis under Uncertainty. *American Economic Review*, **71**, 715–25.

Greenley, D.A., R.G. Walsh and R.A. Young (1981): Option Value: Empirical Evidence from a Case Study of Recreation and Water Quality. *Quarterly Journal of Economics*, **96** (4), 657–73.

Hanemann, W.M. (1994): Valuing the Environment Through Contingent Valuation. *Journal of Economic Perspectives*, **8** (4), 19–34.

Hanemann, W.M. (1991): Willingness to Pay and Willingness to Accept: How Much Can they Differ? *The American Economic Review*, **81** (3), 635–47.

Hanley, N. and A. Munro (1992): *The Effects on Information in Contingent Markets for Environmental Goods*. Queen's Institute for Economic Research, Discussion Paper.

Harrison, G.W. (1993): *General Reactions to the NOAA Report*.

Hausman, J.A. (1993): *Contingent Valuation: A Critical Assessment*. North-Holland, Amsterdam.

Kahneman, D. and A. Tversky (1979): Prospect Theory: An Analysis of Decisions Under Risk. *Econometrica*, **47** (2), 263–91.

Kahneman, D., J.L. Knetsch and R.H. Thaler (1990): Experimental Test of the Endowment Effect and the Coase Theorem. *Journal of Political Economy*, **98** (6), 1325–48.

Knetsch, J.L. and J.A. Sinden (1987): The Persistence of Evaluation Disparities. *The Quarterly Journal of Economics*, August, 691–5.

Knetsch, J.L. and J.A. Sinden (1984): Willingness to Pay and Compensation Demanded: Experimental Evidence of an Unexpected Disparity in Measures of Value. *The Quarterly Journal of Economics*, August, 507–21.

Madariaga, B. and K.E. McConnell (1987): Exploring Existence Value. *Water Resource Research*, **23**, 936–42.

Maddala, G.S. (1983): *Limited-Dependent and Qualitative Variables in Econometrics*. Cambridge University Press, Cambridge.

Mäler, K.-G. (1993): *Contingent Valuation—Does it Provide any Useful Information?* (Comments to the NOAA Report).

Martin, F. (1994): Determining the Size of Museum Subsidies. *Journal of Cultural Economics*, **18**, 255–70.

Marwell, G. and R.E. Armes (1981): Economists Free Ride, Does Anyone Else? Experiments on the Provision of Public Goods. *Journal of Public Economics*, **15**, 295–310.

McConnell, K.E. (1990): Models for Referendum Data: The Structure of Discrete Choice Models for Contingent Valuation. *Journal of Environmental Economics and Management*, **18**, 19–34.

Mitchell, R.C. and R.T. Carson (1989): *Using Surveys to Value Public Goods. The Contingent Valuation Method*. Resources for the Future, Washington, DC.

Morrison, W.G. and E.G. West (1986): Subsidies for the Performing Arts: Evidence on Voter Preference. *Journal of Behavioral Economics*, **16**, 57–72.

O'Hagan, J. (1994): *Dublin Theatre: An Economic Analysis of the "Abbey"*. Paper presented at the 8th International Congress on Cultural Economics, Witten, Germany, August, 1994.

Plummer, M.L. and R.C. Hartman (1986): Option Value: A General Approach. *Economic Inquiry*, **24**, 455–71.

Portney, P.R. (1994): The Contingent Valuation Debate: Why Economists Should Care. *Journal of Economic Perspectives*, **8** (4), 3–17.

Randall, A. (1991): Total and Non-use Values. In: Braden, J.B. and C.D. Kolstad (eds), *Measuring the Demand for Environmental Quality*. North-Holland, Oxford.

Schneider, F. and W.W. Pommerehne (1981): Free Riding and Collective Action: An Experiment in Public Microeconomics. *Quarterly Journal of Economics*, **97**, 689–702.

Schulze, G. and H.W. Ursprung (1996): *La Donna e Mobile—or is She? Voter Preferences and Public Support for the Performing Arts*. Paper presented at the 9th International Conference on Cultural Economics, Boston, MA, May 8–11, 1996.

Sellar, C., J.R. Stoll and J.-P. Chavas (1985): Validation of Empirical Measures of Welfare Change: A Comparison of Nonmarket Techniques. *Land Economics*, **61** (2), 156–75.

Sliberman, J., D.A. Gerlowski and N.A. Williams (1992): Estimating Existence Value for Users and Non Users of New Jersey Beaches. *Land Economics*, **68** (2), 225–36.

Smith, V.K. (1984): A Bound for Option Value. *Land Economics*, **60** (3), 292–6.

Smith, V.K. and W.H. Desvousges (1986): *Measuring Water Quality Benefits*. Kluwer-Nijhoff Publishing, Boston.

Stevens, T.H., J. Echeverria, R.J. Glass, T. Hager and T.A. More (1991): Measuring the Existence Value of Wildlife: What Do CVM Estimates Really Show? *Land Economics*, **67** (4), 390–400.

Sutherland, R.J. and R.G. Walsh (1985): Effect of Distance on the Preservation Value of Water Quality. *Land Economics*, **61**, 281–91.

Throsby, C.D. and G.A. Withers (1983): Measuring the Demand for the Arts as a Public Good: Theory and Empirical Results. In: William, S.H. and J.L. Shanahan. (eds), *Economics of Cultural Decisions*. Abt. Books, Cambridge.

Throsby, C.D. and G.A. Withers (1979): *The Economics of the Performing Arts*. St. Martins Press, New York.

Walsh, R.G., J.B. Loomis and R.A. Gillman (1984): Valuing Option, Existence and Bequest Demands for Wilderness. *Land Economics*, **60** (1), 14–29.

14. Individual preferences and allocation mechanisms for a cultural public good: "Napoli Musei Aperti"

Walter Santagata and Giovanni Signorello

INTRODUCTION

Estimating the economic value for cultural public goods provides basic information for their optimal provision (Green and Laffont, 1979; Starret, 1988) and for designing efficient and fair regulatory policies in the cultural sector. Measuring the total value, i.e. use value and passive-use values, is a difficult exercise and requires non-market techniques such as contingent valuation (CV) (Pommerehne, 1987; Mitchell and Carson, 1989). CV is a survey-based approach, in which representative individuals are asked to report information about their maximum willingness to pay (WTP) to secure or avoid the supposed change in the level of provision of the public good. In the last three decades an intensive research program has been devoted to the refinements in CV. As a result of this effort, CV has advanced and matured to such a point that it is now generally considered a useful and necessary informative tool in economics and policy analysis of public goods (Hanemann, 1994; Navrud, 1992).

This chapter presents some results of a CV study aimed at measuring holistically the total benefits accruing to the local residents from maintaining the provision of *Napoli Musei Aperti*, a cultural public good provided in Naples (Santagata and Signorello, 2000). In the survey we tried to place respondents in an incentive-compatible situation, and attempted to adhere to many of the most accredited devices, such as NOAA panel guidelines (Arrow *et al.*, 1993). Further, in the scenario we designed a particular sequence of valuation questions. Respondents were initially asked a general discrete choice question concerning whether or not they wished to donate some positive payment (payment principle question); then, for those agreeing to donate something, a further single-bounded discrete choice question was asked. Finally, individuals "in the market" were followed up by an open-ended question to state their maximum WTP. However, in this chapter we present only results coming from the single-bounded discrete choice data in order to offer a reliable empirical contribution to the CV literature in the area of cultural goods, and to explore some alternative schemes of cultural policy.

VALUING INDIVIDUAL PREFERENCES

The Cultural Good to be Valued: Napoli Musei Aperti

Napoli Musei Aperti (NMA) is a cultural public good provided by the city of Naples. The program *Napoli Musei Aperti* has been conceived to make possible the visiting and enjoyment of important cultural, historic and artistic monuments and sites located in four central areas of the city, namely in the historic Roman ("Decumano" and "Spaccanapoli") and Spanish quarters. The cultural network includes 29 churches, eight aristocratic palaces, eight historical squares, and one museum. Until the program was started these public cultural goods were closed, not restored and not included in a recommended guided tour.

In 1996 NMA was visited by about 814,000 people, both residents and tourists. The program is publicly provided by means of both local and national public funds. Its total cost is about 2,200,000 ECU (4.3 billion Lit.) per year, which means 2.45 ECU (4800 Lit.) per resident above 18 years old (the minimum age of an Italian voter).

NMA is a mixed public good, subject to congestion. The daily capacity of the good is quite large—far more than the current annual total visitors—and in the past congestion has not been an important consideration. Within this carrying capacity, we can describe NMA as a pure public good with zero marginal cost for additional users.

The Design of the Questionnaire

To measure the value of a good, the analyst has to observe people's choices. In particular, the analyst would observe both the *object of choice* and the *circumstances* of that choice, especially the consequences of such a choice in terms of substitution effects with other goods. The decision made in favor of the object implies that its value is at least equal to what was foregone to obtain it. In a CV survey, the analyst records individual choices in a hypothetical setting. The object of choice is represented by the change in the level of the provision of the public good to be valued, and the circumstances of the choice are the components of the virtual scenario (Smith *et al.*, 1997).

Designing a CV questionnaire with very high content validity represents a challenging task. The key issues are the description of the good to be valued, the payment mechanism, and the context for the valuation. Each component should be described by satisfying both theoretical requirements and the need for the respondents to understand and believe the scenario to be plausible where they are asked to make a hypothetical transaction. The literature offers general warnings and guidelines for designing (and successively administrating) a valid CV survey (Fischoff and Furby, 1988; Arrow *et al.*, 1993). Nevertheless, it is important to point out that the accuracy of final results depends not only on the ability and care of the researcher in designing a good questionnaire, but also on the respondent behaving in such a way as to produce a mutually beneficial outcome. As with any social research method, the validity of any CV study depends on the degree to which the interaction between subjects within the statistical game is co-operative.

The development of the questionnaire used in our CV study involved a focus group, a pre-test, and a review of the proposed questionnaire by other researchers with experience in the design of CV surveys. Another step in questionnaire development was the determination of the bid vector for use in the single-bounded discrete choice elicitation format stage. To acquire the necessary information about the bid range, we conducted a pilot test during June 1997.

The final questionnaire included four sections.

1. Basic information and questions
In the first section we described the NMA program using an illustrated map, and the economic modalities of its provision. Then, we asked questions about past and recent visits to at least one of the cultural sites included in the NMA network.

2. The cultural budget constraint
In the second section, we asked people to reveal how many times they attend theatres, operas, ballets, concerts, museums and cinema. Given the average entrance prices for each item, the interviewer was able to estimate and remind the respondent of his/her personal expenditure on cultural activities in the last 12 months. We introduced this reminder to force the respondents in some way to consider the relevance of budget constraint prior to giving any valuation answer. The budget reminder device provides at least two more sources of information. The first one describes, both in monetary terms and in consumption units, the individual consumption of a significant sub-sample of private and public cultural services provided in Naples. This information was used in the analysis of the payment principle question and the valuation functions. The second source of information deals with free-riding and over-riding behavior. Economic theory states that free-riding is a serious problem when the size of the group is large and the good to be supplied is a public good. Both characteristics are present in the NMA program. To limit free-riding two strategies could be addressed. The first one is the adoption of the dichotomous choice (referendum) elicitation format. As Hohen and Randall (1987) argued, the

referendum format could be an incentive-compatible mechanism. The second strategy consists of reminding people, just prior to the WTP announcement for NMA, of their expenditures on cultural goods. It should be noted that the items of the cultural budget are a sub-set of the whole budget for culture. What is of interest here is to remind people to make a choice between close substitutes. The idea behind this methodological approach is to define thresholds of reliability that could help in discriminating between truthful respondents and respondents who potentially over-ride, free-ride or easy-ride (Cornes and Sandler, 1986). Potential *over-riders* are defined as respondents who state a maximum willingness to pay greater than their yearly cultural expenditures. Potential *easy-riders* are defined as respondents who state a maximum WTP equal to zero but yearly cultural expenditures greater than zero (see Santagata and Signorello, 2000 for further details).

3. Enhancing citizen's trust

The third section of the questionnaire was designed to collect information on voluntary monetary contributions to the continued provision of the NMA program. We constructed the hypothetical scenario stating first the total and *per capita* current public expenditure sustained by city government for the provision of the NMA program, and then the average individual fiscal contribution. Next, we asked individuals to imagine that the local authorities would not be able to fund the NMA program any more because they were forced to invest all their money to support other local social priorities. Then, we pointed out that the program could still be provided if each adult citizen offered a voluntary monetary contribution. We know from experimental economics that one of the most insidious traps of WTP revelation is the actual structure of the provision of a public good (Antoci and Sacco, 1997). Many people do not trust public administrators. In other words, even if people would like to contribute voluntarily, they are prevented by the supposed inefficient behavior on the part of public bureaucrats. Many individuals think that the state will waste their money. Hence to reduce this negative tendency, we proposed a mechanism that would enforce a reasonable confidence in the utilization of the total private contribution. In the questionnaire we stated:

- the total amount of voluntary contribution for NMA would be managed by a non-profit agency;
- every year the citizens would be informed of the way their money has been spent and of the results reached;
- the individual monetary contributions would be collected each year only if their amount were sufficient to bear all the costs for supplying the NMA program, just as it is currently supplied by the Naples local authority. Otherwise, the money would not be collected and the NMA program would be abandoned.

4. Elicitation format

So far, we have illustrated many essential components of the hypothetical
scenario, namely: the source of the change (diversion of the public expenditure towards other local priorities); the reference (NMA program abandoned)
and the target level (NMA program at the current state) of the good; the payment
vehicle (monetary voluntary contribution); the decision-making unit (each
resident over 18 years); the timing of the payment (annual); the participants in
the market (all residents over 18 years); the budget reminder (individual representation of current cultural expenditures); and the rule of the provision of the
good (total contribution should cover total cost). A further essential element of
the scenario is the valuation questions. There are various ways to elicit WTP.
In this survey, we adopted a multilevel questioning strategy in which the single-
bounded discrete choice question was chosen as the primary valuation question.
At the first level, respondents were asked whether or not they agreed to donate
something to maintain the NMA. The aim of this so-called "payment principle
question" was to validate refusals and reduce protest behavior. Only respondents
answering "yes" passed to the second level, where they were asked a single-
bounded discrete choice valuation question. This format, introduced in a seminal
article by Bishop and Heberlein (1979), now dominates the CV literature and
has also been endorsed by the NOAA panel. Its popularity among scholars
stems from its inherent market resemblance. Single-bounded discrete choice
involves asking respondents whether they would be willing to pay (contribute)
specific amounts, and the amount is varied at random across respondents. We
use a vector formed by 10 bid amounts [5000, 7000, 10,000, 15,000, 20,000,
25,000, 30,000, 50,000, 75,000, 100,000 Lit.]. The bid range was chosen to
cover what we perceived, through the open-ended pre-test, to be the likely range
of WTP. Each bid was randomly assigned with equal probability to each
respondent. Given that the single-bounded discrete choice question format
yields data that allow us to calculate only summary statistics (e.g. mean, median,
and other quartiles) of the WTP, we introduced a third valuation question: the
single-bounded discrete choice question was followed up by an open-ended (or
continuous valuation) question. Respondents who agreed to donate the given
bid were asked to specify the maximum amount they would be willing to donate
to the special fund for the continued provision of NMA. Respondents who
refused to pay the given bid were also asked to specify their maximum amount.
In both cases, respondents were prompted to give answers consistent with the
choice made at the previous single-bounded discrete choice stage. In other
words, if the answer to the single-bounded discrete choice was "yes", the
maximum WTP would not be lower than the proposed bid. Vice versa, if the
answer was "no", the maximum WTP must be lower than the assigned bid. To
summarize, each individual was potentially asked to give three valuation
responses: two discrete (yes or no) and one continuous (amount of contribution).

For a sub-sample of respondents, this elicitation scheme generated a hierarchical data set, as we have a multiple response nested within each individual response. For the whole sample, the possible paths of response were as follows (the location of the continuous WTP is indicated in parenthesis):

1. No (WTP = 0).
2. Yes—Yes + continuous amount (WTP ≥ bid).
3. Yes—No + continuous amount (WTP < bid).

It is clear that this combination of WTP questions provides more statistical information for the analyst. However, it has a drawback: the potential anchoring effect of the proposed bid to the open-ended bids.

In the final section of the survey we asked a set of questions to identify the socio-economic profile of the respondent.[1]

The Execution of the Survey

The survey was directly administered in autumn 1997 by a large number of trained interviewers. The training emphasized the need for neutrality, and the nature of the survey. Five hundred individuals were drawn from citizens registered on the electoral roll. The electoral roll is an excellent sample frame since it is a legal requirement in Italy that all adults over 18 be registered. The selection was conducted using a systematic rule, and a quota designed to ensure sex and districts balanced among the respondents. Another sample, of the same size and selected according to the same criteria, was utilized as a substitute to replace non-responding individuals.

To each individual we sent by mail a single page letter on The University of Turin letterhead paper. The letter was designed to motivate respondents by explaining the policy relevance of the questions, the scientific purpose of the survey, the importance of representative participation, and the respect for anonymity. Each letter was addressed to the individual and personally signed by the project director. There was a 75% response rate. The final usable sample was composed of 468 citizens. The response rate for each question was consistently high, except for the questions on delicate issues such as occupation and net personal and household income.

Sample Description

Table 14.1 gives a summary of some socio-economic characteristics of the sample which on average reveals a high knowledge of the NMA program and a wide fruition of sites included in the NMA program. With regard to the other variables, our sample appears representative of the general population over 18 years at 0.05 level of sample error.

Table 14.1   Sample characteristics

VARIABLE	MEAN	STANDARD DEVIATION
SEX	0.49	0.50
AGE	43.33	17.58
EDUC	10.6	4.54
EXPEND	87,890	141,500
KNOW	0.80	0.40
PASTVIS	0.57	0.50
NUMVIS	1.68	3.00
HOUSEHOLD	3.48	2.31

Note: SEX = 1 for male, 0 for female; AGE = age of respondent (continuous variable); EDUC = years of instruction (continuous variable); EXPEND = expenditures in cultural activities (Lit.); KNOW = knowledge of NMA (1 for yes, 0 for no); PASTVIS = visit to at least one of the sites, included in the NMA (1 for yes, 0 for no); NUMVIS = visits to the NMA in the past 12 months (continuous variable); HOUSEHOLD = number of components of household respondent (continuous variable).

Results from Payment Principle Question

226 respondents (48%), out of 468, answered negatively to the payment principle question. This proportion of people who choose not to contribute is unexpectedly high, considering the special features of NMA, which include sites and monuments of great historical and symbolic importance for Naples. We explored why such a large number of respondents decided to stay "out of the market". The primary recorded motive was genuine indifference towards the provision of NMA, and a secondary reason was the assignment of any eventual private contribution to other local social emergencies. Of course a well-known reason could have been strategic behavior. The proportion of protest reasons, such as that government should make the necessary provision out of taxes already paid, was not substantial. Dealing with protest zero bidders is a critical issue. We used the strategy of considering them as real zero bids. This results in conservative estimates of the public's WTP.

The payment principle question splits respondents into two sub-samples, A and B. Sample A includes the proportion $p = 0.52$ of respondents willing to donate something for NMA; sample B includes the proportion $(1 - p) = 0.48$ of respondents not willing to donate anything for NMA.

The discrete yes/no responses to the payment principle question were analyzed by using a probit regression model. To account for the influence of districts where respondents live, we included in the qualitative regression model five dummy variables, as we divided the city of Naples into six homogeneous districts. Table 14.2 shows the estimation results of the "macro" decision of respondents: whether or not to be in the market for NMA. The probit model predicts the actual outcome in 66.3% of all cases. Moreover, among the explanatory variables, only the coefficients of EXPEND and KNOW are significantly different from zero. The sign of the estimated coefficients is positive for all variables except AGE and Q1.

Table 14.2   Probit model for the payment principle question

No. Obs.		468	
Log-Likelihood		−276.5110	
Chi-Squared (12)		95.21660	

Variable	Coefficient	Std. Error	*t*-Ratio
Constant	−1.0550	0.4010	−2.63
EXPEND	0.18907E–05	0.6216E–06	3.04
KNOW	0.91733	0.1832	5.00
NUMVISIT	0.30946E–01	0.2326E–01	1.33
AGE	−0.54683E–02	0.4004E–02	−1.36
SEX	0.11362	0.1278	0.90
EDUC	0.78477E–02	0.1684E–01	0.46
HOUSEHOLD	0.12038E–01	0.2956E–01	0.40
Q1	0.87455E–01	0.3167	0.27
Q2	0.42075	0.3086	1.36
Q3	0.31803	0.3905	0.81
Q4	0.31697	0.3048	1.04
Q5	−0.62976E–01	0.3048	−0.20

Note: Q1, Q2, Q3, Q4, and Q5 are the dummy variables for the six districts.

WTP Estimation

As explained above, respondents who agreed to contribute for the continued existence of NMA were asked a further question on whether they would be willing to donate a specific annual amount (bid) drawn at random from the vector specified previously. Table 14.3 reports the basic data set derived from

the single-bounded discrete choice valuation question for the whole sample
and for the sub-sample A (non-zero bidders).

Table 14.3   Data sets

Bid (Lit.)	Whole sample		Sample A	
	No. of respondents	No. of yes	No. of respondents	No. of yes
5000	56	29	30	29
7000	46	24	26	24
10,000	40	18	18	18
15,000	44	30	31	30
20,000	43	20	26	20
25,000	41	13	17	13
30,000	49	11	23	11
50,000	54	14	23	14
75,000	46	8	22	8
100,000	46	14	26	14
Total	468	181	242	181

The discrete choice data set was analyzed using a spike logit model that
employs all information coming from the two discrete choice valuation
questions. The spike is the probability that WTP is equal to zero. We adopted
a simple univariate linear logit model which, according to the random
maximizing utility framework (Hanemann, 1989), is given by:

$$\text{Prob(yes|Bid)} = \text{Prob(Bid} \geq \text{WTP)} = F_\eta(\Delta V)$$
$$= 1 - G_{\text{WTP}}(\text{Bid}) = [1 + \exp(\alpha - \beta \text{Bid})]^{-1}$$

where F_η is the c.d.f. of the random error $\eta = \varepsilon_0 - \varepsilon_1$, $V = V(1, Y - \text{Bid}) - V(0,Y)$
is the difference in indirect utility function (1 represents the NMA and 0
represents the state of nature without NMA), $G_{\text{WTP}}(\text{Bid})$ is the c.d.f. of the
random variable WTP, α and β are the coefficients to be estimated. In terms of
Hicksian welfare measures, the WTP corresponds to the equivalent surplus.
The estimated survival function $(1 - G_{\text{WTP}}(\text{Bid}))$ can be interpreted as an
aggregate demand curve for the discrete commodity. The log-likelihood
function of spike logit model is shown in Kriström (1997). The results of the
maximum likelihood estimation are presented in Table 14.4.

Estimated coefficients have the expected signs and are significantly different
from zero. The spike, calculated as $[1 + \exp(\alpha)]^{-1}$ is equal to 0.51 which is very

close to the actual proportion of people who declined to donate anything for the provision of NMA. The expected value of the mean WTP, $E(\text{WTP})$, has been calculated using the formula $\ln[1 + \exp(\alpha)]/\beta$ developed by Hanemann (1989) for a WTP distribution truncated at zero in the left side. Its value is equal to Lit. 42,600.

Table 14.4   Estimated logit model

Variable	Coefficients
Constant	0.4281E–01
	(0.460)
Bid	–0.16778E–04
	(–8.970)
Log-likelihood	–433.413
No. Obs.	468

Note: Asymptotic *t*-value in parentheses.

Valuation Function

It is common practice in CV studies to estimate a valuation function, i.e. a function that relates discrete choice or WTP to variables that are supposed to have an influence on the choice or on stated WTP amount. This explorative estimation can serve two purposes. Firstly, it allows us to perform a test of construct (theoretical) validity by determining whether choices or WTP amount are significantly related to covariates suggested by the theory. Secondly, it could be used for transferring the sample results to populations different from the one from which the sample is drawn, and for taking into account non-respondents of the CV survey provided that we know their characteristics.

The multivariate logit equation is shown in Table 14.5. The coefficients on the bid amount BID, expenditure in cultural activities EXPEND, previous knowledge of the NMA program KNOW, and number of past visits to the sites NUMVISIT were statistically significant at the 1% level and of the expected signs. This means that individuals having general and motivated interest in cultural activities and recreation are more likely to contribute towards the continued provision of the NMA program. The ages of respondents and the sizes of their households influenced negatively the attitude towards the contribution for the supply of public cultural goods. The estimated equation correctly predicted a relatively high percentage (82.2%) of responses.

Case studies

Table 14.5   Multivariate logit valuation function

No. Obs.			468
Log-Likelihood			–259.7884
Chi-Squared (13)			104.9909

Variable	Coefficient	Std. Error	t-Ratio
Constant	–1.0784	0.7175	–1.50
BID	–0.19944E–04	0.3959E–05	–5.03
EXPEND	0.33769E–05	0.1046E–05	3.23
KNOW	0.86392	0.3366	2.56
NUMVISIT	0.99128E–01	0.4230E–01	2.34
AGE	–0.98271E–02	0.7063E–02	–1.39
SEX	0.11211	0.2205	0.50
EDUC	0.41723E–01	0.2896E–01	1.44
HOUSEHOLD	–0.44173E–01	0.5071E–01	–0.87
Q1	0.58221E–01	0.5533	0.10
Q2	0.48227	0.5365	0.90
Q3	0.22011	0.6661	0.33
Q4	–0.55400E–01	0.5360	–0.10
Q5	–0.22889E–01	0.5357	–0.04

Note: Q1, Q2, Q3, Q4, and Q5 are the dummy variables for the six districts.

POLICY ANALYSIS

CV is now considered a useful measurement tool in many policy-relevant issues. First, CV can be applied in benefit–cost analysis for the selection of investment programs, when *publicness* is concerned. Second, CV can be applied in the courts for assessing liabilities. The most renowned case concerned the natural resource damage assessment following the Exxon Valdez ecological disaster of March 1989. Third, direct survey techniques, very similar to CV, have been applied to appraise, with reference to individual fiscal preferences, the way national and local governments allocate public expenditures (Throsby and Withers, 1983; Morrison and West, 1986; Piperno and Santagata, 1992; Withers *et al.*, 1994).

A further case for CV as a policy instrument is the private supply of public goods (Andreoni, 1988; Weisbrod, 1988). Given a standard consumer utility function for a public good and a private composite good, the Samuelsonian optimal condition for the efficient supply of the public good requires that the sum of individual marginal WTP equals the marginal cost of producing the public good. When the public good is discrete, like in the present study, total (aggregate) WTP must be equal to or greater than the total (aggregate) cost.

In both cases, the failure of the market mechanism due to free-riding behavior has been stressed, giving rise for a long time to a full rationale for the public provision of public goods (Throsby and Withers, 1986). Nevertheless, following the development of the literature on incentive-compatible mechanisms (Green and Laffont, 1979), the accumulation of empirical evidence from experimental economics (Ledyard, 1995), and the improvements in survey design and CV empirical implementation for controlling and limiting strategic behavior, the revelation of true fiscal preferences may be measured and the private supply of public goods become feasible.

Nevertheless, as far as a cultural good like *Napoli Musei Aperti* is concerned, the more serious problem seems to be individual overvaluation, rather than free-riding behavior with undervaluation. This is because cultural activities are a good charged with positive value and the voluntary contribution is supplied in a hypothetical setting.[2]

Mechanisms Regulating the Provision of a Cultural Public Good

We consider four stylized rules of supply.

Market. The cultural public good is provided through private mechanisms. NMA is like a pure public good when consumed from the outside; but a mixed public good when users are visiting churches and palaces. Exclusion is possible. Admission fees for personal consumption can be charged or total WTP (user and passive-user values) can be extracted by a discriminating monopolist. In the case discussed below the entrepreneur, in a complete information setting, is a perfect discriminating monopolist and aims at profit maximization.

State. The good is provided by public institutions and funding is achieved through direct taxation. The good may be characterized by free access or subject to a public admission fee, whose total amount is less than the total cost.

Non-profit. Provision is granted by patrons, foundations and, less properly, by sponsors. Admission may be free and/or a fee can be charged.

Collective ethic co-operation. The good is provided through voluntary contributions. The admission is free.

Results from the CV study of NMA allow us to compare three of the above systems of regulation (information about the "non-profit institutions" scheme is not available) and to reiterate an interesting finding by Willis (1994) concerning the WTP for Durham Cathedral (see Table 14.6).

Market. The donation maximizing total revenue is Lit. 86,000. Twenty percent of citizens would pay, that is those having a "reservation price" at least equal to Lit. 86,000. Given that the inhabitants of Naples were about one million in 1987 and that the total cost of Napoli Musei Aperti has been 4.3 billion Lit., the aggregate maximum revenue should cover the total costs.

Table 14.6   Comparing allocative mechanisms of "Napoli Musei Aperti"

	Price	Total revenue per 100 citizens (Lit.)	Total cost covered	Excluded per 100 citizens	Excluded 0>WTP<50,000 per 100 citizens	Excluded WTP=0
Market	86,000	1,701,085	Yes	80.2	29.1	51.1
State	(4,800)	(480,000)	Yes	50.1	1.0	51.1
Collective Ethic Cooperation	0	4,260,000	Yes	0	0	0

State. Nobody is excluded from the consumption of the public good and the total cost is covered by taxation. However, 51% of the citizens are charged an average compulsory contribution equal to Lit. 4800, even if their WTP is zero. This could be considered an implicit form of exclusion, or of forced inclusion.

Collective ethic co-operation. Voluntary contribution provides a total revenue equal to Lit. 4,260,000, the amount of the individual WTP per 100 citizens. Nobody is excluded. The total cost is covered by voluntary contribution. As in the CV study of Durham Cathedral (Willis, 1994), the amount of voluntary contribution is greater than the maximum total revenue we could get from the market system. It should be noted that a perfectly discriminating monopolist could get the same outcomes. The difference is that the monopolist would obtain this result by excluding those who reveal a zero WTP.

The system based on the social institution (*Collective ethic co-operation*) seems in the provision of cultural public goods to be superior from several different points of view:

- free admission does not compel anyone to contribute, either through taxation or fees;
- in relative terms, the total revenue is maximized (the whole consumer surplus would be collected);
- the total cost of provision is covered;
- nobody is excluded, either explicitly or implicitly, from the consumption of the good;
- through the voluntary contribution scheme, it is possible to collect money from all components of the total value: use value and passive-use values;
- given that to declare a WTP equal to zero is simply an economic evaluation, it is possible that free entry provides a positive incentive to further consumption of cultural goods.

CONCLUSION

This chapter aimed to test the feasibility of the CV method to assess individual preferences for maintaining "Napoli Musei Aperti", a local cultural public good, and to explore some alternative schemes of cultural policy. The budget reminder device introduced into the questionnaire increased the reliability of the CV method. The estimates of the WTP appeared to have a reasonable size, even if it is well known that the single-bounded discrete choice format overstates the true WTP, especially when hypothetical willingness to donate is concerned.

The policy analysis of the WTP estimates shows that the "collective ethic co-operation", a system of provision based on individual voluntary contributions for a public good, appears to be superior to other systems of regulation.

ACKNOWLEDGEMENTS

The authors are grateful to R. Ready and D. Throsby for their comments. Support for this project was provided by Research Grant No. 96.03902.Ps.15 from Consiglio Nazionale delle Ricerche.

ENDNOTES

1. The WTP questions used are:

   " *To face social emergencies that hit the city, the Naples local authority could decide <u>not to fund the NMA Program any more</u>. Let's imagine that, as happens in other Italian cities of art, every citizen could supply <u>a personal voluntary contribution substituting current public funds provided by the collection of local taxes</u>.*

       – Would you like to offer a yearly voluntary monetary contribution in order to preserve the NMA Program? (yes/no)
   – If yes, given that your expenditure in culture is estimated at Lit. ..., and assuming that it will be unchanged for the next year, would you like to offer yearly Lit. ... (one bid randomly selected from a bid vector)?
   – In any case would you like to tell us which is your maximum WTP? Lit. ..."

   A copy of the full questionnaire is available from the Authors upon request.
2. The results presented in the text are based on the spike-logit model estimates of the discrete choice data. In Santagata and Signorello (2000) we presented a similar analysis using WTP information from open-ended data. Although open WTPs, as expected, are lower than closed WTP estimates, the conclusions about the fairness and efficiency of the three allocative mechanisms examined are equivalent.

REFERENCES

Andreoni J. 1988: "Privately Provided Public Goods in a Large Economy: The Limits of Altruism", *Journal of Public Economics*, 35, 57–73.

Antoci A. and P.-L. Sacco 1997: "Il futuro delle città d'arte: il ruolo della contribuzione volontaria nelle politiche di ammortamento sociale", *Stato e Mercato*, 49.

Arrow K., R. Solow, P.R. Portney, E.E. Leamer, R. Radner and H. Schuman. 1993: Report of the NOA Panel on Contingent Valuation, *Federal Register*, 58, 4601–14.

Bishop R. and T. Heberlein 1979: "Measuring the Values of Extra-Market Goods: Are Indirect Measures Biased?", *American Journal of Agricultural Economics*, 5, 926–30.

Cornes R. and T. Sandler 1986: *The Theory of Externalities, Public Good, and Club Goods*, Cambridge University Press, Cambridge.

Fischoff B. and L. Furby 1988: "Measuring Values: A Conceptual Framework for Interpreting Transactions with Special Reference to Contingent Valuation", *Journal of Risk and Uncertainty*, 1, 147–84.

Green J. and J.J. Laffont 1979: *Incentives in Public Decision Making*, North-Holland, Amsterdam.

Hanemann M. 1989: "Welfare Evaluations in Contingent Valuation Experiments with Discrete Response Data: A Reply", *American Journal of Agricultural Economics*, 4, 1057–61.

Hanemann M. 1994: "Valuing the Environment Through Contingent Valuation", *Journal of Economic Perspective*, 4, 19–43.

Hohen J.P. and A. Randall 1987: "A Satisfactory Benefit Cost Indicator from Contingent Valuation", *Journal of Environmental Economics and Management*, 3, 226–47.

Kriström B. 1997: "Spike Models in Contingent Valuation", *American Journal of Agricultural Economics*, 3, 1013–23.

Ledyard J.O. 1995: "Public Goods: A Survey of Experimental Research", in J. Kagel and A. Roth (eds.), *The Handbook of Experimental Economics*, Princeton University Press, Princeton, NJ, pp. 111–94.

Mitchell R.C. and R.T. Carson 1989: *Using Surveys to Value Public Goods: The Contingent Valuation Method*, Resources for the Future, Washington, DC.

Morrison W.G., and E.G. West 1986: "Subsidies for the Performing Arts: Evidence on Voter Preferences" *Journal of Behavioral Economics*, 15, 57–72.

Navrud S. (ed.) 1992: *Pricing the European Environment*, Oxford University Press, Oxford.

Piperno S. and W. Santagata 1992: "Revealed Preferences for Local Public Goods. The Turin Experiment", in D. King (ed.), *Local Government Economics in Theory and Practice*, Routledge, London.

Pommerehne W.W. 1987: *Proeferenzen fur oeffentliche Guter*, Tubingen.

Santagata W. and G. Signorello 2000: "Contingent Valuation of a Cultural Public Good and Policy Design: The Case of 'Napoli Musei Aperti'", *Journal of Cultural Economics*, 24, (3), 181–204.

Smith V.K., X. Zhang and R.B. Palmquist 1997: "Marine Debris, Beach Quality, and Non-Market Value", *Environmental and Resource Economics*, 10, 223–47.

Starret D.A. 1988: *Foundations of Public Economics*, Cambridge University Press, Cambridge.

Throsby C.D. and G.A. Withers 1983: "Measuring the Demand for the Arts as a Public Good: Theory and Empirical Results", in J.L. Shanahan *et al.* (eds.), *Economic Support for the Arts*, Association for Cultural Economics, Akron, Ohio.
Throsby C.D. and G.A. Withers 1986: "Strategic Bias and Demand for Public Goods", *Journal of Public Economics*, 31, 307–27.
Weisbrod, B.A., 1988: *The Nonprofit Economy*, Harvard University Press, Cambridge.
Willis K.G. 1994: "Paying for Heritage: What Price for Durham Cathedral", *Journal of Environmental Planning and Management*, 3, 267–78.
Withers G., D. Throsby and K. Johnston 1994: *Public Expenditure in Australia*, Australian Government Publishing Service, Canberra.

PART III

Review of Studies

15. Review of existing studies, their policy use and future research needs

David Pearce, Susana Mourato, Ståle Navrud and Richard C. Ready

REVIEW AND CLASSIFICATION OF CULTURAL HERITAGE STUDIES

In spite of the obvious links between questions of the conservation of natural and cultural goods, there have been surprisingly few applications of non-market valuation techniques to cultural assets. Only a small number of studies, using almost exclusively stated preference techniques, have been applied to cultural heritage goods. Many of these studies are described in detail in the previous chapters.

Table 15.1 presents an overview of 27 studies valuing mainly historical buildings, monuments and artifacts. We have also included a few examples of contingent valuation studies of other cultural goods and services, such as museums and performing and visual arts. All of these studies apply stated preference techniques, which are unique in their capability to measure both use and non-use values arising from cultural capital. As is evident from the table, not only is the number of existing studies small, but the studies also span a wide range of goods and situations. Six of the sites studied are part of UNESCO's World Heritage List.

Table 15.2 classifies the studies according to the type of benefit estimated and the type of cultural good/activity studied. Here we have differentiated among different types of cultural heritage goods, including single buildings, groups of buildings, monuments, archaeological areas and artifacts, and other goods including performing arts and museums. It is apparent from this table that cultural heritage is a complex, multifaceted good. Not only is there a diversity of physical assets involved (the columns in Table 15.2), there is also a diversity of services, qualities and policy issues for each (the rows in Table 15.2). The studies listed represent just the first small steps in considering the breadth of cultural heritage goods.

Table 15.1 Review of cultural heritage valuation studies. Studies presented in this book are numbered according to their chapter. Other studies are assigned a letter, for use in Table 15.2.

Study and nature of the asset	WTP (US$)[a]	WTP definition[b]	Annuity (US$)[c]	% zero WTP	% of stated income[d]
Valuing the impacts of road improvements upon Stonehenge, UK. Contingent valuation* (Chapter 7)	20–23: on-site, nationals 6–11: off-site, nationals 0.3–2: on-site, foreigners	Household, annual, 2 years, PC/CA, tax (entry fee for foreigners)	2.3–2.7 0.7–1.3 0.02–0.1	55% 65%	0.08–0.09 0.03–0.06 0.0001–0.000
Valuing aesthetic changes in Lincoln Cathedral due to air pollution, UK. Contingent valuation (Chapter 5)	1–2 per year of soiling, residents of Lincolnshire	Household, annual, DB DC, tax	1–2	<19%	0.005–0.01
Non-Moroccan values for rehabilitating the Fes Medina, Morocco*. Contingent valuation (Chapter 9)	38–70: Fes visitors 22–31: Morocco visitors	Individual, per trip, SB DC, tax	2.4–4.4 1.4–2.0	Approx. 17% Approx. 19%	n.a.
Non-Moroccan values for rehabilitating the Fes Medina, Morocco*. Carson et al., 2001—M Delphi—Contingent Valuation Survey of 30 European environmental economists	6–17: European non-visitors	Household one-time payment, OE, none	0.4–1.1	>15%	n.a.
Valuing access to Durham Cathedral, UK*. Contingent valuation (Chapter 4)	1.4	Individual, per visit, OE, fee	56 (average no. visits = 41)	36%	0.2
Valuing the preservation of Bulgarian monasteries, Bulgaria*. Contingent valuation (Chapter 6)	0.6–1	Household, annual, OE, tax	0.6–1	39%	0.1–0.2

258

Study		Payment vehicle			
Valuing acid deposition injuries to marble monuments in Washington, DC, USA. Contingent valuation (Chapter 11)	16: low impact 23: medium impact 33: high impact	Household, one-time only, CA, none	1.0 1.5 2.1	8% (approx.)	0.003–0.006
Valuing the conservation of Campi Flegrei archaeological park in Napoli, Italy. Contingent valuation (Chapter 10)	216	Individual, Annual, 5 years, SB DC, donation	58	18% (approx.)	0.5
Renovation of historical buildings in Grainger City, Newcastle, UK. Contingent valuation (Chapter 4)	16–22	Household, annual, OE, tax	16–22	47%	n.a.
Recreational value of aboriginal rock paintings, Nopiming Park, Canada. Contingent valuation (Chapter 8)	134	Individual, annual, CB, travel cost	134	n.a.	n.a.
Valuing the right to access two Italian art museums at present charges. Contingent valuation (Chapter 12)	28–33	Individual, annual, SB DC, donation	28–33	18% (approx.)	n.a.
Valuing visitor benefits to Warkworth Castle UK. Contingent valuation. (Chapter 4)	4	Individual, per visit, OE, fee	4 (average no. of visits = 1)	n.a.	0.01
Value of continuing current activities of the Royal Theatre in Copenhagen, Denmark. Contingent valuation (Chapter 13)	9–24	Individual, annual, OE, tax	9–24	18%	n.a.
Maintaining the Napoli Musei Aperti. Contingent valuation (Chapter 14)	11 (users) 4 (non-users)	Household, annual, OE, donation	11 4	34% (users) 67% (non-users)	n.a.

Table 15.1 continued

Study and nature of the asset	WTP (US$)[a]	WTP definition[b]	Annuity (US$)[c]	% zero WTP	% of stated income[d]
Damages from air pollution on the Nidaros Cathedral, Norway. Contingent valuation (Chapter 3)	51: originality preserved 45: restoration—losing originality	Individual, annual, OE, tax and donation	51 45	9–20 % (domestic visitors) 38–49 % (foreign visitors)	n.a.
Damages from traffic-caused air pollution on historical buildings in Neuchatel, Switzerland. Contingent valuation. Grosclaude and Soguel, 1994—A	77–86	Individual, annual, BG, donation	77–86	43%	n.a.
Arts support (theatre, opera, ballet, music, visual arts, crafts). Sydney, Australia. Contingent valuation. Throsby and Withers, 1986—B	18–111	Individual, annual, OE, tax	18–111	n.a.	n.a.
Prehistoric cave paintings preservation programmes (two hypothetical new caves discovery in Peak District, UK). Contingent valuation. Coulton, 1999—C	1 (two caves open to public, none exist in 50 years) 14 (one cave open to public, one cave protected and exists in 50 years)	Individual, one-time, OE, tax	0–1	85% 29%	0–0.00003
Restoring historic core of the city of Split, Croatia Contingent valuation. Pagiola, 1999—D	44 (domestic and foreign tourists) 168 (local residents)	Individual, per visit Individual, annual, DB DC, tax	n.a. 168	n.a. n.a.	n.a

Study	Value	Design		%	
Machu Picchu, Peru* Contingent valuation. Hett and Mourato, 2000—E	47 (foreign tourists) 26 (Peruvians)	Individual, per visit, PC, entry fee	47 26	n.a	0.07 0.26
Picture library, UK. Contingent valuation. EFTEC, 2000—F	12	Individual, annual, PC	12	10%	n.a
History (recorded heritage) centre. Contingent valuation. EFTEC, 2000—G	34 (users, loss of access, but collection protected) 48 (users, loss of access and collection) 18 (non-users, loss of access and loss of collection)	Individual, annual, PC	34 48 18	n.a	n.a
Preservation of the St. Genevieve Academy. Contingent valuation. Whitehead et al., 1998—H	5–6	Household, one-time, PC, donation	0.3–0.36	61%	0.001
Preservation of the Northern Hotel in Fort Collins. Contingent valuation. Kling et al., 2000—I	86 (tax, low information) 126 (tax, high information) 195 (foregone rebate, low information) 434 (foregone rebate, low information)	Household, one-time, DC	5 8 12 26	n.a.	n.a.
Congestion in the British Museum. Conjoint analysis. Maddison and Foster, 2001—J	9 (marginal congestion cost per visitor)	Individual, per visit, CA, entry fee	n.a.	n.a.	0.01
Restoring Stone Town, Zanzibar* Contingent valuation. Bølling and Iversen, 1999—K	20 (tourists)	Individual, per visit, OE/SB DC, arrival fee	n.a.	n.a.	n.a.

Table 15.1 continued

Study and nature of the asset	WTP (US$)[a]	WTP definition[b]	Annuity (US$)[c]	% zero WTP	% of stated income[d]
Rehabilitating Colon Theatre, Buenos Aires, Argentina. Conjoint analysis. Roche Rivera, 1998—L	58 (local residents)	Individual, annual, SB DC, tax	58	n.a.	n.a.

Source: Based partly on Pearce and Mourato (1999) and Pearce *et al.* (2001)

Notes:
* Is or includes a site listed in the UNESCO World Heritage List; n.a. = data not available.
[a] Using average exchange rates for the year of the study.
[b] Individual or household; periodicity; elicitation format (OE: open-ended; PC: payment card; BG: bidding game; SB DC: single-bounded dichotomous choice; DB DC: double-bounded dichotomous choice; CA: conjoint analysis; CB: contingent behaviour); payment vehicle (tax, donation, entry fee, arrival fee, travel cost).
[c] Estimated annuities were calculated for a time horizon of 50 years using a discount rate of 6%.
[d] Gross annual household returns.

Table 15.2 Cultural heritage studies classification. Studies that fit in two categories are listed in both. The number or letter assigned to each study refers to Table 15.1. Studies marked with an asterisk are or include a site listed in the UNESCO World Heritage List

Type of benefit	Type of good				
	Single building	Group of buildings	Monuments	Archaeological areas and artifacts	Other
Protect from air pollution damages	5—Lincoln Cathedral 3—Nidaros Cathedral	A—Historical buildings in Neuchatel	11—Washington, DC monuments		
Restore of preserve from degradation	3—Nidaros Cathedral 5—Lincoln Cathedral H—Northern Hotel, Fort Collins	6—Bulgarian monasteries* 9, M—Fes Medina* 4—Grainger City D—Historic core of Split E—Machu Picchu* K—Stone Town of Zanzibar*		C—Prehistoric cave paintings in UK	L—Colon Theatre
Protect from urban development/infrastructure				7—Stonehenge 10—Campi Flegrei archaeological park	
Gain access	4—Warkworth Castle 4—Durham Cathedral			8—Rock paintings, Nopiming Park C—Prehistoric cave paintings in UK	12—Art galleries in Turin

Table 15.2 continued

Type of benefit	Type of good				
	Single building	Group of buildings	Monuments	Archaeological areas and artifacts	Other
Maintain at present level	I—St. Genevieve Academy				13—Royal Theatre, Copenhagen 14—Napoli Musei Aperti B—Performing and visual arts in Sydney F—Picture library, UK G—History (recorded heritage) centre, UK
Reduction of congestion					J—British Museum

MAIN LESSONS FROM EXISTING EMPIRICAL EVIDENCE

While the conclusions of each study are different, some consistent findings emerge from the studies that have been conducted to date.

(a) *Few economic valuation studies* have been undertaken in the area of cultural heritage (either built or movable heritage). All studies reviewed here use stated preference methods, mainly contingent valuation, and there exist very few applications of revealed preference methods.[1]

(b) The *existing studies vary widely* both in terms of the type of good or activity being analysed and the type of benefit being evaluated. There are some instances where similar goods were evaluated. However, the type of benefit estimated is usually different, as is the sample frame used, making it difficult to make meaningful comparisons among studies.

(c) Generally, the findings suggest that people attribute a *significantly positive value* to the conservation or restoration of cultural assets. The implication is that damages to cultural goods are undesirable and that the public would be willing to pay positive amounts to avoid them or to slow the rate at which they occur.

(d) Several of the studies show a *relatively large proportion of respondents stating a zero WTP* (up to 89%). Some of these responses can be considered protests against some aspect of the survey instrument (i.e. a dislike of paying taxes or a rejection of the contingent scenario) and thus are not a reflection of people's true preferences. Others, however, are 'genuine' zero values arising from budget constraints, lack of interest in cultural issues and from the fact that cultural heritage preservation is typically ranked low amongst competing public issues, as is shown consistently by attitudinal questions. Hence, the welfare of a significant proportion of the population seems to be unaffected by changes in cultural goods/activities. In some instances, the positive estimated values are driven by a minority of the population, typically, the users of the cultural good and the richer and more educated segments of the population. This finding has important implications for the funding of cultural heritage goods. For example, in instances where more than two thirds of the population express a zero WTP, the imposition of a tax may be infeasible; targeted voluntary donations or entry fees may provide more appropriate means of extracting existing values (although the former invites free-riding behaviour); or, if a tax mechanism is used, care must be taken to ensure that the distributional effects are taken into account with off-setting expenditures.

(e) *Values for users (visitors or residents) are invariably higher than for non-users.* This indicates that there can be significant values from recreational and educational visits. A number of issues should be taken into account when designing pricing mechanisms: the implications of the current focus on making heritage available to the general public, and the possible trade-off between access and conservation that suggests the importance of calculating congestion costs and tourist 'carrying capacity' of a site. However, user values alone may not be enough to deliver sustainability for the large majority of cultural goods and services.

(f) *Non-visitor benefits are positive.* In cases where the relevant population benefiting from improvement or maintenance of the cultural good is thought to be very large, possibly crossing national borders, the total aggregated benefit can be very large. This is the case when unique and charismatic cultural heritage goods are at stake. However, the available evidence also suggests that the proportion of those stating zero WTP is largest amongst non-users.

(g) The issue of *competing cultural goods and of part–whole bias* (when the value of a group of cultural goods is not significantly different from a smaller subset of those goods) has been insufficiently addressed by the existing studies. This issue may be less of a problem for flagship cultural goods with no substitutes (e.g. the Pyramids in Egypt), but may be very severe when cultural goods perceived as being non-unique are being evaluated (e.g. historical buildings, castles, churches and cathedrals). If this bias exists, the estimated values for a particular cultural good may reflect a desire to preserve all similar goods, and thus overstate the value of the good.

(h) Little attention has been given to the *periodicity of the elicited WTP values.* While it is difficult to compare values across studies of different goods, there appears to be a pattern where less periodic payments result in lower WTP amounts. This could be an indication of temporal embedding, where respondents may give lump-sum amounts that are lower than the present value of periodic WTP values using market discount rates. Tests for this kind of bias should be incorporated in studies using one-off or very periodic payments.

(i) Finally, we see authors dedicating a great deal of attention to presenting an *accurate description of the good* to be valued, presented in a form that is meaningful to the respondent. This has two components. First, it is of critical importance that the level of provision of the good matches expert assessments of the with-project situation. For example, when valuing impacts from air pollution, it is necessary to match the valuation scenarios with projections made by atmospheric and materials scientists. Second, these differing levels of quality must be presented in a way that respondents can understand. Several of the studies included photographs and maps to help in this regard.

It is striking to note that all of these conclusions apply equally to studies that value environmental goods. There, we have an equally diverse set of goods that can have values that are highly site-specific, though far more environmental valuation studies have been conducted to date than cultural heritage valuation studies. There too we often see a combination of large use values per person held by a few visitors and small non-use values per household held by a large population of non-visitors. Likewise, in environmental valuation, we face part–whole and embedding issues requiring careful construction and pretesting of the survey instrument. Finally, presenting an accurate and meaningful description of the good to be valued is equally important when valuing environmental goods, and we see many of the same types of visual aids in use.

While the valuation of cultural heritage goods is certainly challenging, it is no more challenging, or fundamentally different from, the valuation of an environmental good that has a significant non-use component. Indeed, in one of the studies listed (Bølling and Iversen 1999), the authors valued both a cultural heritage good and an environmental good in the same survey. We expect non-market valuation techniques to perform equally well for cultural heritage goods as for environmental goods, where literally thousands of studies have been conducted.

Still, it is somewhat surprising that more studies have not been conducted using either the travel cost method or the hedonic pricing method. Chapter 2 discusses the challenges of applying these techniques to cultural heritage goods, but we do see some potential for their use.

POLICY USE OF CULTURAL HERITAGE VALUES

There are clear potential policy uses of the value estimates generated by the studies discussed here. First, valuation estimates are useful for evaluating whether to undertake projects to protect or restore cultural heritage goods. For example, the study valuing road removal at Stonehenge (Chapter 7) provided benefit estimates that could then be compared to estimates of the cost of road construction and removal. It is interesting to note that after completion of that valuation study, the decision was indeed made to go ahead with the project. Both the valuation study of the Fes Medina (Chapter 9) and of buildings in Split, Croatia were conducted as part of project analyses conducted by the World Bank, and will be used to evaluate continued funding for those projects.

Second, valuation estimates are also useful for determining the level of investment in ongoing activities to provide or protect cultural heritage goods.

Here, the studies of the Nidaros and Lincoln Cathedrals (Chapters 3 and 5) are good examples, where the study results can be used to determine how much effort and resources should be devoted to restoring and preserving the appearance of the cathedrals. Similarly, the study of marble monuments in Washington, DC (Chapter 11) helps inform EPA decisions about air quality regulation. More studies are needed that value different levels of provision or quality of cultural heritage goods.

Third, valuation results can inform decisions when choices have to be made among competing objectives within cultural heritage. The Nidaros Cathedral study (Chapter 3) provides information about public preferences over the aesthetics of the building and the degree to which the outside of the building is original. The Stonehenge study (Chapter 7) contrasts values of on-site users and values of passing motorists.

Fourth, valuation results can be very useful in informing decisions about the funding of cultural heritage goods. Not only do the study results show the diversity in values held by the population, they can also be used to predict what will happen if increased reliance is placed on entrance fees. Two of the studies (Durham Cathedral, Chapter 4 and Napoli Musei Aperti, Chapter 14) found that revenues from access fees might be lower than revenues from voluntary donations, because they exclude a large number of users with low WTP.

FUTURE RESEARCH NEEDS

Table 15.2 shows clearly the most pressing research need in this area—more studies are needed on the diverse array of cultural heritage goods. Still, we are not hopeful that we will ever reach a point where 'enough' studies have been conducted. One lesson we can take from the environmental valuation literature is that *benefit transfer*, that is the application of values estimated at one site to policy issues at a geographically different but similar type of site, is often unreliable. Environmental values and cultural heritage values are naturally highly site- and good-specific. We do not anticipate that there will ever be a catalogue of values from which decision makers can select an appropriate number for the new policy issue they face.

It may turn out that groups of cultural heritage goods have similar values. To date, there are too few studies to judge the extent to which values for cultural heritage vary. Whether value estimates will vary much from site to site and good to good is still an open empirical question. We can state, however, that for benefit transfer to work at all, it must be between sites that are very similar, both in the physical good being valued, the change in the good and the population holding the values.

We would like to see new valuation studies designed to address specific policy problems, rather than provide general values for the goods. Knowing the amount that a visitor is willing to pay to gain entry into a cathedral does not help us decide whether to restore damaged portions. Similarly, we would like to see more emphasis on research into trade-offs among competing objectives, for example between access and deterioration due to that access. Non-market valuation techniques are uniquely well suited for considering issues that involve trade-offs between use values and non-use values.

CONCLUSION

The valuation studies described in previous chapters were selected to show the heterogeneity of our cultural heritage and the policy issues that arise regarding its preservation. Together with the other studies listed in Table 15.1 they clearly show that non-market valuation techniques can be successfully applied to cultural heritage objects of local, national and even global significance (e.g. UNESCO World Heritage Sites), and objects that have different functions including objects with multiple functions (e.g. churches and monasteries which are both tourist attractions and have important religious functions). The existing studies also cover both developed and less developed countries, and transition economies. Some of the studies were conducted to inform policy decisions, and have proved useful in cost–benefit analyses of restoration and preservation programmes for cultural heritage, as well as infrastructure projects and air pollution policies with impacts on cultural heritage. The information generated by such studies can be a valuable complement to expert judgement. We expect to see an increased use of these non-market valuation techniques to help inform policies regarding cultural heritage in the future, in much the same way as these techniques are now contributing to formulating environmental policy.

ENDNOTE

1. For applications of the travel cost method on performing arts, see e.g. Martin (1994) and Forrest *et al.* (2000).

REFERENCES

Bølling, J. and V. Iversen. 1999. *Tourists' Willingness to Pay for Restoration of Stone Town to its Original State and Stopping Habitat Destruction in Jozani Forest Reserve, Zanzibar*. Master's Thesis, Department of Economics and Social Sciences, Agricultural University of Norway, Ås, Norway.

Carson, R.C., M. Connoway and S. Navrud, 2001: How to value cultrual heritage of global significance. A delphi contingent valuation study. Note. Department of Economics, University of California, San Diego, La Jolla.

Coulton, J.C. 1999. *Optimal Cultural Heritage Allocation: A Model and Contingent Valuation Study.* M.Sc. Thesis, Environmental and Resource Economics Program, University College London, September 1999, 38 pp. + appendices.

EFTEC (Economics for the Environment Consultancy). 2000. *Valuing Our Recorded Heritage, Final Report.* Report to the Museums and Galleries Commission, London.

Forrest, D., K. Grime and R. Woods, 2000. Is it worth subsidising regional repertory theatre, *Oxford Economic Papers*, **52**, 381–97

Grosclaude, P. and N. Soguel. 1994. Valuing damage to historic buildings using a contingent market: a case study of road traffic externalities, *Journal of Environmental Planning and Management*, **37**(3), 279–87.

Hett, T. and S. Mourato 2000. *Sustainable Management of Machu Picchu: a Stated Preference Approach.* Paper submitted to Conference on Sustainability, Tourism and the Environment, Dublin.

Kling, R., C. Revier and K. Sable (2000). *Estimating the Public Good Value of Preserving A Local Historic Landmark: The Role of Non-Substitutability and Information in Contingent Valuation.* Paper presented to the Association for Cultural Economics Conference in Minneapolis.

Maddison, D. and T. Foster 2001. *Valuing Congestion in the British Museum.* Mimeo, Department of Economics, University College London.

Martin, F. 1994. Determining the size of museum subsides, *Journal of Cultural Economics*, **18**, 255–70.

Pagiola, S. 1999. *Valuing the Benefits of Investments in Cultural Heritage: The Historic Core of Split.* Paper presented at the World Bank Economists' Forum, Alexandria, 3–4 May 1999.

Pearce, D.W. and S. Mourato 1999. *The Economics of Cultural Heritage.* Report to the World Bank, Washington, DC.

Pearce, D., D. Maddison and M. Pollicino 2001. *Economics and Cultural Heritage. Towards an economic approach to valuing and conserving cultural assets.* Centre for Cultural Economics and Management, University College London.

Roche Rivera, H. 1998. *The Willingness-to-Pay for a Public Mixed Good: The Colon Theatre in Argentina.* Paper presented at the Tenth International Conference on Cultural Economics, 14–17 June 1998, Barcelona.

Throsby, C. and G. Withers. 1986. Strategic bias and the demand for public goods, *Journal of Public Economics*, **31**, 307–27.

Whitehead J., C.M. Chambers and P.E. Chambers. 1998. Contingent valuation of quasi-public goods: validity, reliability, and application to valuing a historic site, *Public Finance Review*, **26**, 137–54.

Index